Quick & Simple
Tower Dual Basket Air Fryer Cookbook

350 Easy, Affordable, Delicious, Healthy & Mouthwatering Air Fryer Recipes for Everyday

Mark Aziz

Copyright © 2023 by   All rights reserved.

The content contained within this book may not be reproduced, duplicated, or transmitted without direct written permission from the author or the publisher. Under no circumstances will any blame or legal responsibility be held against the publisher, or author, for any damages, reparation, or monetary loss due to the information contained within this book, either directly or indirectly.

Legal Notice: This book is copyright protected. It is only for personal use. You cannot amend, distribute, sell, use, quote or paraphrase any part, or the content within this book, without the consent of the author or publisher.

Disclaimer Notice: Please note the information contained within this document is for educational and entertainment purposes only. All effort has been executed to present accurate, up to date, reliable, complete information. No warranties of any kind are declared or implied. Readers acknowledge that the author is not engaged in the rendering of legal, financial, medical, or professional advice. The content within this book has been derived from various sources. Please consult a licensed professional before attempting any techniques outlined in this book. By reading this document, the reader agrees that under no circumstances is the author responsible for any losses, direct or indirect, that are incurred as a result of the use of the information contained within this document, including, but not limited to, errors, omissions, or inaccuracies.

Table of Contents

Table of Contents 3
Chapter 1: Introduction 7
History of the Tower Dual Basket Air Fryer 7
Benefits of the Tower Dual Basket Air Fryer 7
Features of the Tower Dual Basket Air Fryer 7
Tips for Using the Tower Dual Basket Air Fryer 7
Cleaning and Maintenance of the Tower Dual Basket Air Fryer 8

Chapter 2: Measurement Conversions 9
BASIC KITCHEN CONVERSIONS & EQUIVALENTS 9

Chapter 3: Appetizers And Snacks Recipes 10
Italian Bruschetta With Mushrooms & Cheese 11
Cayenne-spiced Roasted Pecans 11
Crispy Breaded Beef Cubes 11
Buffalo Cauliflower 11
Cheesy Spinach Dip(1) 11
Zucchini Chips 12
Beef And Mango Skewers 12
Buffalo French Fries 12
Zucchini Chips With Cheese 12
Cholula Avocado Fries 12
Buffalo Bites 13
Awesome Lemony Green Beans 13
Za'atar Garbanzo Beans 13
Zucchini With Parmesan Cheese 13
Tomato & Basil Bruschetta 13
Hot Cheese Bites 14
Rosemary Garlic Goat Cheese 14
Kale Chips With Tex-mex Dip 14
Okra Chips 14
Cuban Sliders 14
Garlic Edamame 14
Bacon Pickle Spear Rolls 15
Delicious Zucchini Crackers 15
Cinnamon Apple Crisps 15
Bacon Butter 15
Corn With Coriander And Parmesan Cheese 15
Eggplant Chips 16
Veggie Salmon Nachos 16
Arancini With Sun-dried Tomatoes And Mozzarella ... 16
Pork Pot Stickers With Yum Yum Sauce 16
Apple Rollups 17
Crispy Cajun Dill Pickle Chips 17
Spicy Kale Chips With Yogurt Sauce 17
Crispy & Healthy Kale Chips 18
Olive & Pepper Tapenade 18
Cinnamon Sweet Potato Fries 18
Simple Curried Sweet Potato Fries 18
Baked Ricotta 18
Cajun Sweet Potato Tots 19
Fried Goat Cheese 19
No-guilty Spring Rolls 19
Jalapeño & Mozzarella Stuffed Mushrooms 19
Potato Pastries 20
Bbq Pork Ribs 20
Korean Brussels Sprouts 20

Chapter 4: Bread And Breakfast Recipes 21
Spinach And Mushroom Mini Quiche 22
Pancake For Two 22
Vegetarian Quinoa Cups 22
Strawberry Tarts 22
Dill Eggs In Wonton 23
English Scones 23
English Pumpkin Egg Bake 23
Strawberry And Peach Toast 23
Spinach With Scrambled Eggs 23
Bacon And Broccoli Bread Pudding 24
Eggless Mung Bean Tart 24
Chives Omelet 24
Cherry Beignets 24
Sourdough Croutons 25
Orange Trail Oatmeal 25
Bunless Breakfast Turkey Burgers 25
Cinnamon Pear Oat Muffins 25
Cheddar Soufflés 25
Egg Peppers Cups 26
Cornflakes Toast Sticks 26
Carrot Orange Muffins 26
Simple Cheddar-omelet 26
Mixed Pepper Hash With Mozzarella Cheese 27
Vegetable Quiche 27
Cheddar Biscuits With Nutmeg 27
Medium Rare Simple Salt And Pepper Steak 27
Spinach Bacon Spread 27
Apple & Turkey Breakfast Sausages 28
Yummy Bagel Breakfast 28
Ham And Corn Muffins 28
Parmesan Sausage Egg Muffins 28
Chicken Scotch Eggs 28

Banana-strawberry Cakecups 29	Eggs Salad 30
Tomatoes Hash With Cheddar Cheese 29	Holiday Breakfast Casserole 30
Baked Eggs 29	Mushroom & Cavolo Nero Egg Muffins 30
Western Omelet 29	Creamy Eggs And Leeks 31
Chocolate Almond Crescent Rolls 29	Cheddar & Egg Scramble 31
Baked Parmesan Eggs With Kielbasa 30	Breakfast Chimichangas 31
Turkey Casserole With Cheddar Cheese 30	

Chapter 5: Vegetable Side Dishes Recipes 32

Roasted Eggplant Slices 33	Roasted Thyme Asparagus 38
Lemony Cabbage Slaw 33	Air Fried Broccoli 38
Speedy Baked Caprese With Avocado 33	Stuffed Bell Peppers With Mayonnaise 38
Caraway Seed Pretzel Sticks 33	Rice And Eggplant Bowl 38
Simple Green Bake 33	Lemon Broccoli 38
Sweet And Spicy Tofu 33	Hot Okra Wedges 39
Steamed Green Veggie Trio 34	Brown Rice And Goat Cheese Croquettes 39
Mashed Potato Tots 34	Curried Brussels Sprouts 39
Blistered Tomatoes 34	Parmesan Asparagus 39
Roasted Fennel Salad 35	Truffle Vegetable Croquettes 40
Basic Corn On The Cob 35	Garlic Provolone Asparagus 40
Creole Seasoned Okra 35	Lemon Fennel With Sunflower Seeds 40
Scalloped Potatoes 35	Garlicky Mushrooms With Parsley 40
Awesome Chicken Taquitos 35	Rosemary Potato Salad 40
Cheddar-garlic Drop Biscuits 35	Simple Taro Fries 41
Green Beans And Potatoes Recipe 36	Avocado Fries 41
Turkish Mutabal (eggplant Dip) 36	Rich Spinach Chips 41
Baked Jalapeño And Cheese Cauliflower Mash 36	Air Fried Bell Peppers With Onion 41
Corn Pakodas 36	Buttery Stuffed Tomatoes 41
Mediterranean Air Fried Veggies 36	Yellow Squash 42
Ratatouille 37	Fingerling Potatoes 42
Open-faced Sandwich 37	Spicy Corn On The Cob 42
Cholula Onion Rings 37	Air-fried Potato Salad 42
French Fries 37	Rosemary Roasted Potatoes With Lemon 43
Creamy Spinach With Nutmeg 37	Pancetta Mushroom & Onion Sautée 43

Chapter 6: Vegetarians Recipes 44

Crispy Wings With Lemony Old Bay Spice 45	Sesame Orange Tofu With Snow Peas 48
Vegan Buddha Bowls(2) 45	Ricotta Veggie Potpie 49
Veggie Burgers 45	Mexican Twice Air-fried Sweet Potatoes 49
Pizza Portobello Mushrooms 45	Caramelized Carrots 49
Corn On The Cob 46	Breaded Avocado Tacos 49
Lentil Fritters 46	Bell Pepper & Lentil Tacos 50
Spinach And Artichoke–stuffed Peppers 46	Golden Fried Tofu 50
Falafels 46	Easy Glazed Carrots 50
Italian Seasoned Easy Pasta Chips 46	Buttered Broccoli 50
Asparagus, Mushroom And Cheese Soufflés 47	Spicy Celery Sticks 50
Curried Cauliflower 47	Tacos 51
Vegetarian Eggplant "pizzas" 47	Two-cheese Grilled Sandwiches 51
Sweet Corn Bread 47	Basil Tomatoes 51
Broccoli & Parmesan Dish 48	Thyme Lentil Patties 51
Cheesy Enchilada Stuffed Baked Potatoes 48	Kale & Lentils With Crispy Onions 51

Chapter 7: Poultry Recipes 52

Crispy Duck With Cherry Sauce 53	Chicken Strips 53
Mediterranean Stuffed Chicken Breasts 53	Barbecued Chicken Thighs 54
Fried Herbed Chicken Wings 53	Simple Chicken Shawarma 54

Recipe	Page
Turkey & Rice Frittata	54
Chicken & Fruit Biryani	54
Nashville Hot Chicken	54
Paprika Duck	55
Spice Chicken Pieces	55
Breaded Chicken Patties	55
Crispy Chicken Cordon Bleu	56
Chicken Tenderloins With Parmesan Cheese	56
Perfect Grill Chicken Breast	56
Herb-roasted Turkey Breast	56
Indian-style Chicken With Raita	57
Flavorful Spiced Chicken Pieces	57
Chicken Fajita Poppers	57
German Chicken Frikadellen	57
Curried Chicken With Fruit	57
Cal-mex Turkey Patties	58
Mediterranean Fried Chicken	58
Chicken & Pepperoni Pizza	58
Lemon Parmesan Chicken	58
Parmesan Crusted Chicken Cordon Bleu	59
Duck Breast With Figs	59
Chicken Salad With White Dressing	59
Parmesan Chicken Meatloaf	60
Honey Rosemary Chicken	60
Parmesan Chicken Fingers	60
Chicken Wings With Bbq Sauce	61
Chicken Fajitas	61
Crispy Chicken Parmesan	61
Cheese Turkey Meatloaf	61
Chipotle Drumsticks	62
Vip´s Club Sandwiches	62
Orange Curried Chicken Stir-fry	62
Sesame Chicken Tenders	62
Fiesta Chicken Plate	63
Celery Chicken Mix	63
Buffalo Chicken Taquitos	63
Turkey And Cranberry Quesadillas	63
Lemon-pepper Chicken Wings	64
Chicken Burgers With Blue Cheese Sauce	64
Gluten-free Nutty Chicken Fingers	64
Cinnamon Chicken Thighs	64
Crispy Chicken Strips	65
Katsu Chicken Thighs	65
Korean-style Chicken Bulgogi	65

Chapter 8: Beef, pork & Lamb Recipes 66

Recipe	Page
Tasty Pork Chops	67
Marinated Beef And Vegetable Stir Fry	67
Breaded Italian Pork Chops	67
Sweet And Spicy Pork Ribs	67
Sweet And Sour Pork	67
Garlic Steak With Cheese Butter	68
Bbq Pork Chops With Vegetables	68
Tender Pork Ribs With Bbq Sauce	68
Parmesan-crusted Pork Chops	69
Potato And Prosciutto Salad	69
Beef And Pork Sausage Meatloaf	69
Spiced Pork Chops	69
Mexican-style Shredded Beef	69
Barbecued Baby Back Ribs	70
Cinnamon-stick Kofta Skewers	70
Korean Short Ribs	70
Crispy Steak Subs	70
Steak Fajitas With Vegetables	71
Better-than-chinese-take-out Pork Ribs	71
Country-style Pork Ribs	71
Easy Tex-mex Chimichangas	71
Grilled Steak With Salsa	72
Simple Rib-eye Steak	72
Albóndigas	72
Marinated Rib-eye Steak With Herb Roasted Mushrooms	72
Salty Lamb Chops	73
Original Köttbullar	73
Rice And Meatball Stuffed Bell Peppers	73
Honey Pork Links	73
Avocado Buttered Flank Steak	74
Bacon Wrapped Pork With Apple Gravy	74
Fajita Flank Steak Rolls	74
Crispy Lamb Shoulder Chops	74
Beef Kebabs	75
Pork Meatballs	75
Flank Steak With Tamari Sauce	75
Cheeseburgers	75
Lamb Meatballs	76
Garlic And Oregano Lamb Chops	76
Juicy Beef Kabobs With Sour Cream	76
Steak Bites And Spicy Dipping Sauce	76
Bacon With Shallot And Greens	77
Air Fried London Broil	77
Sweet-and-sour Polish Sausage	77
Creole Pork Chops	77
Bourbon-bbq Sauce Marinated Beef Bbq	77
Mini Meatloaves With Pancetta	77
Beef Taco Chimichangas	78
Homemade Pork Gyoza	78
Tender Country Ribs	78

Chapter 9: Fish And Seafood Recipes 79

Recipe	Page
Southwestern Prawns With Asparagus	80
Mustard-crusted Fish Fillets	80
Ham Tilapia	80
Air Fried Mussels With Parsley	80
Fish Nuggets With Broccoli Dip	80
Potato Chip-crusted Cod	81
Lime Bay Scallops	81
Easy Scallops With Lemon Butter	81

Cilantro Sea Bass 81
Seafood Spring Rolls 81
Tortilla-crusted With Lemon Filets 82
Blackened Red Snapper 82
Thyme Scallops 82
Mediterranean Sea Scallops 82
Caribbean Skewers 83
Kid's Flounder Fingers 83
Cod Nuggets 83
Italian Shrimp 83
Breaded Parmesan Perch 83
Korean-style Fried Calamari 83
Cajun Fish Cakes 84
Lemon-dill Salmon With Green Beans 84
Sesame-crusted Tuna Steaks 84
Tuna Wraps 84
Snow Crab Legs 85
Collard Green & Cod Packets 85
Cajun Fish Sticks 85

Creole Tilapia With Garlic Mayo 85
Tilapia Teriyaki 85
Crab Rangoon 86
Lemon Butter–dill Salmon 86
Old Bay Cod Fish Fillets 86
Spicy Halibut Steak 86
Easy Air Fried Salmon 86
Crispy Smelts 87
Maple Butter Salmon 87
Trimmed Mackerel With Spring Onions 87
Lobster Tails 87
Shrimp "scampi" 87
Spanish Garlic Shrimp 88
Lemon Shrimp And Zucchinis 88
Maryland-style Crab Cakes 88
Fried Shrimp 88
Old Bay Fish 'n' Chips 89
Fried Catfish Nuggets 89

Chapter 10: Desserts And Sweets Recipes *90*

Cranberries Pudding 91
Chocolate Coconut Brownies 91
Toasted Coconut Flakes 91
Simple & Tasty Brownies 91
Giant Vegan Chocolate Chip Cookie 91
Buttery Shortbread Sticks 92
Chocolate Croissants 92
Glazed Donuts 92
Molten Chocolate Almond Cakes 92
Mixed Berry Crumble 93
Graham Cracker Cheesecake 93
Almond Shortbread Cookies 93
Peanut Butter-banana Roll-ups 94
Zucchini Bread With Chocolate Chips 94
Cinnamon Crunch S'mores 94
Vegan Brownie Bites 94
Hasselback Apple Crisp 94
Sage Cream 95

Apple-blueberry Hand Pies 95
Dark Chocolate Cream Galette 95
Coconut Cream Roll-ups 96
Apple Pie Crumble 96
Chocolate Molten Cake 96
Chocolate Banana Brownie 96
Butter Cheesecake 96
Grilled Spiced Fruit 97
Curry Peaches, Pears, And Plums 97
Plum Apple Crumble With Cranberries 97
Chocolate-almond Candies 97
Honey Donuts 98
Easy-to-make Almond Cookies 98
Tasty Berry Cobbler 98
Coconut Rice Cake 98
Low-carb Peanut Butter Cookies 98
Zucchini Bars With Cream Cheese 99

Recipes Index *100*

Chapter 1: Introduction

History of the Tower Dual Basket Air Fryer

Tower Housewares has been a UK-based company producing various kitchen appliances and utensils for over a century. With a history of innovation, the introduction of the Tower Dual Basket Air Fryer is a relatively recent addition to their product line, reflecting the company's commitment to adapting to modern cooking trends and consumer needs. The dual-basket air fryer is an evolution of the traditional single-basket design, created to offer more versatility and efficiency in cooking.

Benefits of the Tower Dual Basket Air Fryer

The Tower Dual Basket Air Fryer presents numerous advantages, building on the well-known benefits of air fryers with added flexibility:

1. **Dual Cooking Zones:** It allows simultaneous cooking of two different food items with separate timers and temperature controls, making meal prep more efficient.
2. **Healthier Options:** Like all air fryers, it uses significantly less oil than traditional frying methods, which can lead to healthier meals.
3. **Space-Saving:** Despite the dual baskets, it's designed to be compact and suitable for various kitchen sizes.
4. **Energy Efficiency:** It cooks food quickly and is generally more energy-efficient than using a conventional oven, especially for small to medium quantities of food.

Features of the Tower Dual Basket Air Fryer

The Tower Dual Basket Air Fryer is equipped with a variety of features that enhance its functionality:

- **Independent Baskets:** Each basket operates independently, so different foods can be cooked at their respective temperatures and times.
- **Sync and Match:** Some models have the ability to synchronize the finish times of both baskets, so different foods are ready to serve at the same time.
- **Touchscreen Interface:** An intuitive control panel makes it easy to select functions, adjust times, and temperatures.
- **Variety of Functions:** Besides air frying, it offers options to roast, bake, and dehydrate, among other functions.
- **Pre-set Programs:** With various pre-set programs, cooking common dishes is straightforward and convenient.

Tips for Using the Tower Dual Basket Air Fryer

To optimize the use of the Tower Dual Basket Air Fryer, keep in mind the following tips:

1. **Utilize Dual Baskets:** Plan meals that make the most of both baskets. For example, meat in one and vegetables in the other.
2. **Preheat for Best Results:** If recommended by the manufacturer, preheating can lead to crisper and more evenly cooked food.
3. **Shake or Turn Food:** This ensures even

cooking and browning.

4. **Use Little to No Oil:** Take advantage of the health benefits by minimizing oil use. When you do use oil, opt for a spray to coat food lightly.

5. **Experiment:** Don't be afraid to try different recipes and functions. The more you use it, the better you'll understand how it works with various foods.

Cleaning and Maintenance of the Tower Dual Basket Air Fryer

Maintaining the Tower Dual Basket Air Fryer is essential for its durability and performance:

- **Follow Manufacturer's Instructions:** Adhere to the cleaning instructions provided in the manual.
- **Regular Cleaning:** Wipe down the interior and exterior after each use, and wash baskets in soapy water or a dishwasher if they are dishwasher-safe.
- **Avoid Harsh Chemicals:** To protect non-stick surfaces, avoid using abrasive cleaners or metal utensils.
- **Check for Food Residue:** Ensure no food is stuck to the heating elements or the baskets.
- **Perform Regular Checks:** Inspect your air fryer regularly for any signs of wear and tear, especially on the baskets and their coatings.

Chapter 2: Measurement Conversions

BASIC KITCHEN CONVERSIONS & EQUIVALENTS

DRY MEASUREMENTS CONVERSION CHART
3 TEASPOONS = 1 TABLESPOON = 1/16 CUP
6 TEASPOONS = 2 TABLESPOONS = 1/8 CUP
12 TEASPOONS = 4 TABLESPOONS = 1/4 CUP
24 TEASPOONS = 8 TABLESPOONS = 1/2 CUP
36 TEASPOONS = 12 TABLESPOONS = 3/4 CUP
48 TEASPOONS = 16 TABLESPOONS = 1 CUP

METRIC TO US COOKING CONVERSIONS
OVEN TEMPERATURES
120 °C = 250 °F
160 °C = 320 °F
180° C = 360 °F
205 °C = 400 °F
220 °C = 425 °F

LIQUID MEASUREMENTS CONVERSION CHART
8 FLUID OUNCES = 1 CUP = 1/2 PINT = 1/4 QUART
16 FLUID OUNCES = 2 CUPS = 1 PINT = 1/2 QUART
32 FLUID OUNCES = 4 CUPS = 2 PINTS = 1 QUART = 1/4 GALLON
128 FLUID OUNCES = 16 CUPS = 8 PINTS = 4 QUARTS = 1 GALLON

BAKING IN GRAMS
1 CUP FLOUR = 140 GRAMS
1 CUP SUGAR = 150 GRAMS
1 CUP POWDERED SUGAR = 160 GRAMS
1 CUP HEAVY CREAM = 235 GRAMS

VOLUME
1 MILLILITER = 1/5 TEASPOON
5 ML = 1 TEASPOON
15 ML = 1 TABLESPOON
240 ML = 1 CUP OR 8 FLUID OUNCES
1 LITER = 34 FL. OUNCES

WEIGHT
1 GRAM = .035 OUNCES
100 GRAMS = 3.5 OUNCES
500 GRAMS = 1.1 POUNDS
1 KILOGRAM = 35 OUNCES

US TO METRIC COOKING CONVERSIONS
1/5 TSP = 1 ML
1 TSP = 5 ML
1 TBSP = 15 ML
1 FL OUNCE = 30 ML
1 CUP = 237 ML
1 PINT (2 CUPS) = 473 ML
1 QUART (4 CUPS) = .95 LITER
1 GALLON (16 CUPS) = 3.8 LITERS
1 OZ = 28 GRAMS
1 POUND = 454 GRAMS

BUTTER
1 CUP BUTTER = 2 STICKS = 8 OUNCES = 230 GRAMS = 8 TABLESPOONS

WHAT DOES 1 CUP EQUAL
1 CUP = 8 FLUID OUNCES
1 CUP = 16 TABLESPOONS
1 CUP = 48 TEASPOONS
1 CUP = 1/2 PINT
1 CUP = 1/4 QUART
1 CUP = 1/16 GALLON
1 CUP = 240 ML

BAKING PAN CONVERSIONS
1 CUP ALL-PURPOSE FLOUR = 4.5 OZ
1 CUP ROLLED OATS = 3 OZ 1 LARGE EGG = 1.7 OZ
1 CUP BUTTER = 8 OZ 1 CUP MILK = 8 OZ
1 CUP HEAVY CREAM = 8.4 OZ
1 CUP GRANULATED SUGAR = 7.1 OZ
1 CUP PACKED BROWN SUGAR = 7.75 OZ
1 CUP VEGETABLE OIL = 7.7 OZ
1 CUP UNSIFTED POWDERED SUGAR = 4.4 OZ

BAKING PAN CONVERSIONS
9-INCH ROUND CAKE PAN = 12 CUPS
10-INCH TUBE PAN = 16 CUPS
11-INCH BUNDT PAN = 12 CUPS
9-INCH SPRINGFORM PAN = 10 CUPS
9 X 5 INCH LOAF PAN = 8 CUPS
9-INCH SQUARE PAN = 8 CUPS

Chapter 3: Appetizers And Snacks Recipes

Italian Bruschetta With Mushrooms & Cheese

Servings: 4
Cooking Time: 25 Minutes
Ingredients:
- ½ cup button mushrooms, chopped
- ½ baguette, sliced
- 1 garlic clove, minced
- 3 oz sliced Parmesan cheese
- 1 tbsp extra virgin olive oil
- Salt and pepper to taste

Directions:
1. Preheat air fryer to 350°F. Add the mushrooms, olive oil, salt, pepper, and garlic to a mixing bowl and stir thoroughly to combine. Divide the mushroom mixture between the bread slices, drizzling all over the surface with olive oil, then cover with Parmesan slices. Place the covered bread slices in the greased frying basket and Bake for 15 minutes. Serve and enjoy!

Cayenne-spiced Roasted Pecans

Servings: 4
Cooking Time: 15 Minutes
Ingredients:
- ¼ tsp chili powder
- Salt and pepper to taste
- ⅛ tsp cayenne pepper
- 1 tsp cumin powder
- 1 tsp cinnamon powder
- ⅛ tsp garlic powder
- ⅛ tsp onion powder
- 1 cup raw pecans
- 2 tbsp butter, melted
- 1 tsp honey

Directions:
1. Preheat air fryer to 300°F. Whisk together black pepper, chili powder, salt, cayenne pepper, cumin, garlic powder, cinnamon, and onion powder. Set to the side. Toss pecans, butter, and honey in a medium bowl, then toss in the spice mixture. Pour pecans in the frying basket and toast for 3 minutes. Stir the pecans and toast for another 3 to 5 minutes until the nuts are crisp. Cool and serve.

Crispy Breaded Beef Cubes

Servings: 4
Cooking Time: 12 To 16 Minutes
Ingredients:
- 1 pound (454 g) sirloin tip, cut into 1-inch cubes
- 1 cup cheese pasta sauce
- 1½ cups soft bread crumbs
- 2 tablespoons olive oil
- ½ teaspoon dried marjoram

Directions:
1. Preheat the air fryer to 360°F (182°C).
2. In a medium bowl, toss the beef with the pasta sauce to coat.
3. In a shallow bowl, combine the bread crumbs, oil, and marjoram, and mix well. Drop the beef cubes, one at a time, into the bread crumb mixture to coat thoroughly.
4. Air fry the beef in two batches for 6 to 8 minutes, shaking the basket once during cooking time, until the beef is at least 145°F (63°C) and the outside is crisp and brown.
5. Serve hot.

Buffalo Cauliflower

Servings: 6
Cooking Time: 12 Minutes
Ingredients:
- 1 large head of cauliflower, washed and cut into medium-size florets
- ½ cup all-purpose flour
- ¼ cup melted butter
- 3 tablespoons hot sauce
- ½ teaspoon garlic powder
- ½ cup blue cheese dip or ranch dressing (optional)

Directions:
1. Preheat the air fryer to 350°F.
2. Make sure the cauliflower florets are dry, and then coat them in flour.
3. Liberally spray the air fryer basket with an olive oil mist. Place the cauliflower into the basket, making sure not to stack them on top of each other. Depending on the size of your air fryer, you may need to do this in two batches.
4. Cook for 6 minutes, then shake the basket, and cook another 6 minutes.
5. While cooking, mix the melted butter, hot sauce, and garlic powder in a large bowl.
6. Carefully remove the cauliflower from the air fryer. Toss the cauliflower into the butter mixture to coat. Repeat Steps 2–4 for any leftover cauliflower. Serve warm with the dip of your choice.

Cheesy Spinach Dip(1)

Servings: 6
Cooking Time: 35 Minutes
Ingredients:
- ½ can refrigerated breadstick dough
- 8 oz feta cheese, cubed
- ¼ cup sour cream
- ½ cup baby spinach
- ½ cup grated Swiss cheese
- 2 green onions, chopped
- 2 tbsp melted butter
- 4 tsp grated Parmesan cheese

Directions:
1. Preheat air fryer to 320°F. Blend together feta, sour cream, spinach, Swiss cheese, and green onions in a bowl. Spread into the pan and Bake until hot, about 8 minutes. Unroll six of the breadsticks and cut in half crosswise to make 12 pieces. Carefully stretch each piece and tie into a loose knot. Tuck in the ends to prevent burning.

2. When the dip is ready, remove the pan from the air fryer and place each bread knot on top of the dip until the dip is covered. Brush melted butter on each knot and sprinkle with Parmesan. Bake until the knots are golden, 8-13 minutes. Serve warm.

Zucchini Chips

Servings: 3
Cooking Time: 17 Minutes
Ingredients:
- 1½ small Zucchini, washed but not peeled, and cut into ¼-inch-thick rounds
- Olive oil spray
- ¼ teaspoon Table salt

Directions:
1. Preheat the air fryer to 375°F.
2. Lay some paper towels on your work surface. Set the zucchini rounds on top, then set more paper towels over the rounds. Press gently to remove some of the moisture. Remove the top layer of paper towels and lightly coat the rounds with olive oil spray on both sides.
3. When the machine is at temperature, set the rounds in the basket, overlapping them a bit as needed. Air-fry for 15 minutes, tossing and rearranging the rounds at the 5- and 10-minute marks, until browned, soft, yet crisp at the edges.
4. Gently pour the contents of the basket onto a wire rack. Cool for at least 10 minutes or up to 2 hours before serving.

Beef And Mango Skewers

Servings: 4
Cooking Time: 4 To 7 Minutes
Ingredients:
- ¾ pound (340 g) beef sirloin tip, cut into 1-inch cubes
- 2 tablespoons balsamic vinegar
- 1 tablespoon olive oil
- 1 tablespoon honey
- ½ teaspoon dried marjoram
- Pinch of salt
- Freshly ground black pepper, to taste
- 1 mango

Directions:
1. Preheat the air fryer to 390ºF (199ºC).
2. Put the beef cubes in a medium bowl and add the balsamic vinegar, olive oil, honey, marjoram, salt, and pepper. Mix well, then massage the marinade into the beef with your hands. Set aside.
3. To prepare the mango, stand it on end and cut the skin off, using a sharp knife. Then carefully cut around the oval pit to remove the flesh. Cut the mango into 1-inch cubes.
4. Thread metal skewers alternating with three beef cubes and two mango cubes.
5. Roast the skewers in the air fryer basket for 4 to 7 minutes, or until the beef is browned and at least 145ºF (63ºC).
6. Serve hot.

Buffalo French Fries

Servings: 6
Cooking Time: 35 Minutes
Ingredients:
- 3 large russet potatoes
- 2 tbsp buffalo sauce
- 2 tbsp extra-virgin olive oil
- Salt and pepper to taste

Directions:
1. Preheat air fryer to 380°F. Peel and cut potatoes lengthwise into French fries. Place them in a bowl, then coat with olive oil, salt and pepper. Air Fry them for 10 minutes. Shake the basket, then cook for five minutes. Serve drizzled with Buffalo sauce immediately.

Zucchini Chips With Cheese

Servings: 8
Cooking Time: 13 Minutes
Ingredients:
- 2 zucchinis, thinly sliced
- 4 tablespoons almond flour
- 2 oz. Parmesan
- 2 eggs, beaten
- ½ teaspoon white pepper
- Cooking spray

Directions:
1. Prepare your clean air fryer and preheat it to 355 degrees F/ 180 degrees C.
2. Thoroughly mix up almond flour, Parmesan and white pepper in a large bowl.
3. After that, dip the zucchini slices in the egg and coat in the almond flour mixture.
4. Place the prepared zucchini slices in the preheated air fryer and cook them for 10 minutes.
5. Flip the vegetables on another side and cook them for 3 minutes more or until crispy.
6. Serve and enjoy.

Cholula Avocado Fries

Servings: 2
Cooking Time: 20 Minutes
Ingredients:
- 1 egg, beaten
- ¼ cup flour
- 2 tbsp ground flaxseed
- ¼ tsp Cholula sauce
- Salt to taste
- 1 avocado, cut into fries

Directions:
1. Preheat air fryer to 375ºF. Mix the egg and Cholula sauce in a bowl. In another bowl, combine the remaining ingredients, except for the avocado. Submerge avocado slices in the egg mixture and dredge them into the flour to coat. Place the fries in the lightly greased frying basket and Air Fry for 5 minutes. Serve immediately.

Buffalo Bites

Servings: 16
Cooking Time: 12 Minutes
Ingredients:
- 1 pound ground chicken
- 8 tablespoons buffalo wing sauce
- 2 ounces Gruyère cheese, cut into 16 cubes
- 1 tablespoon maple syrup

Directions:
1. Mix 4 tablespoons buffalo wing sauce into all the ground chicken.
2. Shape chicken into a log and divide into 16 equal portions.
3. With slightly damp hands, mold each chicken portion around a cube of cheese and shape into a firm ball. When you have shaped 8 meatballs, place them in air fryer basket.
4. Cook at 390°F for approximately 5minutes. Shake basket, reduce temperature to 360°F, and cook for 5 minutes longer.
5. While the first batch is cooking, shape remaining chicken and cheese into 8 more meatballs.
6. Repeat step 4 to cook second batch of meatballs.
7. In a medium bowl, mix the remaining 4 tablespoons of buffalo wing sauce with the maple syrup. Add all the cooked meatballs and toss to coat.
8. Place meatballs back into air fryer basket and cook at 390°F for 2 minutes to set the glaze. Skewer each with a toothpick and serve.

Awesome Lemony Green Beans

Servings: 4
Cooking Time: 12 Minutes
Ingredients:
- 1 lemon, juiced
- 1-pound green beans, washed and destemmed
- ¼ teaspoon extra virgin olive oil
- Salt to taste
- Black pepper to taste

Directions:
1. At 400 degrees F/ 205 degrees C, preheat your air fryer.
2. Put the green beans in your air fryer basket and drizzle the lemon juice over them.
3. Sprinkle on the black pepper and salt.
4. Pour in the oil, and toss to coat the green beans well.
5. Cook for almost 10-12 minutes and serve warm.

Za'atar Garbanzo Beans

Servings: 6
Cooking Time: 12 Minutes
Ingredients:
- One 14.5-ounce can garbanzo beans, drained and rinsed
- 1 tablespoon extra-virgin olive oil
- 6 teaspoons za'atar seasoning mix
- 2 tablespoons chopped parsley
- Salt and pepper, to taste

Directions:
1. Preheat the air fryer to 390°F.
2. In a medium bowl, toss the garbanzo beans with olive oil and za'atar seasoning.
3. Pour the beans into the air fryer basket and cook for 12 minutes, or until toasted as you like. Stir every 3 minutes while roasting.
4. Remove the beans from the air fryer basket into a serving bowl, top with fresh chopped parsley, and season with salt and pepper.

Zucchini With Parmesan Cheese

Servings: 6
Cooking Time: 30 Minutes
Ingredients:
- 6 medium zucchini, cut into sticks
- 6 tablespoons Parmesan cheese, grated
- 4 egg whites, beaten
- ½-teaspoon garlic powder
- 1 cup bread crumbs
- Pepper to taste
- Salt to taste

Directions:
1. At 400 degrees F/ 205 degrees C, heat your air fryer in advance.
2. Mix up the beaten egg whites with some salt and pepper in a suitable bowl.
3. In another bowl, add the garlic powder, bread crumbs, and Parmesan cheese and combine well.
4. Before rolling in the bread crumbs, dredge each zucchini stick in the egg whites.
5. Place the coated zucchini in the basket of your air fryer and for 20 minutes at 400 degrees F/ 205 degrees C.

Tomato & Basil Bruschetta

Servings: 4
Cooking Time: 15 Minutes
Ingredients:
- 3 red tomatoes, diced
- ½ ciabatta loaf
- 1 garlic clove, minced
- 1 fresh mozzarella ball, sliced
- 1 tbsp olive oil
- 10 fresh basil, chopped
- 1 tsp balsamic vinegar
- Pinch of salt

Directions:
1. Preheat air fryer to 370°F. Mix tomatoes, olive oil, salt, vinegar, basil, and garlic in a bowl until well combined. Cut the loaf into 6 slices, about 1-inch thick. Spoon the tomato mixture over the bread and top with one mozzarella slice. Repeat for all bruschettas. Put the bruschettas in the foil-lined frying basket and Bake for 5 minutes until golden. Serve.

Hot Cheese Bites

Servings: 6
Cooking Time: 30 Minutes + Cooling Time
Ingredients:
- 1/3 cup grated Velveeta cheese
- 1/3 cup shredded American cheese
- 4 oz cream cheese
- 2 jalapeños, finely chopped
- ½ cup bread crumbs
- 2 egg whites
- ½ cup all-purpose flour

Directions:
1. Preheat air fryer to 400°F. Blend the cream cheese, Velveeta, American cheese, and jalapeños in a bowl. Form the mixture into 1-inch balls. Arrange them on a sheet pan and freeze for 15 minutes.
2. Spread the flour, egg, and bread crumbs in 3 separate bowls. Once the cheese balls are removed from the freezer, dip them first in flour, then in the egg and finally in the crumbs. Air Fry for 8 minutes in the previously greased frying basket. Flip the balls and cook for another 4 minutes until crispy. Serve warm.

Rosemary Garlic Goat Cheese

Servings: 4
Cooking Time: 20 Minutes
Ingredients:
- 2 peeled garlic cloves roasted
- 1 ½ cups goat cheese
- ½ cup grated Parmesan
- 1 egg, beaten
- 1 tbsp olive oil
- 1 tbsp apple cider vinegar
- Salt and pepper to taste
- 1 tsp chopped rosemary

Directions:
1. Preheat air fryer to 350°F. Carefully squeeze the garlic into a bowl and mash it with a fork until a paste is formed. Stir in goat cheese, Parmesan, egg, olive oil, vinegar, salt, black pepper, and rosemary. Spoon the mixture into a baking dish, and place the dish in the frying basket. Air Fry for 7 minutes. Serve warm.

Kale Chips With Tex-mex Dip

Servings: 8
Cooking Time: 5 To 6 Minutes
Ingredients:
- 1 cup Greek yogurt
- 1 tablespoon chili powder
- ⅓ cup low-sodium salsa, well drained
- 1 bunch curly kale
- 1 teaspoon olive oil
- ¼ teaspoon coarse sea salt

Directions:
1. In a small bowl, combine the yogurt, chili powder, and drained salsa; refrigerate.
2. Rinse the kale thoroughly, and pat dry. Remove the stems and ribs from the kale, using a sharp knife. Cut or tear the leaves into 3-inch pieces.
3. Toss the kale with the olive oil in a large bowl.
4. Air-fry the kale in small batches until the leaves are crisp. This should take 5 to 6 minutes. Shake the basket once during cooking time.
5. As you remove the kale chips, sprinkle them with a bit of the sea salt.
6. When all of the kale chips are done, serve with the dip.

Okra Chips

Servings: 4
Cooking Time: 16 Minutes
Ingredients:
- 1¼ pounds Thin fresh okra pods, cut into 1-inch pieces
- 1½ tablespoons Vegetable or canola oil
- ¾ teaspoon Coarse sea salt or kosher salt

Directions:
1. Preheat the air fryer to 400°F.
2. Toss the okra, oil, and salt in a large bowl until the pieces are well and evenly coated.
3. When the machine is at temperature, pour the contents of the bowl into the basket. Air-fry, tossing several times, for 16 minutes, or until crisp and quite brown.
4. Pour the contents of the basket onto a wire rack. Cool for a couple of minutes before serving.

Cuban Sliders

Servings: 8
Cooking Time: 8 Minutes
Ingredients:
- 8 slices ciabatta bread, ¼-inch thick
- cooking spray
- 1 tablespoon brown mustard
- 6-8 ounces thin sliced leftover roast pork
- 4 ounces thin deli turkey
- ⅓ cup bread and butter pickle slices
- 2–3 ounces Pepper Jack cheese slices

Directions:
1. Spray one side of each slice of bread with butter or olive oil cooking spray.
2. Spread brown mustard on other side of each slice.
3. Layer pork roast, turkey, pickles, and cheese on 4 of the slices. Top with remaining slices.
4. Cook at 390°F for approximately 8minutes. The sandwiches should be golden brown.
5. Cut each slider in half to make 8 portions.

Garlic Edamame

Servings: 4
Cooking Time: 10 Minutes
Ingredients:
- Olive oil
- 1 (16-ounce) bag frozen edamame in pods

- ½ teaspoon salt
- ½ teaspoon garlic salt
- ¼ teaspoon freshly ground black pepper
- ½ teaspoon red pepper flakes (optional)

Directions:
1. Spray a fryer basket lightly with olive oil.
2. In a medium bowl, add the frozen edamame and lightly spray with olive oil. Toss to coat.
3. In a small bowl, mix together the salt, garlic salt, black pepper, and red pepper flakes (if using). Add the mixture to the edamame and toss until evenly coated.
4. Place half the edamame in the fryer basket. Do not overfill the basket.
5. Air fry for 5 minutes. Shake the basket and cook until the edamame is starting to brown and get crispy, 3 to 5 more minutes.
6. Repeat with the remaining edamame and serve immediately.

Bacon Pickle Spear Rolls

Servings: 4
Cooking Time: 20 Minutes
Ingredients:
- 4 dill pickle spears, sliced in half
- 8 bacon slices, halved
- 1 cup avocado mayonnaise

Directions:
1. Use a bacon slice to wrap a pickle spear.
2. Arrange the wraps in the basket of air fryer and cook them for 20 minutes at 400 degrees F/ 205 degrees C.
3. After dividing into bowls and serve as a snack with the mayonnaise.

Delicious Zucchini Crackers

Servings:12
Cooking Time: 20 Minutes
Ingredients:
- 1 cup zucchini, grated
- 2 tablespoons flax meal
- 1 teaspoon salt
- 3 tablespoons almond flour
- ¼ teaspoon baking powder
- ¼ teaspoon chili flakes
- 1 tablespoon xanthan gum
- 1 tablespoon butter, softened
- 1 egg, beaten
- Cooking spray

Directions:
1. Squeeze the zucchini to remove the vegetable juice and transfer to a large bowl.
2. Thoroughly mix up the flax meal, salt, almond flour, baking powder, chili flakes and xanthan gum.
3. Add butter and egg. Knead the non- sticky dough.
4. Place the mixture on the baking paper and cover with another baking paper.
5. Roll up the dough into the flat square.
6. After this, remove the baking paper from the dough surface.
7. Cut it on medium size crackers.
8. Prepare the air fryer basket by lining it with baking paper, and then put the crackers inside it.
9. Spray them with cooking spray. Cook them for 20 minutes at 355 degrees F/ 180 degrees C.
10. Serve and enjoy.

Cinnamon Apple Crisps

Servings: 1
Cooking Time: 22 Minutes
Ingredients:
- 1 large apple
- ½ teaspoon ground cinnamon
- 2 teaspoons avocado oil or coconut oil

Directions:
1. Preheat the air fryer to 300°F.
2. Using a mandolin or knife, slice the apples to ¼-inch thickness. Pat the apples dry with a paper towel or kitchen cloth. Sprinkle the apple slices with ground cinnamon. Spray or drizzle the oil over the top of the apple slices and toss to coat.
3. Place the apple slices in the air fryer basket. To allow for even cooking, don't overlap the slices; cook in batches if necessary.
4. Cook for 20 minutes, shaking the basket every 5 minutes. After 20 minutes, increase the air fryer temperature to 330°F and cook another 2 minutes, shaking the basket every 30 seconds. Remove the apples from the basket before they get too dark.
5. Spread the chips out onto paper towels to cool completely, at least 5 minutes. Repeat with the remaining apple slices until they're all cooked.

Bacon Butter

Servings:5
Cooking Time: 2 Minutes
Ingredients:
- ½ cup butter
- 3 oz bacon, chopped

Directions:
1. Preheat the air fryer to 400°F and put the bacon inside. Cook it for 8 minutes. Stir the bacon every 2 minutes. Meanwhile, soften the butter in the oven and put it in the butter mold. Add cooked bacon and churn the butter. Refrigerate the butter for 30 minutes.

Corn With Coriander And Parmesan Cheese

Servings: 2
Cooking Time: 15 Minutes
Ingredients:
- 2 ears corn, husked and cleaned
- 1 tablespoon melted butter
- 1 tablespoon fresh coriander, finely chopped
- 2 tablespoons Parmesan cheese, finely chopped

Directions:

1. Butter the corn and then arrange the corn in the air fryer.
2. Cook for 14 minutes at 400 degrees F/ 205 degrees C.
3. When done, serve warm and top with the Parmesan cheese and fresh coriander.
4. Bon appétit!

Eggplant Chips

Servings:4
Cooking Time: 25 Minutes
Ingredients:
- 1 eggplant, sliced
- 1 teaspoon garlic powder
- 1 tablespoon olive oil

Directions:
1. Mix the garlic powder and olive oil well.
2. Brush every eggplant slice with a garlic powder mixture.
3. Place the eggplant slices in the cooking pan of your air fryer. Cook them for 15 minutes at 400 degrees F/ 205 degrees C.
4. When the time is up, flip the eggplant slices and cook the other side for 10 minutes.
5. Serve and enjoy!

Veggie Salmon Nachos

Servings:6
Cooking Time: 9 To 12 Minutes
Ingredients:
- 2 ounces (57 g) baked no-salt corn tortilla chips
- 1 (5-ounce / 142-g) baked salmon fillet, flaked
- ½ cup canned low-sodium black beans, rinsed and drained
- 1 red bell pepper, chopped
- ½ cup grated carrot
- 1 jalapeño pepper, minced
- ⅓ cup shredded low-sodium low-fat Swiss cheese
- 1 tomato, chopped

Directions:
1. Preheat the air fryer to 360°F (182°C).
2. In a baking pan, layer the tortilla chips. Top with the salmon, black beans, red bell pepper, carrot, jalapeño, and Swiss cheese.
3. Bake in the air fryer for 9 to 12 minutes, or until the cheese is melted and starts to brown.
4. Top with the tomato and serve.

Arancini With Sun-dried Tomatoes And Mozzarella

Servings: 6
Cooking Time: 15 Minutes
Ingredients:
- 1 tablespoon olive oil
- ½ small onion, finely chopped
- 1 cup Arborio rice
- ¼ cup white wine or dry vermouth
- 1 cup vegetable or chicken stock
- 1½ cups water
- 1 teaspoon salt
- freshly ground black pepper
- ⅓ cup grated Parmigiano-Reggiano cheese
- 2 to 3 ounces mozzarella cheese
- 2 eggs, lightly beaten
- ¼ cup chopped oil-packed sun-dried tomatoes
- 1½ cups Italian seasoned breadcrumbs, divided
- olive oil
- marinara sauce, for serving

Directions:
1. .Start by cooking the Arborio rice.
2. Stovetop Method: Preheat a medium saucepan over medium heat. Add the olive oil and sauté the onion until it starts to become tender – about 5 minutes. Add the rice and stir well to coat all the grains of rice. Add the white wine or vermouth. Let this simmer and get absorbed by the rice. Then add the stock and water, cover, reduce the heat to low and simmer for 20 minutes.
3. Pressure-Cooker Method: Preheat the pressure cooker using the BROWN setting. Add the oil and cook the onion for a few minutes. Add the rice, wine, stock, water, salt and freshly ground black pepper, give everything one good stir and lock the lid in place. Pressure cook on HIGH for 7 minutes. Reduce the pressure with the QUICK-RELEASE method and carefully remove the lid.
4. Taste the rice to make sure it is tender. Season with salt and freshly ground black pepper and stir in the grated Parmigiano-Reggiano cheese. Spread the rice out onto a baking sheet to cool.
5. While the rice is cooling, cut the mozzarella into ¾-inch cubes.
6. Once the rice has cooled, combine the rice with the eggs, sun-dried tomatoes and ½ cup of the breadcrumbs. Place the remaining breadcrumbs in a shallow dish. Shape the rice mixture into 12 balls. Press a hole in the rice ball with your finger and push one or two cubes of mozzarella cheese into the hole. Mold the rice back into a ball, enclosing the cheese. Roll the finished rice balls in the breadcrumbs and place them on a baking sheet while you make the remaining rice balls. Spray or brush the rice balls with olive oil.
7. Preheat the air fryer to 380°F.
8. Cook 6 arancini at a time. Air-fry for 10 minutes. Gently turn the arancini over, brush or spray with oil again and air-fry for another 5 minutes. Serve warm with the marinara sauce.

Pork Pot Stickers With Yum Yum Sauce

Servings: 48
Cooking Time: 8 Minutes
Ingredients:
- 1 pound ground pork
- 2 cups shredded green cabbage
- ¼ cup shredded carrot

- ½ cup finely chopped water chestnuts
- 2 teaspoons minced fresh ginger
- ¼ cup hoisin sauce
- 2 tablespoons soy sauce
- 1 tablespoon sesame oil
- freshly ground black pepper
- 3 scallions, minced
- 48 round dumpling wrappers (or wonton wrappers with the corners cut off to make them round)
- 1 tablespoon vegetable oil
- soy sauce, for serving
- Yum Yum Sauce:
- 1½ cups mayonnaise
- 2 tablespoons sugar
- 3 tablespoons rice vinegar
- 1 teaspoon soy sauce
- 2 tablespoons ketchup
- 1½ teaspoons paprika
- ¼ teaspoon ground cayenne pepper
- ¼ teaspoon garlic powder

Directions:
1. Preheat a large sauté pan over medium-high heat. Add the ground pork and brown for a few minutes. Remove the cooked pork to a bowl using a slotted spoon and discard the fat from the pan. Return the cooked pork to the sauté pan and add the cabbage, carrots and water chestnuts. Sauté for a minute and then add the fresh ginger, hoisin sauce, soy sauce, sesame oil, and freshly ground black pepper. Sauté for a few more minutes, just until cabbage and carrots are soft. Then stir in the scallions and transfer the pork filling to a bowl to cool.
2. Make the pot stickers in batches of 1 Place 12 dumpling wrappers on a flat surface. Brush a little water around the perimeter of the wrappers. Place a rounded teaspoon of the filling into the center of each wrapper. Fold the wrapper over the filling, bringing the edges together to form a half moon, sealing the edges shut. Brush a little more water on the top surface of the sealed edge of the pot sticker. Make pleats in the dough around the sealed edge by pinching the dough and folding the edge over on itself. You should have about 5 to 6 pleats in the dough. Repeat this three times until you have 48 pot stickers. Freeze the pot stickers for 2 hours (or as long as 3 weeks in an airtight container).
3. Preheat the air fryer to 400°F.
4. Air-fry the pot stickers in batches of 16. Brush or spray the pot stickers with vegetable oil just before putting them in the air fryer basket. Air-fry for 8 minutes, turning the pot stickers once or twice during the cooking process.
5. While the pot stickers are cooking, combine all the ingredients for the Yum Yum sauce in a bowl. Serve the pot stickers warm with the Yum Yum sauce and soy sauce for dipping.

Apple Rollups

Servings: 8
Cooking Time: 5 Minutes
Ingredients:
- 8 slices whole wheat sandwich bread
- 4 ounces Colby Jack cheese, grated
- ½ small apple, chopped
- 2 tablespoons butter, melted

Directions:
1. Remove crusts from bread and flatten the slices with rolling pin. Don't be gentle. Press hard so that bread will be very thin.
2. Top bread slices with cheese and chopped apple, dividing the ingredients evenly.
3. Roll up each slice tightly and secure each with one or two toothpicks.
4. Brush outside of rolls with melted butter.
5. Place in air fryer basket and cook at 390°F for 5minutes, until outside is crisp and nicely browned.

Crispy Cajun Dill Pickle Chips

Servings:16
Cooking Time: 10 Minutes
Ingredients:
- ¼ cup all-purpose flour
- ½ cup panko bread crumbs
- 1 large egg, beaten
- 2 teaspoons Cajun seasoning
- 2 large dill pickles, sliced into 8 rounds each
- Cooking spray

Directions:
1. Preheat the air fryer to 390°F (199°C).
2. Place the all-purpose flour, panko bread crumbs, and egg into 3 separate shallow bowls, then stir the Cajun seasoning into the flour.
3. Dredge each pickle chip in the flour mixture, then the egg, and finally the bread crumbs. Shake off any excess, then place each coated pickle chip on a plate.
4. Spritz the air fryer basket with cooking spray, then place 8 pickle chips in the basket and air fry for 5 minutes, or until crispy and golden brown. Repeat this process with the remaining pickle chips.
5. Remove the chips and allow to slightly cool on a wire rack before serving.

Spicy Kale Chips With Yogurt Sauce

Servings:4
Cooking Time: 5 Minutes
Ingredients:
- 1 cup Greek yogurt
- 3 tablespoons lemon juice
- 2 tablespoons honey mustard
- ½ teaspoon dried oregano
- 1 bunch curly kale
- 2 tablespoons olive oil
- ½ teaspoon salt
- ⅛ teaspoon pepper

Directions:

1. In a small bowl, combine the yogurt, lemon juice, honey mustard, and oregano, and set aside.
2. Remove the stems and ribs from the kale with a sharp knife. Cut the leaves into 2- to 3-inch pieces.
3. Toss the kale with olive oil, salt, and pepper. Massage the oil into the leaves with your hands.
4. Air-fry the kale in batches until crisp, about 5 minutes, shaking the basket once during cooking time. Serve with the yogurt sauce.

Crispy & Healthy Kale Chips

Servings: 2
Cooking Time: 5 Minutes
Ingredients:
- 1 bunch of kale, remove stem and cut into pieces
- 1/2 tsp garlic powder
- 1 tsp olive oil
- 1/2 tsp salt

Directions:
1. Preheat the air fryer to 370°F.
2. Add all ingredients into the large bowl and toss well.
3. Transfer kale mixture into the air fryer basket and cook for 3 minutes.
4. Shake basket well and cook for 2 minutes more.
5. Serve and enjoy.

Olive & Pepper Tapenade

Servings: 4
Cooking Time: 10 Minutes
Ingredients:
- 1 red bell pepper
- 3 tbsp olive oil
- ½ cup black olives, chopped
- 1 garlic clove, minced
- ½ tsp dried oregano
- 1 tbsp white wine juice

Directions:
1. Preheat air fryer to 380°F. Lightly brush the outside of the bell pepper with some olive oil and put it in the frying basket. Roast for 5 minutes. Combine the remaining olive oil with olives, garlic, oregano, and white wine in a bowl. Remove the red pepper from the air fryer, then gently slice off the stem and discard the seeds. Chop into small pieces. Add the chopped pepper to the olive mixture and stir all together until combined. Serve and enjoy!

Cinnamon Sweet Potato Fries

Servings: 5
Cooking Time: 30 Minutes
Ingredients:
- 3 sweet potatoes
- 2 tsp butter, melted
- 1 tsp cinnamon
- Salt and pepper to taste

Directions:

1. Preheat air fryer to 400°F. Peel the potatoes and slice them thinly crosswise. Transfer the slices to a large bowl. Toss with butter, cinnamon, salt, and pepper until fully coated. Place half of the slices into the air fryer. Stacking is ok. Air Fry for 10 minutes. Shake the basket, and cook for another 10 -12 minutes until crispy. Serve hot.

Simple Curried Sweet Potato Fries

Servings: 3
Cooking Time: 20 Minutes
Ingredients:
- 2 small sweet potatoes, peel and cut into fry shape
- ¼ teaspoon coriander
- ½ teaspoon curry powder
- 2 tablespoons olive oil
- ¼ teaspoon salt

Directions:
1. Add all the recipe ingredients into the suitable mixing bowl and toss well.
2. Grease its air fryer basket with cooking spray.
3. Transfer sweet potato fries in the air fryer basket.
4. Cook for 20 minutes at 370 degrees F/ 185 degrees C. Shake halfway through.
5. Serve and enjoy.

Baked Ricotta

Servings: 2
Cooking Time: 15 Minutes
Ingredients:
- 1 (15-ounce / 425-g) container whole milk Ricotta cheese
- 3 tablespoons grated Parmesan cheese, divided
- 2 tablespoons extra-virgin olive oil
- 1 teaspoon chopped fresh thyme leaves
- 1 teaspoon grated lemon zest
- 1 clove garlic, crushed with press
- ¼ teaspoon salt
- ¼ teaspoon pepper
- Toasted baguette slices or crackers, for serving

Directions:
1. Preheat the air fryer to 380ºF (193ºC).
2. To get the baking dish in and out of the air fryer, create a sling using a 24-inch length of foil, folded lengthwise into thirds.
3. Whisk together the Ricotta, 2 tablespoons of the Parmesan, oil, thyme, lemon zest, garlic, salt, and pepper. Pour into a baking dish. Cover the dish tightly with foil.
4. Place the sling under dish and lift by the ends into the air fryer, tucking the ends of the sling around the dish. Bake for 10 minutes. Remove the foil cover and sprinkle with the remaining 1 tablespoon of the Parmesan. Air fry for 5 more minutes, or until bubbly at edges and the top is browned.
5. Serve warm with toasted baguette slices or crackers.

Cajun Sweet Potato Tots

Servings:
Cooking Time: 31 Minutes
Ingredients:
- 2 sweet potatoes, peeled
- ½ teaspoon Cajun seasoning
- Salt

Directions:
1. Add water in large pot and bring to boil. Add sweet potatoes in pot and boil for almost 15 minutes. Drain well.
2. Grated boil sweet potatoes into a suitable bowl using a grated.
3. Add Cajun seasoning and salt in grated sweet potatoes and mix until well combined.
4. Grease its air fryer basket with cooking spray.
5. Make small tot of sweet potato mixture and place in air fryer basket.
6. Cook at almost 400 degrees F/ 205 degrees C for 8 minutes. Turn tots to another side and cook for 8 minutes more.
7. Serve and enjoy.

Fried Goat Cheese

Servings: 3
Cooking Time: 4 Minutes
Ingredients:
- 7 ounces 1- to 1½-inch-diameter goat cheese log
- 2 Large egg(s)
- 1¾ cups Plain dried bread crumbs (gluten-free, if a concern)
- Vegetable oil spray

Directions:
1. Slice the goat cheese log into ½-inch-thick rounds. Set these flat on a small cutting board, a small baking sheet, or a large plate. Freeze uncovered for 30 minutes.
2. Preheat the air fryer to 400°F.
3. Set up and fill two shallow soup plates or small pie plates on your counter: one in which you whisk the egg(s) until uniform and the other for the bread crumbs.
4. Take the goat cheese rounds out of the freezer. With clean, dry hands, dip one round in the egg(s) to coat it on all sides. Let the excess egg slip back into the rest, then dredge the round in the bread crumbs, turning it to coat all sides, even the edges. Repeat this process—egg, then bread crumbs—for a second coating. Coat both sides of the round and its edges with vegetable oil spray, then set it aside. Continue double-dipping, double-dredging, and spraying the remaining rounds.
5. Place the rounds in one layer in the basket. Air-fry undisturbed for 4 minutes, or until lightly browned and crunchy. Do not overcook. Some of the goat cheese may break through the crust. A few little breaks are fine but stop the cooking before the coating reaches structural failure.
6. Remove the basket from the machine and set aside for 3 minutes. Use a nonstick-safe spatula, and maybe a flatware fork for balance, to transfer the rounds to a wire rack. Cool for 5 minutes more before serving.

No-guilty Spring Rolls

Servings: 6
Cooking Time: 20 Minutes
Ingredients:
- 2 cups shiitake mushrooms, thinly sliced
- 4 cups green cabbage, shredded
- 4 tsp sesame oil
- 6 garlic cloves, minced
- 1 tbsp grated ginger
- 1 cup grated carrots
- Salt to taste
- 16 rice paper wraps
- ½ tsp ground cumin
- ½ tsp ground coriander

Directions:
1. Warm the sesame oil in a pan over medium heat. Add garlic, ginger, mushrooms, cabbage, carrots, cumin, coriander, and salt and stir-fry for 3-4 minutes or until the cabbage is wilted. Remove from heat. Get a piece of rice paper, wet with water, and lay it on a flat, non-absorbent surface. Place ¼ cup of the filling in the middle, then fold the bottom over the filling and fold the sides in. Roll up to make a mini burrito. Repeat until you have the number of spring rolls you want.
2. Preheat air fryer to 390°F. Place the spring rolls in the greased frying basket. Spray the tops with cooking oil and Air Fry for 8-10 minutes until golden. Serve immediately.

Jalapeño & Mozzarella Stuffed Mushrooms

Servings: 4
Cooking Time: 30 Minutes
Ingredients:
- 16 button mushrooms
- 1/3 cup salsa
- 3 garlic cloves, minced
- 1 onion, finely chopped
- 1 jalapeño pepper, minced
- ⅛ tsp cayenne pepper
- 3 tbsp shredded mozzarella
- 2 tsp olive oil

Directions:
1. Preheat air fryer to 350°F. Cut the stem off the mushrooms, then slice them finely. Set the caps aside. Combine the salsa, garlic, onion, jalapeño, cayenne, and mozzarella cheese in a bowl, then add the stems. Fill the mushroom caps with the mixture, making sure to overfill so the mix is coming out of the top. Drizzle with olive oil. Place the caps in the air fryer and Bake for 8-12 minutes.

The filling should be hot and the mushrooms soft. Serve warm.

Potato Pastries

Servings: 8
Cooking Time: 37 Minutes
Ingredients:
- 2 large potatoes, peeled
- 1 tablespoon olive oil
- ½ cup carrot, peeled and chopped
- ½ cup onion, chopped
- 2 garlic cloves, minced
- 1 tablespoon fresh ginger, minced
- ½ cup green peas, shelled
- Salt and ground black pepper, as needed
- 3 puff pastry sheets

Directions:
1. Boil water in a suitable pan, then put the potatoes and cook for about 15-20 minutes
2. Drain the potatoes well and then mash the potatoes.
3. Heat the oil over medium heat in a skillet, then add the carrot, onion, ginger, garlic and sauté for about 4-5 minutes.
4. Then drain all the fat from the skillet.
5. Stir in the mashed potatoes, peas, salt and black pepper. Continue to cook for about 1-2 minutes.
6. Remove the potato mixture from heat and set aside to cool completely.
7. After placing the puff pastry onto a smooth surface, cut each puff pastry sheet into four pieces and cut each piece into a round shape.
8. Add about 2 tablespoons of veggie filling over each pastry round.
9. Use your wet finger to moisten the edges.
10. To seal the filling, fold each pastry round in half.
11. Firmly press the edges with a fork.
12. Set the temperature setting to 390 degrees F/ 200 degrees C.
13. Arrange the pastries in the basket of your air fryer and air fry for about 5 minutes at 390 minutes.
14. Work in 2 batches.
15. Serve.

Bbq Pork Ribs

Servings:2
Cooking Time: 35 Minutes
Ingredients:
- 1 tablespoon kosher salt
- 1 tablespoon dark brown sugar
- 1 tablespoon sweet paprika
- 1 teaspoon garlic powder
- 1 teaspoon onion powder
- 1 teaspoon poultry seasoning
- ½ teaspoon mustard powder
- ½ teaspoon freshly ground black pepper
- 2¼ pounds (1 kg) individually cut St. Louis–style pork spareribs

Directions:
1. Preheat the air fryer to 350ºF (177ºC).
2. In a large bowl, whisk together the salt, brown sugar, paprika, garlic powder, onion powder, poultry seasoning, mustard powder, and pepper. Add the ribs and toss. Rub the seasonings into them with your hands until they're fully coated.
3. Arrange the ribs in the air fryer basket, standing up on their ends and leaned up against the wall of the basket and each other. Roast for 35 minutes, or until the ribs are tender inside and golden brown and crisp on the outside. Transfer the ribs to plates and serve hot.

Korean Brussels Sprouts

Servings: 4
Cooking Time: 20 Minutes
Ingredients:
- 1 lb Brussels sprouts
- 1 ½ tbsp maple syrup
- 1 ½ tsp white miso
- 1 tsp toasted sesame oil
- 1 ½ tsp soy sauce
- 2 garlic cloves, minced
- 1 tsp grated fresh ginger
- ½ tsp Gochugaru chili flakes

Directions:
1. Preheat air fryer to 390°F. Place the Brussels sprouts in the greased basket, spray with oil and Air Fry for 10-14 minutes, tossing once until crispy, tender, and golden.
2. In a bowl, combine maple syrup and miso. Whisk until smooth. Add the sesame oil, soy sauce, garlic, ginger, and Gochugaru flakes. Stir well. When the Brussels sprouts are done, add them to the bowl and toss with the sauce. Serve immediately.

Chapter 4: Bread And Breakfast Recipes

Spinach And Mushroom Mini Quiche

Servings:4
Cooking Time: 15 Minutes
Ingredients:
- 1 teaspoon olive oil, plus more for spraying
- 1 cup coarsely chopped mushrooms
- 1 cup fresh baby spinach, shredded
- 4 eggs, beaten
- ½ cup shredded Cheddar cheese
- ½ cup shredded mozzarella cheese
- ¼ teaspoon salt
- ¼ teaspoon black pepper

Directions:
1. Spray 4 silicone baking cups with olive oil and set aside.
2. In a medium sauté pan over medium heat, warm 1 teaspoon of olive oil. Add the mushrooms and sauté until soft, 3 to 4 minutes.
3. Add the spinach and cook until wilted, 1 to 2 minutes. Set aside.
4. In a medium bowl, whisk together the eggs, Cheddar cheese, mozzarella cheese, salt, and pepper.
5. Gently fold the mushrooms and spinach into the egg mixture.
6. Pour ¼ of the mixture into each silicone baking cup.
7. Place the baking cups into the fryer basket and air fry for 5 minutes. Stir the mixture in each ramekin slightly and air fry until the egg has set, an additional 3 to 5 minutes.

Pancake For Two

Servings:2
Cooking Time: 30 Minutes
Ingredients:
- 1 cup blanched finely ground almond flour
- 2 tablespoons granular erythritol
- 1 tablespoon salted butter, melted
- 1 large egg
- ⅓ cup unsweetened almond milk
- ½ teaspoon vanilla extract

Directions:
1. In a large bowl, mix all ingredients together, then pour half the batter into an ungreased 6" round nonstick baking dish.
2. Place dish into air fryer basket. Adjust the temperature to 320°F and set the timer for 15 minutes. The pancake will be golden brown on top and firm, and a toothpick inserted in the center will come out clean when done. Repeat with remaining batter.
3. Slice in half in dish and serve warm.

Vegetarian Quinoa Cups

Servings: 6
Cooking Time: 25 Minutes
Ingredients:
- 1 carrot, chopped
- 1 zucchini, chopped
- 4 asparagus, chopped
- ¾ cup quinoa flour
- 2 tbsp lemon juice
- ¼ cup nutritional yeast
- ¼ tsp garlic powder
- Salt and pepper to taste

Directions:
1. Preheat air fryer to 340°F. Combine the vegetables, quinoa flour, water, lemon juice, nutritional yeast, garlic powder, salt, and pepper in a medium bowl, and mix well. Divide the mixture between 6 cupcake molds. Place the filled molds into the air fryer and Bake for 20 minutes, or until the tops are lightly browned and a toothpick inserted into the center comes out clean. Serve cooled.

Strawberry Tarts

Servings: 6
Cooking Time: 10 Minutes
Ingredients:
- 2 refrigerated piecrusts
- ½ cup strawberry preserves
- 1 teaspoon cornstarch
- Cooking oil spray
- ½ cup low-fat vanilla yogurt
- 1-ounce cream cheese, at room temperature
- 3 tablespoons confectioners' sugar
- Rainbow sprinkles, for decorating

Directions:
1. Place the piecrusts on a flat surface.
2. Cut each piecrust into 3 rectangles using a knife or pizza cutter, for 6 in total.
3. In a suitable bowl, mix cornstarch and the preserves. Mix well.
4. Scoop 1 tablespoon of the strawberry filling onto the top ½ of each piece of piecrust.
5. Fold the bottom of each piece to enclose the filling inside.
6. Press along the edges of each tart to seal using the back of a fork.
7. At 350 degrees F/ 175 degrees C, preheat your air fryer.
8. Once your air fryer is preheated, spray the crisper plate with cooking oil.
9. Work in batches, spray the breakfast tarts with cooking oil and place them into the basket in a single layer.
10. Set the air fryer's temperature to 375 degrees F/ 190 degrees C, and set the time to 10 minutes.
11. 1
12. Repeat the same steps with remaining ingredients. 1
13. In a suitable bowl, stir together the cream cheese, yogurt, and confectioners' sugar. 1
14. Top the breakfast tarts with the frosting and garnish with sprinkles.

Dill Eggs In Wonton

Servings: 4
Cooking Time: 4 Minutes
Ingredients:
- 2 eggs, hard-boiled, peeled
- 1 tablespoon cream cheese
- 1 tablespoon fresh dill, chopped
- 1 teaspoon ground black pepper
- 4 wontons wrap
- 1 egg white, whisked
- 1 teaspoon sesame oil

Directions:
1. Before cooking, heat your air fryer to 395 degrees F/ 200 degrees C.
2. Grease the air fryer basket with sesame oil.
3. Chop the hard-boiled eggs and in a bowl, mix together with dill, ground pepper, and cream cheese.
4. Separate the egg mixture onto wonton wraps and roll them into rolls.
5. Use the whisked egg white to brush the wontons.
6. Arrange the wontons evenly on the greased air fryer basket.
7. Cook in your air fryer at 395 degrees F/ 200 degrees C for 2 minutes from each side or until golden brown flip to the other side.

English Scones

Servings: 8
Cooking Time: 8 Minutes
Ingredients:
- 2 cups all-purpose flour
- 1 tablespoon baking powder
- ½ teaspoon salt
- 2 tablespoons sugar
- ¼ cup unsalted butter
- ⅔ cup plus 1 tablespoon whole milk, divided

Directions:
1. Preheat the air fryer to 380°F.
2. In a large bowl, whisk together the flour, baking powder, salt, and sugar. Using a pastry blender or your fingers, cut in the butter until pea-size crumbles appear. Make a well in the center and pour in ⅔ cup of the milk. Quickly mix the batter until a ball forms. Knead the dough 3 times.
3. Place the dough onto a floured surface and, using your hands or a rolling pin, flatten the dough until it's ¾ inch thick. Using a biscuit cutter or drinking glass, cut out 10 circles, reforming the dough and flattening as needed to use up the batter.
4. Brush the tops lightly with the remaining 1 tablespoon of milk.
5. Place the scones into the air fryer basket. Cook for 8 minutes or until golden brown and cooked in the center.

English Pumpkin Egg Bake

Servings: 2
Cooking Time: 10 Minutes
Ingredients:
- 2 eggs
- ½ cup milk
- 2 cups flour
- 2 tablespoons cider vinegar
- 2 teaspoons baking powder
- 1 tablespoon sugar
- 1 cup pumpkin purée
- 1 teaspoon cinnamon powder
- 1 teaspoon baking soda
- 1 tablespoon olive oil

Directions:
1. Preheat the air fryer to 300°F (149°C).
2. Crack the eggs into a bowl and beat with a whisk. Combine with the milk, flour, cider vinegar, baking powder, sugar, pumpkin purée, cinnamon powder, and baking soda, mixing well.
3. Grease a baking tray with oil. Add the mixture and transfer into the air fryer. Bake for 10 minutes.
4. Serve warm.

Strawberry And Peach Toast

Servings: 4
Cooking Time: 2 Minutes
Ingredients:
- 2-4 slices bread
- Strawberries, as needed
- 1 peach, corned and sliced
- 1 teaspoon sugar
- Cooking spray
- ¼ cup cream cheese
- 1 teaspoon cinnamon

Directions:
1. Prepare all the recipe ingredients from the list.
2. Spray both sides of the bread with olive oil. Place in the preheated air fryer basket and Cook at almost 375 degrees F/ 190 degrees C for 1 minute on each side.
3. Slice strawberries and peaches and prepare the rest of the ingredients.
4. Spread toast thickly of cream cheese, garnish with strawberries and peach, sprinkle with almonds and cinnamon mixture if you like.
5. Serve with smoothies, coffee or tea.

Spinach With Scrambled Eggs

Servings: 2
Cooking Time: 10 Minutes
Ingredients:
- 2 tablespoons olive oil
- 4 eggs, whisked
- 5 ounces (142 g) fresh spinach, chopped
- 1 medium tomato, chopped

Quick & Simple Tower Dual Basket Air Fryer Cookbook

- 1 teaspoon fresh lemon juice
- ½ teaspoon coarse salt
- ½ teaspoon ground black pepper
- ½ cup of fresh basil, roughly chopped

Directions:
1. Grease a baking pan with the oil, tilting it to spread the oil around. Preheat the air fryer to 280ºF (138ºC).
2. Mix the remaining ingredients, apart from the basil leaves, whisking well until everything is completely combined.
3. Bake in the air fryer for 10 minutes.
4. Top with fresh basil leaves before serving.

Bacon And Broccoli Bread Pudding

Servings: 4
Cooking Time: 48 Minutes
Ingredients:
- ½ pound (227 g) thick cut bacon, cut into ¼-inch pieces
- 3 cups brioche bread, cut into ½-inch cubes
- 2 tablespoons butter, melted
- 3 eggs
- 1 cup milk
- ½ teaspoon salt
- Freshly ground black pepper, to taste
- 1 cup frozen broccoli florets, thawed and chopped
- 1½ cups grated Swiss cheese

Directions:
1. Preheat the air fryer to 400ºF (204ºC).
2. Air fry the bacon for 8 minutes until crispy, shaking the basket a few times to help it air fry evenly. Remove the bacon and set it aside on a paper towel.
3. Air fry the brioche bread cubes for 2 minutes to dry and toast lightly.
4. Butter a cake pan. Combine all the ingredients in a large bowl and toss well. Transfer the mixture to the buttered cake pan, cover with aluminum foil and refrigerate the bread pudding overnight, or for at least 8 hours.
5. Remove the cake pan from the refrigerator an hour before you plan to bake and let it sit on the countertop to come to room temperature.
6. Preheat the air fryer to 330ºF (166ºC). Transfer the covered cake pan to the basket of the air fryer, lowering the pan into the basket. Fold the ends of the aluminum foil over the top of the pan before returning the basket to the air fryer.
7. Air fry for 20 minutes. Remove the foil and air fry for an additional 20 minutes. If the top browns a little too much before the custard has set, simply return the foil to the pan. The bread pudding has cooked through when a skewer inserted into the center comes out clean.
8. Serve warm.

Eggless Mung Bean Tart

Servings: 2
Cooking Time: 20 Minutes
Ingredients:
- 2 tsp soy sauce
- 1 tsp lime juice
- 1 large garlic clove, minced or pressed
- ½ tsp red chili flakes
- ½ cup mung beans, soaked
- Salt and pepper to taste
- ½ minced shallot
- 1 green onion, chopped

Directions:
1. Preheat the air fryer to 390°F. Add the soy sauce, lime juice, garlic, and chili flakes to a bowl and stir. Set aside. Place the drained beans in a blender along with ½ cup of water, salt, and pepper. Blend until smooth. Stir in shallot and green onion, but do not blend.
2. Pour the batter into a greased baking pan. Bake for 15 minutes in the air fryer until golden. A knife inserted in the center should come out clean. Once cooked, cut the "quiche" into quarters. Drizzle with sauce and serve.

Chives Omelet

Servings: 4
Cooking Time: 20 Minutes
Ingredients:
- 6 eggs, whisked
- 1 cup chives, chopped
- Cooking spray
- 1 cup mozzarella, shredded
- Salt and black pepper to the taste

Directions:
1. In a bowl, mix all the ingredients except the cooking spray and whisk well. Grease a pan that fits your air fryer with the cooking spray, pour the eggs mix, spread, put the pan into the machine and cook at 350°F for 20 minutes. Divide the omelet between plates and serve for breakfast.

Cherry Beignets

Servings: 4
Cooking Time: 25 Minutes
Ingredients:
- 2 tsp baking soda
- 1 ½ cups flour
- ¼ tsp salt
- 3 tbsp brown sugar
- 4 tsp chopped dried cherries
- ½ cup buttermilk
- 1 egg
- 3 tbsp melted lard

Directions:
1. Preheat air fryer to 330°F. Combine baking soda, flour, salt, and brown sugar in a bowl. Then stir in dried cherries. In a small bowl, beat together buttermilk and

egg until smooth. Pour in with the dry ingredients and stir until just moistened.
2. On a floured work surface, pat the dough into a square. Divide it by cutting into 16 pieces. Lightly brush with melted lard. Arrange the squares in the frying basket, without overlapping. Air Fry until puffy and golden brown, 5-8 minutes. Serve.

Sourdough Croutons

Servings: 4
Cooking Time: 6 Minutes
Ingredients:
- 4 cups cubed sourdough bread, 1-inch cubes
- 1 tablespoon olive oil
- 1 teaspoon fresh thyme leaves
- ¼ teaspoon salt
- Freshly ground black pepper, to taste

Directions:
1. Combine all ingredients in a bowl.
2. Preheat the air fryer to 400ºF (204ºC).
3. Toss the bread cubes into the air fryer and air fry for 6 minutes, shaking the basket once or twice while they cook.
4. Serve warm.

Orange Trail Oatmeal

Servings: 4
Cooking Time: 20 Minutes
Ingredients:
- 1 ½ cups quick-cooking oats
- 1/3 cup light brown sugar
- 1 egg
- 1 tsp orange zest
- 1 tbsp orange juice
- 2 tbsp whole milk
- 2 tbsp honey
- 2 tbsp butter, melted
- 2 tsp dried cranberries
- 1 tsp dried blueberries
- 1/8 tsp ground nutmeg
- Salt to taste
- ¼ cup pecan pieces

Directions:
1. Preheat air fryer at 325ºF. Combine the oats, sugar, egg, orange zest, orange juice, milk, honey, butter, dried cranberries, dried blueberries, nutmeg, salt, and pecan in a bowl. Press mixture into a greased cake pan. Place cake pan in the frying basket and Roast for 8 minutes. Let cool onto for 5 minutes before slicing. Serve.

Bunless Breakfast Turkey Burgers

Servings: 4
Cooking Time: 15 Minutes
Ingredients:
- 1 pound ground turkey breakfast sausage
- ½ teaspoon salt
- ¼ teaspoon ground black pepper
- ¼ cup seeded and chopped green bell pepper
- 2 tablespoons mayonnaise
- 1 medium avocado, peeled, pitted, and sliced

Directions:
1. In a large bowl, mix sausage with salt, black pepper, bell pepper, and mayonnaise. Form meat into four patties.
2. Place patties into ungreased air fryer basket. Adjust the temperature to 370°F and set the timer for 15 minutes, turning patties halfway through cooking. Burgers will be done when dark brown and they have an internal temperature of at least 165°F.
3. Serve burgers topped with avocado slices on four medium plates.

Cinnamon Pear Oat Muffins

Servings: 6
Cooking Time: 30 Minutes + Cooling Time
Ingredients:
- ½ cup apple sauce
- 1 large egg
- 1/3 cup brown sugar
- 2 tbsp butter, melted
- ½ cup milk
- 11/3 cups rolled oats
- 1 tsp ground cinnamon
- ½ tsp baking powder
- Pinch of salt
- ½ cup diced peeled pears

Directions:
1. Preheat the air fryer to 350°F. Place the apple sauce, egg, brown sugar, melted butter, and milk into a bowl and mix to combine. Stir in the oats, cinnamon, baking powder, and salt and mix well, then fold in the pears.
2. Grease 6 silicone muffin cups with baking spray, then spoon the batter in equal portions into the cups. Put the muffin cups in the frying basket and Bake for 13-18 minutes or until set. Leave to cool for 15 minutes. Serve.

Cheddar Soufflés

Servings: 4
Cooking Time: 12 Minutes
Ingredients:
- 3 large eggs, whites and yolks separated
- ¼ teaspoon cream of tartar
- ½ cup shredded sharp Cheddar cheese
- 3 ounces cream cheese, softened

Directions:
1. In a large bowl, beat egg whites together with cream of tartar until soft peaks form, about 2 minutes.
2. In a separate medium bowl, beat egg yolks, Cheddar, and cream cheese together until frothy, about 1 minute. Add egg yolk mixture to whites, gently folding until combined.

3. Pour mixture evenly into four 4" ramekins greased with cooking spray. Place ramekins into air fryer basket. Adjust the temperature to 350°F and set the timer for 12 minutes. Eggs will be browned on the top and firm in the center when done. Serve warm.

Egg Peppers Cups

Servings: 12
Cooking Time: 12 Minutes
Ingredients:
- 6 green bell peppers
- 12 eggs
- ½ teaspoon ground black pepper
- ½ teaspoon chili flakes

Directions:
1. Before cooking, heat your air fryer to 395 degrees F/ 200 degrees C.
2. While preheating, cut the green bell peppers into halves and remove the seeds.
3. In the bell pepper halves, whisk the eggs.
4. Sprinkle the top with chili flakes and ground black pepper.
5. Arrange evenly the bell pepper halves onto a suitable baking pan.
6. Cook the egg pepper cups in the preheated air fryer for 4 minutes. (2 to 3 halves per batch)

Cornflakes Toast Sticks

Servings: 4
Cooking Time: 6 Minutes
Ingredients:
- 2 eggs
- ½ cup milk
- ⅛ teaspoon salt
- ½ teaspoon pure vanilla extract
- ¾ cup crushed cornflakes
- 6 slices sandwich bread, each slice cut into 4 strips
- Maple syrup, for dipping
- Cooking spray

Directions:
1. Preheat the air fryer to 390ºF (199ºC).
2. In a small bowl, beat together the eggs, milk, salt, and vanilla.
3. Put crushed cornflakes on a plate or in a shallow dish.
4. Dip bread strips in egg mixture, shake off excess, and roll in cornflake crumbs.
5. Spray both sides of bread strips with oil.
6. Put bread strips in air fryer basket in a single layer.
7. Air fry for 6 minutes or until golden brown.
8. Repeat steps 5 and 6 to air fry remaining French toast sticks.
9. Serve with maple syrup.

Carrot Orange Muffins

Servings: 12
Cooking Time: 12 Minutes
Ingredients:
- 1½ cups all-purpose flour
- ½ cup granulated sugar
- ½ teaspoon ground cinnamon
- 2 teaspoons baking powder
- ¼ teaspoon baking soda
- ½ teaspoon salt
- 2 large eggs
- ¼ cup vegetable oil
- ⅓ cup orange marmalade
- 2 cups grated carrots

Directions:
1. Preheat the air fryer to 320°F.
2. In a large bowl, whisk together the flour, sugar, cinnamon, baking powder, baking soda, and salt; set aside.
3. In a separate bowl, whisk together the eggs, vegetable oil, orange marmalade, and grated carrots.
4. Make a well in the dry ingredients; then pour the wet ingredients into the well of the dry ingredients. Using a rubber spatula, mix the ingredients for 1 minute or until slightly lumpy.
5. Using silicone muffin liners, fill 6 muffin liners two-thirds full.
6. Carefully place the muffin liners in the air fryer basket and bake for 12 minutes (or until the tops are browned and a toothpick inserted in the center comes out clean). Carefully remove the muffins from the basket and repeat with remaining batter.
7. Serve warm.

Simple Cheddar-omelet

Servings: 2
Cooking Time: 10 Minutes
Ingredients:
- 4 eggs
- 4 tablespoons cheddar, grated cheese
- ½ green onions, sliced
- ¼ tablespoon black pepper
- 1 tablespoon olive oil

Directions:
1. Prepare all the recipe ingredients from the list.
2. Whisk the eggs along with the black pepper.
3. Preheat the air fryer at about 350 degrees F/ 175 degrees C.
4. Sprinkle your air fryer basket with olive oil and add the egg mixture and the green onions.
5. Air fry for 8 to 10 min. Top with the cheddar, grated cheese.
6. Serve and Enjoy.

Mixed Pepper Hash With Mozzarella Cheese

Servings: 4
Cooking Time: 20 Minutes
Ingredients:
- 1 red bell pepper, cut into strips
- 1 green bell pepper, cut into strips
- 1 orange bell pepper, cut into strips
- 4 eggs, whisked
- Salt and black pepper to the taste
- 2 tablespoons mozzarella, shredded
- Cooking spray

Directions:
1. Mix the all the bell peppers, pepper, salt, and the eggs in a mixing bowl.
2. Toss well to combine.
3. Before cooking, heat your air fryer to 350 degrees F/ 175 degrees C.
4. Gently grease a baking pan that fits in your air fryer with cooking spray.
5. Pour in the egg mixture and spread it well.
6. Top the mixture with Mozzarella and cook in the preheated air fryer for 20 minutes.
7. When cooked, remove from the air fryer and serve hot on plates.
8. Enjoy your breakfast!

Vegetable Quiche

Servings: 2 Servings
Cooking Time: 20 Minutes
Ingredients:
- 2 large eggs
- ½ cup of heavy cream
- 6–8 small broccoli florets
- 2 tablespoons of grated cheddar
- Pinch of salt and black pepper, to taste

Directions:
1. Preheat your air fryer to 325°F. Lightly grease two 5-inch ceramic dishes with oil.
2. Put eggs, heavy cream, salt, and black pepper into a mixing bowl. Whisk it well.
3. Put broccoli florets on the dish's bottom and pour the egg mixture over them.
4. Cook it at 325°F for 10 minutes.* Check the readiness using a toothpick; it should come out clean after inserting in the center.
5. Serve warm and enjoy your Vegetable Quiche!

Cheddar Biscuits With Nutmeg

Servings: 4
Cooking Time: 8 Minutes
Ingredients:
- ½ cup almond flour
- ¼ cup Cheddar cheese, shredded
- ¾ teaspoon salt
- 1 egg, beaten
- 1 tablespoon mascarpone
- 1 tablespoon coconut oil, melted
- ¾ teaspoon baking powder
- ½ teaspoon apple cider vinegar
- ¼ teaspoon ground nutmeg

Directions:
1. Mix the almond flour, baking powder, salt, and ground nutmeg in a big bowl.
2. Place apple cider vinegar, egg, mascarpone, and coconut oil inside the bowl.
3. Add in cheese and make a dough. Knead until soft.
4. Divide into small balls to make the biscuits.
5. Before cooking, heat your air fryer to 400 degrees F/ 205 degrees C.
6. Prepare your air fryer basket by lining it with parchment paper.
7. Transfer the cheese biscuits onto the parchment paper. Cook the cheese biscuits in your air fryer at 400 degrees F/ 205 degrees C until golden brown, for 8 minutes or more.
8. Halfway cooking, check the biscuits to avoid burning.
9. Serve.

Medium Rare Simple Salt And Pepper Steak

Servings: 3
Cooking Time: 30 Minutes
Ingredients:
- 1 ½ pounds skirt steak
- Salt and pepper to taste

Directions:
1. Preheat the air fryer at 390°F.
2. Place the grill pan accessory in the air fryer.
3. Season the skirt steak with salt and pepper.
4. Place on the grill pan and cook for 15 minutes per batch.
5. Flip the meat halfway through the cooking time.

Spinach Bacon Spread

Servings: 4
Cooking Time: 10 Minutes
Ingredients:
- 2 tablespoons coconut cream
- 3 cups spinach leaves
- 2 tablespoons cilantro
- 2 tablespoons bacon, cooked and crumbled
- Salt and black pepper to the taste

Directions:
1. Combine coconut cream, spinach leaves, salt, and black pepper in a suitable baking pan.
2. Transfer the baking pan into your air fryer and cook at 360 degrees F/ 180 degrees C for 10 minutes.
3. When cooked, transfer to a blender and pulse well.
4. To serve, sprinkle the bacon on the top of the mixture.

Apple & Turkey Breakfast Sausages

Servings: 4
Cooking Time: 15 Minutes
Ingredients:
- ½ tsp coriander seeds, crushed
- 1 tbsp chopped rosemary
- 1 tbsp chopped thyme
- Salt and pepper to taste
- 1 tsp fennel seeds, crushed
- ¾ tsp smoked paprika
- ½ tsp garlic powder
- ½ tsp shallot powder
- ⅛ tsp red pepper flakes
- 1 pound ground turkey
- ½ cup minced apples

Directions:
1. Combine all of the seasonings in a bowl. Add turkey and apple and blend seasonings in well with your hands. Form patties about 3 inches in diameter and ¼ inch thick.
2. Preheat air fryer to 400°F. Arrange patties in a single layer on the greased frying basket. Air Fry for 10 minutes, flipping once until brown and cooked through. Serve.

Yummy Bagel Breakfast

Servings: 5-6
Cooking Time: 6 Minutes
Ingredients:
- 2 bagels, make halves
- 4 teaspoons butter

Directions:
1. On a flat kitchen surface, plug your air fryer and turn it on.
2. Preheat your air fryer for about 4-5 minutes to 370 degrees F/ 185 degrees C.
3. Gently coat your air frying basket with cooking oil or spray.
4. Place the bagels to the basket.
5. Transfer the basket in the air fryer. Let it cook for the next 3 minutes.
6. Remove the basket; spread the butter over the bagels and cook for 3 more minutes.
7. Serve warm!

Ham And Corn Muffins

Servings: 8
Cooking Time: 6 Minutes
Ingredients:
- ¾ cup yellow cornmeal
- ¼ cup flour
- 1½ teaspoons baking powder
- ¼ teaspoon salt
- 1 egg, beaten
- 2 tablespoons canola oil
- ½ cup milk
- ½ cup shredded sharp Cheddar cheese
- ½ cup diced ham

Directions:
1. Preheat the air fryer to 390°F (199°C).
2. In a medium bowl, stir together the cornmeal, flour, baking powder, and salt.
3. Add the egg, oil, and milk to dry ingredients and mix well.
4. Stir in shredded cheese and diced ham.
5. Divide batter among 8 parchment-paper-lined muffin cups.
6. Put 4 filled muffin cups in air fryer basket and bake for 5 minutes.
7. Reduce temperature to 330°F (166°C) and bake for 1 minute or until a toothpick inserted in center of the muffin comes out clean.
8. Repeat steps 6 and 7 to bake remaining muffins.
9. Serve warm.

Parmesan Sausage Egg Muffins

Servings: 4
Cooking Time: 20 Minutes
Ingredients:
- 6 ounces (170 g) Italian sausage, sliced
- 6 eggs
- ⅛ cup heavy cream
- Salt and ground black pepper, to taste
- 3 ounces (85 g) Parmesan cheese, grated

Directions:
1. Preheat the air fryer to 350°F (177°C). Grease a muffin pan.
2. Put the sliced sausage in the muffin pan.
3. Beat the eggs with the cream in a bowl and season with salt and pepper.
4. Pour half of the mixture over the sausages in the pan.
5. Sprinkle with cheese and the remaining egg mixture.
6. Bake in the preheated air fryer for 20 minutes or until set.
7. Serve immediately.

Chicken Scotch Eggs

Servings: 4
Cooking Time: 25 Minutes
Ingredients:
- 1 lb ground chicken
- 2 tsp Dijon mustard
- 2 tsp grated yellow onion
- 1 tbsp chopped chives
- 1 tbsp chopped parsley
- ⅛ tsp ground nutmeg
- 1 lemon, zested
- Salt and pepper to taste
- 4 hard-boiled eggs, peeled
- 1 egg, beaten
- 1 cup bread crumbs

- 2 tsp olive oil

Directions:
1. Preheat air fryer to 350°F. In a bowl, mix the ground chicken, mustard, onion, chives, parsley, nutmeg, salt, lemon zest and pepper. Shape into 4 oval balls and form the balls evenly around the boiled eggs. Submerge them in the beaten egg and dip in the crumbs. Brush with olive oil. Place the scotch eggs in the frying basket and Air Fry for 14 minutes, flipping once. Serve hot.

Banana-strawberry Cakecups

Servings: 6
Cooking Time: 25 Minutes
Ingredients:
- ½ cup mashed bananas
- ¼ cup maple syrup
- ½ cup Greek yogurt
- 1 tsp vanilla extract
- 1 egg
- 1 ½ cups flour
- 1 tbsp cornstarch
- ½ tsp baking soda
- ½ tsp baking powder
- ½ tsp salt
- ½ cup strawberries, sliced

Directions:
1. Preheat air fryer to 360°F. Place the mashed bananas, maple syrup, yogurt, vanilla, and egg in a large bowl and mix until smooth. Sift in 1 ½ cups of the flour, baking soda, baking powder, and salt, then stir to combine.
2. In a small bowl, toss the strawberries with the cornstarch. Fold the mixture into the muffin batter. Divide the mixture evenly between greased muffin cups and place into the air frying basket. Bake for 12-15 minutes until golden brown on top and a toothpick inserted into the middle of one of the muffins comes out clean. Leave to cool for 5 minutes. Serve and enjoy!

Tomatoes Hash With Cheddar Cheese

Servings: 4
Cooking Time: 25 Minutes
Ingredients:
- 2 tablespoons olive oil
- 1-pound tomatoes, chopped
- ½ pound cheddar, shredded
- 1½ tablespoons chives, chopped
- Salt and black pepper to the taste
- 6 eggs, whisked

Directions:
1. Gently grease a baking pan that fits in your air fryer with oil.
2. Before cooking, heat your air fryer with the baking pan to 350 degrees F/ 175 degrees C.
3. Add the whisked eggs, salt, chopped tomatoes, and pepper in the baking pan and whisk to combine well.
4. Top the mixture with the shredded cheddar cheese.
5. Sprinkle over with the chopped chives.
6. Cook in the preheated air fryer at 350 degrees F/ 175 degrees C for 25 minutes.
7. When cooked, remove from the air fryer.
8. Serve on plates and enjoy your breakfast.

Baked Eggs

Servings: 4
Cooking Time: 6 Minutes
Ingredients:
- 4 large eggs
- ⅛ teaspoon black pepper
- ⅛ teaspoon salt

Directions:
1. Preheat the air fryer to 330°F. Place 4 silicone muffin liners into the air fryer basket.
2. Crack 1 egg at a time into each silicone muffin liner. Sprinkle with black pepper and salt.
3. Bake for 6 minutes. Remove and let cool 2 minutes prior to serving.

Western Omelet

Servings: 2
Cooking Time: 22 Minutes
Ingredients:
- ¼ cup chopped onion
- ¼ cup chopped bell pepper, green or red
- ¼ cup diced ham
- 1 teaspoon butter
- 4 large eggs
- 2 tablespoons milk
- ⅛ teaspoon salt
- ¾ cup grated sharp Cheddar cheese

Directions:
1. Place onion, bell pepper, ham, and butter in air fryer baking pan. Cook at 390°F for 1 minute and stir. Continue cooking 5 minutes, until vegetables are tender.
2. Beat together eggs, milk, and salt. Pour over vegetables and ham in baking pan. Cook at 360°F for 15 minutes or until eggs set and top has browned slightly.
3. Sprinkle grated cheese on top of omelet. Cook 1 minute or just long enough to melt the cheese.

Chocolate Almond Crescent Rolls

Servings: 4
Cooking Time: 8 Minutes
Ingredients:
- 1 tube of crescent roll dough
- ⅔ cup semi-sweet or bittersweet chocolate chunks
- 1 egg white, lightly beaten
- ¼ cup sliced almonds
- powdered sugar, for dusting
- butter or oil

Directions:
1. Preheat the air fryer to 350°F.

2. Unwrap the crescent roll dough and separate it into triangles with the points facing away from you. Place a row of chocolate chunks along the bottom edge of the dough. Roll the dough up around the chocolate and then place another row of chunks on the dough. Roll again and finish with one or two chocolate chunks. Be sure to leave the end free of chocolate so that it can adhere to the rest of the roll.
3. Brush the tops of the crescent rolls with the lightly beaten egg white and sprinkle the almonds on top, pressing them into the crescent dough so they adhere.
4. Brush the bottom of the air fryer basket with butter or oil and transfer the crescent rolls to the basket. Air-fry at 350°F for 8 minutes. Remove and let the crescent rolls cool before dusting with powdered sugar and serving.

Baked Parmesan Eggs With Kielbasa

Servings: 4
Cooking Time: 8 Minutes
Ingredients:
- 4 eggs
- 1 tablespoon heavy cream
- 1 ounce Parmesan, grated
- 1 teaspoon dried parsley
- 3 ounces kielbasa, chopped
- 1 teaspoon coconut oil

Directions:
1. Add the coconut oil in a suitable baking pan and melt it in your air fryer at 385 degrees F/ 195 degrees C for about 2 to 3 minutes.
2. At the same time in a mixing bowl, whisk the eggs and add heavy cream and the dried parsley.
3. Whisk them together.
4. Add the chopped kielbasa in the melted coconut oil.
5. Cook at 385 degrees F/ 195 degrees C for 4 minutes.
6. When cooked, add Parmesan and the whisked egg mixture and use a fork to stir them together.
7. Cook for 4 or more minutes, halfway through cooking scramble the mixture.

Turkey Casserole With Cheddar Cheese

Servings: 4
Cooking Time: 25 Minutes
Ingredients:
- 4 turkey breast, skinless, boneless, cut into strips and browned
- 2 teaspoons olive oil
- 2 cups almond milk
- 2 cups cheddar cheese, shredded
- 2 eggs, whisked
- Salt and black pepper to the taste
- 1 tablespoon chives, chopped

Directions:
1. Mix the milk, cheese, pepper, salt, chives, and the eggs in a mixing bowl.
2. Gently grease a baking pan that fits in your air fryer.
3. Before cooking, heat your air fryer with the baking pan to 330 degrees F/ 165 degrees C.
4. Add the turkey pieces onto the baking pan. Spread flat on the baking pan.
5. Pour in the egg mixture and toss for a while.
6. Cook in the preheated air fryer for 25 minutes.
7. Serve immediately and enjoy your breakfast.

Eggs Salad

Servings: 4
Cooking Time: 10 Minutes
Ingredients:
- 1 tablespoon lime juice
- 4 eggs, hard boiled, peeled and sliced
- 2 cups baby spinach
- Salt and black pepper to the taste
- 3 tablespoons heavy cream
- 2 tablespoons olive oil

Directions:
1. In your Air Fryer, mix the spinach with cream, eggs, salt and pepper, cover and cook at 360°F for 6 minutes. Transfer this to a bowl, add the lime juice and oil, toss and serve for breakfast.

Holiday Breakfast Casserole

Servings:2
Cooking Time: 25 Minutes
Ingredients:
- ¼ cup cooked spicy breakfast sausage
- 5 eggs
- 2 tbsp heavy cream
- ½ tsp ground cumin
- Salt and pepper to taste
- ½ cup feta cheese crumbles
- 1 tomato, diced
- 1 can green chiles, including juice
- 1 zucchini, diced

Directions:
1. Preheat air fryer to 325°F. Mix all ingredients in a bowl and pour into a greased baking pan. Place the pan in the frying basket and Bake for 14 minutes. Let cool for 5 minutes before slicing. Serve right away.

Mushroom & Cavolo Nero Egg Muffins

Servings: 6
Cooking Time: 20 Minutes
Ingredients:
- 8 oz baby Bella mushrooms, sliced
- 6 eggs, beaten
- 1 garlic clove, minced
- Salt and pepper to taste

- ½ tsp chili powder
- 1 cup cavolo nero
- 2 scallions, diced

Directions:
1. Preheat air fryer to 320°F. Place the eggs, garlic, salt, pepper, and chili powder in a bowl and beat until well combined. Fold in the mushrooms, cavolo nero, and scallions. Divide the mixture between greased muffin cups. Place into the air fryer and Bake for 12-15 minutes, or until the eggs are set. Cool for 5 minutes. Enjoy!

Creamy Eggs And Leeks

Servings: 2
Cooking Time: 7 Minutes
Ingredients:
- 2 leeks, chopped
- 4 eggs, whisked
- ¼ cup Cheddar cheese, shredded
- ½ cup Mozzarella cheese, shredded
- 1 teaspoon avocado oil

Directions:
1. Before cooking, heat your air fryer to 400 degrees F/ 205 degrees C.
2. Using avocado oil, grease your air fryer basket.
3. Combine the whisked eggs with the remaining ingredients.
4. Cook in your air fryer for 7 minutes.
5. When they are cooked, remove from the air fryer and serve warm.

Cheddar & Egg Scramble

Servings: 4
Cooking Time: 20 Minutes
Ingredients:
- 8 eggs
- ¼ cup buttermilk
- ¼ cup milk
- Salt and pepper to taste
- 3 tbsp butter, melted
- 1 cup grated cheddar
- 1 tbsp minced parsley

Directions:
1. Preheat the air fryer to 350°F. Whisk the eggs with buttermilk, milk, salt, and pepper until foamy and set aside. Put the melted butter in a cake pan and pour in the egg mixture. Return the pan into the fryer and cook for 7 minutes, stirring occasionally. Stir in the cheddar cheese and cook for 2-4 more minutes or until the eggs have set. Remove the cake pan and scoop the eggs into a serving plate. Scatter with freshly minced parsley and serve.

Breakfast Chimichangas

Servings: 4
Cooking Time: 8 Minutes
Ingredients:
- Four 8-inch flour tortillas
- ½ cup canned refried beans
- 1 cup scrambled eggs
- ½ cup grated cheddar or Monterey jack cheese
- 1 tablespoon vegetable oil
- 1 cup salsa

Directions:
1. Lay the flour tortillas out flat on a cutting board. In the center of each tortilla, spread 2 tablespoons refried beans. Next, add ¼ cup eggs and 2 tablespoons cheese to each tortilla.
2. To fold the tortillas, begin on the left side and fold to the center. Then fold the right side into the center. Next fold the bottom and top down and roll over to completely seal the chimichanga. Using a pastry brush or oil mister, brush the tops of the tortilla packages with oil.
3. Preheat the air fryer to 400°F for 4 minutes. Place the chimichangas into the air fryer basket, seam side down, and air fry for 4 minutes. Using tongs, turn over the chimichangas and cook for an additional 2 to 3 minutes or until light golden brown.

Chapter 5: Vegetable Side Dishes Recipes

Roasted Eggplant Slices

Servings: 1
Cooking Time: 15 Minutes
Ingredients:
- 1 large eggplant, sliced
- 2 tablespoons olive oil
- ¼ teaspoon salt
- ½ teaspoon garlic powder

Directions:
1. Preheat the air fryer to 390ºF (199ºC).
2. Apply the olive oil to the slices with a brush, coating both sides. Season each side with sprinklings of salt and garlic powder.
3. Put the slices in the air fryer and roast for 15 minutes.
4. Serve immediately.

Lemony Cabbage Slaw

Servings: 4
Cooking Time: 20 Minutes
Ingredients:
- 1 green cabbage head, shredded
- Juice of ½ lemon
- A pinch of salt and black pepper
- ½ cup coconut cream
- ½ teaspoon fennel seeds
- 1 tablespoon mustard

Directions:
1. Combine all the ingredients in a suitable baking pan.
2. Cook in your air fryer at 350 degrees F/ 175 degrees C for 20 minutes.
3. Serve on plates as a side dish.

Speedy Baked Caprese With Avocado

Servings: 4
Cooking Time: 15 Minutes
Ingredients:
- 4 oz fresh mozzarella
- 8 cherry tomatoes
- 2 tsp olive oil
- 2 halved avocados, pitted
- ¼ tsp salt
- 2 tbsp basil, torn

Directions:
1. Preheat air fryer to 375ºF. In a bowl, combine tomatoes and olive oil. Set aside. Add avocado halves, cut sides up, in the frying basket, scatter tomatoes around halves, and Bake for 7 minutes. Divide avocado halves between 4 small plates, top each with 2 tomatoes and sprinkle with salt. Cut mozzarella cheese and evenly distribute over tomatoes. Scatter with the basil to serve.

Caraway Seed Pretzel Sticks

Servings: 4
Cooking Time: 30 Minutes
Ingredients:
- ½ pizza dough
- 1 tsp baking soda
- 2 tbsp caraway seeds
- 1 cup of hot water
- Cooking spray

Directions:
1. Preheat air fryer to 400°F. Roll out the dough, on parchment paper, into a rectangle, then cut it into 8 strips. Whisk the baking soda and 1 cup of hot water until well dissolved in a bowl. Submerge each strip, shake off any excess, and stretch another 1 to 2 inches. Scatter with caraway seeds and let rise for 10 minutes in the frying basket. Grease with cooking spray and Air Fry for 8 minutes until golden brown, turning once. Serve.

Simple Green Bake

Servings: 4
Cooking Time: 15 Minutes
Ingredients:
- 1 cup asparagus, chopped
- 2 cups broccoli florets
- 1 tbsp olive oil
- 1 tbsp lemon juice
- 1 cup green peas
- 2 tbsp honey mustard
- Salt and pepper to taste

Directions:
1. Preheat air fryer to 330°F. Add asparagus and broccoli to the frying basket. Drizzle with olive oil and lemon juice and toss. Bake for 6 minutes. Remove the basket and add peas. Steam for another 3 minutes or until the vegetables are hot and tender. Pour the vegetables into a serving dish. Drizzle with honey mustard and season with salt and pepper. Toss and serve warm.

Sweet And Spicy Tofu

Servings: 3
Cooking Time: 23 Minutes
Ingredients:
- For Tofu:
- 1 (14-ounce) block firm tofu, pressed and cubed
- ½ cup arrowroot flour
- ½ teaspoon sesame oil
- For Sauce:
- 4 tablespoons low-sodium soy sauce
- 1½ tablespoons rice vinegar
- 1½ tablespoons chili sauce
- 1 tablespoon agave nectar
- 2 large garlic cloves, minced
- 1 teaspoon fresh ginger, peeled and grated
- 2 scallions (green part), chopped

Directions:
1. Mix arrowroot flour, sesame oil, and tofu together in a bowl.

2. Before cooking, heat your air fryer to 360 degrees F/ 180 degrees C.
3. Gently grease an air fryer basket.
4. Place the tofu evenly on the air fryer basket in a layer.
5. Cook in your air fryer for 20 minutes. Halfway through cooking, shake the air fryer basket once.
6. To make the sauce, add soy sauce, rice vinegar, chili sauce, agave nectar, garlic, and ginger in a bowl. Beat the mixture to combine well.
7. When the tofu has cooked, remove from the air fryer and transfer to a skillet.
8. Add the sauce and heat the skillet over medium heat. Cook for about 3 minutes. Stir the meal from time to time.
9. Add the scallions to garnish and serve hot.

Steamed Green Veggie Trio

Servings: 4
Cooking Time: 9 Minutes
Ingredients:
- 2 cups broccoli florets
- 1 cup green beans
- 1 tablespoon olive oil
- 1 tablespoon lemon juice
- 1 cup frozen baby peas
- 2 tablespoons honey mustard
- Pinch salt
- Freshly ground black pepper

Directions:
1. Put the broccoli and green beans in the basket of the air fryer. Put 2 tablespoons water in the air fryer pan. Sprinkle the vegetables with the olive oil and lemon juice, and toss.
2. Steam for 6 minutes, then remove the basket from the air fryer and add the peas.
3. Steam for 3 minutes or until the vegetables are hot and tender.
4. Transfer the vegetables to a serving dish and drizzle with the honey mustard and sprinkle with salt and pepper. Toss and serve.

Mashed Potato Tots

Servings: 18
Cooking Time: 10 Minutes
Ingredients:
- 1 medium potato or 1 cup cooked mashed potatoes
- 1 tablespoon real bacon bits
- 2 tablespoons chopped green onions, tops only
- ¼ teaspoon onion powder
- 1 teaspoon dried chopped chives
- salt
- 2 tablespoons flour
- 1 egg white, beaten
- ½ cup panko breadcrumbs
- oil for misting or cooking spray

Directions:
1. If using cooked mashed potatoes, jump to step 4.
2. Peel potato and cut into ½-inch cubes. (Small pieces cook more quickly.) Place in saucepan, add water to cover, and heat to boil. Lower heat slightly and continue cooking just until tender, about 10minutes.
3. Drain potatoes and place in ice cold water. Allow to cool for a minute or two, then drain well and mash.
4. Preheat air fryer to 390°F.
5. In a large bowl, mix together the potatoes, bacon bits, onions, onion powder, chives, salt to taste, and flour. Add egg white and stir well.
6. Place panko crumbs on a sheet of wax paper.
7. For each tot, use about 2 teaspoons of potato mixture. To shape, drop the measure of potato mixture onto panko crumbs and push crumbs up and around potatoes to coat edges. Then turn tot over to coat other side with crumbs.
8. Mist tots with oil or cooking spray and place in air fryer basket, crowded but not stacked.
9. Cook at 390°F for 10 minutes, until browned and crispy.
10. Repeat steps 8 and 9 to cook remaining tots.

Blistered Tomatoes

Servings: 20
Cooking Time: 15 Minutes
Ingredients:
- 1½ pounds Cherry or grape tomatoes
- Olive oil spray
- 1½ teaspoons Balsamic vinegar
- ¼ teaspoon Table salt
- ¼ teaspoon Ground black pepper

Directions:
1. Put the basket in a drawer-style air fryer, or a baking tray in the lower third of a toaster oven–style air fryer. Place a 6-inch round cake pan in the basket or on the tray for a small batch, a 7-inch round cake pan for a medium batch, or an 8-inch round cake pan for a large one. Heat the air fryer to 400°F with the pan in the basket. When the machine is at temperature, keep heating the pan for 5 minutes more.
2. Place the tomatoes in a large bowl, coat them with the olive oil spray, toss gently, then spritz a couple of times more, tossing after each spritz, until the tomatoes are glistening.
3. Pour the tomatoes into the cake pan and air-fry undisturbed for 10 minutes, or until they split and begin to brown.
4. Use kitchen tongs and a nonstick-safe spatula, or silicone baking mitts, to remove the cake pan from the basket. Toss the hot tomatoes with the vinegar, salt, and pepper. Cool in the pan for a few minutes before serving.

Roasted Fennel Salad

Servings: 3
Cooking Time: 20 Minutes
Ingredients:
- 3 cups (about ¾ pound) Trimmed fennel, roughly chopped
- 1½ tablespoons Olive oil
- ¼ teaspoon Table salt
- ¼ teaspoon Ground black pepper
- 1½ tablespoons White balsamic vinegar

Directions:
1. Preheat the air fryer to 400°F.
2. Toss the fennel, olive oil, salt, and pepper in a large bowl until the fennel is well coated in the oil.
3. When the machine is at temperature, pour the fennel into the basket, spreading it out into as close to one layer as possible. Air-fry for 20 minutes, tossing and rearranging the fennel pieces twice so that any covered or touching parts get exposed to the air currents, until golden at the edges and softened.
4. Pour the fennel into a serving bowl. Add the vinegar while hot. Toss well, then cool a couple of minutes before serving. Or serve at room temperature.

Basic Corn On The Cob

Servings: 4
Cooking Time: 15 Minutes
Ingredients:
- 3 ears of corn, shucked and halved
- 2 tbsp butter, melted
- Salt and pepper to taste
- 1 tsp minced garlic
- 1 tsp paprika

Directions:
1. Preheat air fryer at 400°F. Toss all ingredients in a bowl. Place corn in the frying basket and Bake for 7 minutes, turning once. Serve immediately.

Creole Seasoned Okra

Servings: 4
Cooking Time: 25 Minutes
Ingredients:
- 1 teaspoon olive oil, plus more for spraying
- 12 ounces frozen sliced okra
- 1 to 2 teaspoons Creole seasoning

Directions:
1. Spray a fryer basket lightly with olive oil.
2. In a medium bowl, toss the frozen okra with 1 teaspoon of olive oil and the Creole seasoning.
3. Place the okra into the fryer basket. You may need to cook them in batches.
4. Air fry until the okra is browned and crispy, 20 to 25 minutes, making sure to shake the basket and lightly spray with olive oil every 5 minutes.

Scalloped Potatoes

Servings: 4
Cooking Time: 20 Minutes
Ingredients:
- 2 cups pre-sliced refrigerated potatoes
- 3 cloves garlic, minced
- Pinch salt
- Freshly ground black pepper
- ¾ cup heavy cream

Directions:
1. Layer the potatoes, garlic, salt, and pepper in a 6-by-6-by-2-inch baking pan. Slowly pour the cream over all.
2. Bake for 15 minutes, until the potatoes are golden brown on top and tender. Check their state and, if needed, bake for 5 minutes until browned.

Awesome Chicken Taquitos

Servings: 4
Cooking Time: 12 Minutes
Ingredients:
- 1 cup shredded mozzarella cheese
- ¼ cup salsa
- ¼ cup Greek yogurt
- Salt and black pepper
- 8 flour tortillas

Directions:
1. In a suitable bowl, mix chicken, cheese, salsa, sour cream, salt, and black pepper.
2. Spray 1 side of the tortilla with cooking spray.
3. Lay 2 tablespoon of the chicken mixture at the center of the non-oiled side the tortillas.
4. Roll tightly around the mixture. Arrange taquitos on your air fryer basket.
5. Cook for almost 12 minutes at 380 degrees F/ 195 degrees C.
6. Serve.

Cheddar-garlic Drop Biscuits

Servings: 10
Cooking Time: 10 Minutes
Ingredients:
- 2 cups all-purpose flour
- 1 tablespoon baking powder
- 1 teaspoon salt
- ½ teaspoon garlic powder
- ¾ cup sour cream
- ¾ cup salted butter, melted, divided
- 1 cup shredded Cheddar cheese

Directions:
1. Preheat the air fryer to 400°F.
2. In a large bowl, mix flour, baking powder, salt, garlic powder, sour cream, and ½ cup butter until well combined. Gently stir in Cheddar.
3. Using your hands, form dough into ten even-sized balls.

4. Place balls in the air fryer basket, working in batches as necessary. Cook 10 minutes until golden and crispy on the edges.
5. Remove biscuits from the air fryer and brush with remaining ¼ cup melted butter to serve.

Green Beans And Potatoes Recipe

Servings: 5
Cooking Time: 25 Minutes
Ingredients:
- 2 lbs. green beans
- 6 new potatoes; halved
- Salt and black pepper to the taste
- 6 bacon slices; cooked and chopped.
- A drizzle of olive oil

Directions:
1. In a bowl; mix green beans with potatoes, salt, pepper and oil, toss, transfer to your air fryer and cook at 390 °F, for 15 minutes. Divide among plates and serve with bacon sprinkled on top.

Turkish Mutabal (eggplant Dip)

Servings: 2
Cooking Time: 40 Minutes
Ingredients:
- 1 medium eggplant
- 2 tbsp tahini
- 2 tbsp lemon juice
- 1 tsp garlic powder
- ¼ tsp sumac
- 1 tsp chopped parsley

Directions:
1. Preheat air fryer to 400°F. Place the eggplant in a pan and Roast for 30 minutes, turning once. Let cool for 5-10 minutes. Scoop out the flesh and place it in a bowl. Squeeze any excess water; discard the water. Mix the flesh, tahini, lemon juice, garlic, and sumac until well combined. Scatter with parsley and serve.

Baked Jalapeño And Cheese Cauliflower Mash

Servings: 6
Cooking Time: 15 Minutes
Ingredients:
- 1 steamer bag cauliflower florets, cooked according to package instructions
- 2 tablespoons salted butter, softened
- 2 ounces cream cheese, softened
- ½ cup shredded sharp Cheddar cheese
- ¼ cup pickled jalapeños
- ½ teaspoon salt
- ¼ teaspoon ground black pepper

Directions:
1. Place cooked cauliflower into a food processor with remaining ingredients. Pulse twenty times until cauliflower is smooth and all ingredients are combined.
2. Spoon mash into an ungreased 6" round nonstick baking dish. Place dish into air fryer basket. Adjust the temperature to 380°F and set the timer for 15 minutes. The top will be golden brown when done. Serve warm.

Corn Pakodas

Servings: 5
Cooking Time: 8 Minutes
Ingredients:
- 1 cup flour
- ¼ teaspoon baking soda
- ¼ teaspoon salt
- ½ teaspoon curry powder
- ½ teaspoon red chili powder
- ¼ teaspoon turmeric powder
- ¼ cup water
- 10 cobs baby corn, blanched
- Cooking spray

Directions:
1. Preheat the air fryer to 425°F (218°C).
2. Cover the air fryer basket with aluminum foil and sprtiz with the cooking spray.
3. In a bowl, combine all the ingredients, save for the corn. Stir with a whisk until well combined.
4. Coat the corn in the batter and put inside the air fryer.
5. Air fry for 8 minutes until a golden brown color is achieved.
6. Serve hot.

Mediterranean Air Fried Veggies

Servings: 4
Cooking Time: 6 Minutes
Ingredients:
- 1 large zucchini, sliced
- 1 cup cherry tomatoes, halved
- 1 parsnip, sliced
- 1 green pepper, sliced
- 1 carrot, sliced
- 1 teaspoon mixed herbs
- 1 teaspoon mustard
- 1 teaspoon garlic purée
- 6 tablespoons olive oil
- Salt and ground black pepper, to taste

Directions:
1. Preheat the air fryer to 400°F (204°C).
2. Combine all the ingredients in a bowl, making sure to coat the vegetables well.
3. Transfer to the air fryer and air fry for 6 minutes, ensuring the vegetables are tender and browned.
4. Serve immediately.

Ratatouille

Servings: 4
Cooking Time: 25 Minutes
Ingredients:
- 1 sprig basil
- 1 sprig flat-leaf parsley
- 1 sprig mint
- 1 tablespoon coriander powder
- 1 teaspoon capers
- ½ lemon, juiced
- Salt and ground black pepper, to taste
- 2 eggplants, sliced crosswise
- 2 red onions, chopped
- 4 cloves garlic, minced
- 2 red peppers, sliced crosswise
- 1 fennel bulb, sliced crosswise
- 3 large zucchinis, sliced crosswise
- 5 tablespoons olive oil
- 4 large tomatoes, chopped
- 2 teaspoons herbs de Provence

Directions:
1. Blend the basil, parsley, coriander, mint, lemon juice and capers, with a little salt and pepper. Make sure all ingredients are well-incorporated.
2. Preheat the air fryer to 400ºF (204ºC).
3. Coat the eggplant, onions, garlic, peppers, fennel, and zucchini with olive oil.
4. Transfer the vegetables into a baking dish and top with the tomatoes and herb purée. Sprinkle with more salt and pepper, and the herbs de Provence.
5. Air fry for 25 minutes.
6. Serve immediately.

Open-faced Sandwich

Servings: 4
Cooking Time: 25 Minutes
Ingredients:
- 1 can chickpeas, drained and rinsed
- 1 medium-sized head of cauliflower
- 1 tbsp. extra-virgin olive oil
- 2 ripe avocados, mashed
- 2 tbsps. lemon juice
- 4 flatbreads, toasted
- salt and pepper to taste

Directions:
1. Before cooking, heat your air fryer to 425 degrees F/ 220 degrees C.
2. Cut the cauliflower head into florets. Combine chickpea, olive oil, lemon juice, and the cauliflower together in a mixing bowl.
3. Transfer the mixture inside the air fryer basket.
4. Cook in your air fryer for 25 minutes.
5. When cooked, spread the mixture on half of the flatbread and then add avocado mash.
6. To season, add more salt and pepper as you like.
7. Serve the meal with hot sauce.

Cholula Onion Rings

Servings: 4
Cooking Time: 30 Minutes
Ingredients:
- 1 large Vidalia onion
- ½ cup chickpea flour
- 1/3 cup milk
- 2 tbsp lemon juice
- 2 tbsp Cholula hot sauce
- 1 tsp allspice
- 2/3 cup bread crumbs

Directions:
1. Preheat air fryer to 380°F. Cut ½-inch off the top of the onion's root, then cut into ½-inch thick rings. Set aside. Combine the chickpea flour, milk, lemon juice, hot sauce, and allspice in a bowl. In another bowl, add in breadcrumbs. Submerge each ring into the flour batter until well coated, then dip into the breadcrumbs, and Air Fry for 14 minutes until crispy, turning once. Serve.

French Fries

Servings: 4
Cooking Time: 25 Minutes
Ingredients:
- 2 cups fresh potatoes
- 2 teaspoons oil
- ½ teaspoon salt

Directions:
1. Cut potatoes into ½-inch-wide slices, then lay slices flat and cut into ½-inch sticks.
2. Rinse potato sticks and blot dry with a clean towel.
3. In a bowl or sealable plastic bag, mix the potatoes, oil, and salt together.
4. Pour into air fryer basket.
5. Cook at 390°F for 10 minutes. Shake basket to redistribute fries and continue cooking for approximately 15 minutes, until fries are golden brown.

Creamy Spinach With Nutmeg

Servings: 2
Cooking Time: 15 Minutes
Ingredients:
- 10 ounces frozen spinach, thawed
- ¼ cup parmesan cheese, shredded
- ½ teaspoon ground nutmeg
- 1 teaspoon black pepper
- 4 ounces cream cheese, diced
- 2 teaspoons garlic, minced
- 1 small onion, chopped
- 1 teaspoon salt

Directions:
1. Spray 6-inch pan with cooking spray and set aside.

Quick & Simple Tower Dual Basket Air Fryer Cookbook

2. In a suitable bowl, mix together spinach, cream cheese, garlic, onion, nutmeg, black pepper, and salt.
3. Pour spinach mixture into the prepared pan.
4. Place dish in air fryer basket and air fry the mixture at 350 degrees F/ 175 degrees C for almost 10 minutes.
5. Open air fryer basket and sprinkle parmesan cheese on top of spinach mixture and air fry them at 400 degrees F/ 205 degrees C for 5 minutes more.
6. Serve and enjoy.

Roasted Thyme Asparagus

Servings: 4
Cooking Time: 20 Minutes
Ingredients:
- 1 lb asparagus, trimmed
- 2 tsp olive oil
- 3 garlic cloves, minced
- 2 tbsp balsamic vinegar
- ½ tsp dried thyme
- ½ red chili, finely sliced

Directions:
1. Preheat air fryer to 380°F. Put the asparagus and olive oil in a bowl and stir to coat, then put them in the frying basket. Toss some garlic over the asparagus and Roast for 4-8 minutes until crisp-tender. Spritz with balsamic vinegar and toss in some thyme leaves. Top with red chili slices and serve.

Air Fried Broccoli

Servings: 4
Cooking Time: 7 Minutes
Ingredients:
- 4 cups broccoli florets
- ¼ cup water
- 1 tablespoon olive oil
- ¼ teaspoon black pepper
- ⅛ teaspoon kosher salt

Directions:
1. Add broccoli, oil, black pepper, and salt in a suitable bowl and toss well.
2. Add ¼ cup of water into the bottom of air fryer under the basket.
3. Transfer broccoli into the air fryer basket and cook for 7 minutes at 400 degrees F/ 205 degrees C.
4. Serve and enjoy.

Stuffed Bell Peppers With Mayonnaise

Servings: 2
Cooking Time: 15 Minutes
Ingredients:
- 2 red bell peppers, tops and seeds removed
- 2 yellow bell peppers, tops and seeds removed
- Black pepper and salt, to taste
- 1 cup cream cheese
- 4 tablespoons mayonnaise
- 2 pickles, chopped

Directions:
1. Arrange the black peppers in the lightly greased cooking basket. Cook in the preheated air fryer at about 400 degrees F/ 205 degrees C for almost 15 minutes, flipping them once halfway through the cooking time.
2. Season with black pepper and salt.
3. Then, in a suitable mixing bowl, combine the cream cheese with the mayonnaise and chopped pickles.
4. Stuff the black pepper with the cream cheese mixture and serve.
5. Enjoy!

Rice And Eggplant Bowl

Servings:4
Cooking Time: 10 Minutes
Ingredients:
- ¼ cup sliced cucumber
- 1 teaspoon salt
- 1 tablespoon sugar
- 7 tablespoons Japanese rice vinegar
- 3 medium eggplants, sliced
- 3 tablespoons sweet white miso paste
- 1 tablespoon mirin rice wine
- 4 cups cooked sushi rice
- 4 spring onions
- 1 tablespoon toasted sesame seeds

Directions:
1. Coat the cucumber slices with the rice wine vinegar, salt, and sugar.
2. Put a dish on top of the bowl to weight it down completely.
3. In a bowl, mix the eggplants, mirin rice wine, and miso paste. Allow to marinate for half an hour.
4. Preheat the air fryer to 400°F (204°C).
5. Put the eggplant slices in the air fryer and air fry for 10 minutes.
6. Fill the bottom of a serving bowl with rice and top with the eggplants and pickled cucumbers.
7. Add the spring onions and sesame seeds for garnish. Serve immediately.

Lemon Broccoli

Servings: 3
Cooking Time: 20 Minutes
Ingredients:
- 1 tablespoon butter
- 2 teaspoons vegetable bouillon granules
- 1 large head broccoli
- 1 tablespoon fresh lemon juice
- 3 garlic cloves, sliced
- ½ teaspoon fresh lemon zest, finely grated
- ½ teaspoon red pepper flakes, crushed

Directions:

1. Before cooking, heat your air fryer to 355 degrees F/ 180 degrees C.
2. Using cooking spray, lightly grease a suitable baking pan. Cut the broccoli into bite-sized pieces.
3. In the baking pan, add bouillon granules, lemon juice, and butter.
4. Cook in your air fryer for 1½ minutes. Then add garlic and stir.
5. Cook for about 30 seconds and add lemon zest, red pepper flakes, and broccoli.
6. Cook for about 18 minutes.
7. When cooked, remove from the air fryer and serve hot in a bowl.

Hot Okra Wedges

Servings: 2
Cooking Time: 35 Minutes
Ingredients:
- 1 cup okra, sliced
- 1 cup breadcrumbs
- 2 eggs, beaten
- A pinch of black pepper
- 1 tsp crushed red peppers
- 2 tsp hot Tabasco sauce

Directions:
1. Preheat air fryer to 350°F. Place the eggs and Tabasco sauce in a bowl and stir thoroughly; set aside. In a separate mixing bowl, combine the breadcrumbs, crushed red peppers, and pepper. Dip the okra into the beaten eggs, then coat in the crumb mixture. Lay the okra pieces on the greased frying basket. Air Fry for 14-16 minutes, shaking the basket several times during cooking. When ready, the okra will be crispy and golden brown. Serve.

Brown Rice And Goat Cheese Croquettes

Servings: 3
Cooking Time: 8 Minutes
Ingredients:
- ¾ cup Water
- 6 tablespoons Raw medium-grain brown rice, such as brown Arborio
- ½ cup Shredded carrot
- ¼ cup Walnut pieces
- 3 tablespoons (about 1½ ounces) Soft goat cheese
- 1 tablespoon Pasteurized egg substitute, such as Egg Beaters (gluten-free, if a concern)
- ¼ teaspoon Dried thyme
- ¼ teaspoon Table salt
- ¼ teaspoon Ground black pepper
- Olive oil spray

Directions:
1. Combine the water, rice, and carrots in a small saucepan set over medium-high heat. Bring to a boil, stirring occasionally. Cover, reduce the heat to very low, and simmer very slowly for 45 minutes, or until the water has been absorbed and the rice is tender. Set aside, covered, for 10 minutes.
2. Scrape the contents of the saucepan into a food processor. Cool for 10 minutes.
3. Preheat the air fryer to 400°F.
4. Put the nuts, cheese, egg substitute, thyme, salt, and pepper into the food processor. Cover and pulse to a coarse paste, stopping the machine at least once to scrape down the inside of the canister.
5. Uncover the food processor; scrape down and remove the blade. Using wet, clean hands, form the mixture into two 4-inch-diameter patties for a small batch, three 4-inch-diameter patties for a medium batch, or four 4-inch-diameter patties for a large one. Generously coat both sides of the patties with olive oil spray.
6. Set the patties in the basket with as much air space between them as possible. Air-fry undisturbed for 8 minutes, or until brown and crisp.
7. Use a nonstick-safe spatula to transfer the croquettes to a wire rack. Cool for 5 minutes before serving.

Curried Brussels Sprouts

Servings: 4
Cooking Time:15 To 17 Minutes
Ingredients:
- 1 pound Brussels sprouts, ends trimmed, discolored leaves removed, halved lengthwise
- 2 teaspoons olive oil
- 3 teaspoons curry powder, divided
- 1 tablespoon freshly squeezed lemon juice

Directions:
1. In a large bowl, toss the Brussels sprouts with the olive oil and 1 teaspoon of curry powder. Transfer to the air fryer basket. Roast for 12 minutes, shaking the basket once during cooking.
2. Sprinkle with the remaining 2 teaspoons of the curry powder and the lemon juice. Shake again. Roast for 3 to 5 minutes more, or until the Brussels sprouts are browned and crisp (see Tip). Serve immediately.

Parmesan Asparagus

Servings: 2
Cooking Time: 5 Minutes
Ingredients:
- 1 bunch asparagus, stems trimmed
- 1 teaspoon olive oil
- salt and freshly ground black pepper
- ¼ cup coarsely grated Parmesan cheese
- ½ lemon

Directions:
1. Preheat the air fryer to 400°F.
2. Toss the asparagus with the oil and season with salt and freshly ground black pepper.

3. Transfer the asparagus to the air fryer basket and air-fry at 400°F for 5 minutes, shaking the basket to turn the asparagus once or twice during the cooking process.
4. When the asparagus is cooked to your liking, sprinkle the asparagus generously with the Parmesan cheese and close the air fryer drawer again. Let the asparagus sit for 1 minute in the turned-off air fryer. Then, remove the asparagus, transfer it to a serving dish and finish with a grind of black pepper and a squeeze of lemon juice.

Truffle Vegetable Croquettes

Servings: 4
Cooking Time: 40 Minutes
Ingredients:
- 2 cooked potatoes, mashed
- 1 cooked carrot, mashed
- 1 tbsp onion, minced
- 2 eggs, beaten
- 2 tbsp melted butter
- 1 tbsp truffle oil
- ½ tbsp flour
- Salt and pepper to taste

Directions:
1. Preheat air fryer to 350°F. Sift the flour, salt, and pepper in a bowl and stir to combine. Add the potatoes, carrot, onion, butter, and truffle oil to a separate bowl and mix well. Shape the potato mixture into small bite-sized patties. Dip the potato patties into the beaten eggs, coating thoroughly, then roll in the flour mixture to cover all sides. Arrange the croquettes in the greased frying basket and Air Fry for 14-16 minutes. Halfway through cooking, shake the basket. The croquettes should be crispy and golden. Serve hot and enjoy!

Garlic Provolone Asparagus

Servings: 3
Cooking Time: 5 Minutes
Ingredients:
- 9 ounces Asparagus
- ¼ teaspoon chili powder
- ¼ teaspoon garlic powder
- 1 teaspoon olive oil
- 4 Provolone cheese slices

Directions:
1. Sprinkle the trimmed asparagus with garlic powder and chili powder.
2. Before cooking, heat your air fryer to 400 degrees F/ 205 degrees C.
3. Transfer the asparagus in the air fryer basket.
4. Sprinkle with olive oil.
5. Cook the asparagus in your air fryer for 3 minutes.
6. Sprinkle the Provolone cheese on the top and continue cooking for 3 or more minutes.

Lemon Fennel With Sunflower Seeds

Servings: 4
Cooking Time: 15 Minutes
Ingredients:
- 1 pound fennel, cut into small wedges
- A pinch of salt and black pepper
- 3 tablespoons olive oil
- Salt and black pepper to the taste
- Juice of ½ lemon
- 2 tablespoons sunflower seeds

Directions:
1. Mix fennel wedges, salt, black pepper, olive oil, and lemon in a suitable baking pan.
2. Cook the mixture in your air fryer at 400 degrees F/ 205 degrees C for 15 minutes.
3. When cooked, sprinkle on top with the sunflower seeds.
4. Serve on plates as a side dish.

Garlicky Mushrooms With Parsley

Servings: 2
Cooking Time: 12 Minutes
Ingredients:
- 8 ounces mushrooms, sliced
- 1 tablespoon parsley, chopped
- 1 teaspoon soy sauce
- ½ teaspoon garlic powder
- 1 tablespoon olive oil
- Black pepper
- Salt

Directions:
1. Add all the recipe ingredients into the mixing bowl and toss well.
2. Transfer mushrooms in air fryer basket and cook at almost 380 degrees F/ 195 degrees C for almost 10-12 minutes. Shake basket halfway through.
3. Serve and enjoy.

Rosemary Potato Salad

Servings: 4
Cooking Time: 30 Minutes
Ingredients:
- 3 tbsp olive oil
- 2 lb red potatoes, halved
- Salt and pepper to taste
- 1 red bell pepper, chopped
- 2 green onions, chopped
- 1/3 cup lemon juice
- 3 tbsp Dijon mustard
- 1 tbsp rosemary, chopped

Directions:
1. Preheat air fryer to 350°F. Add potatoes to the frying basket and drizzle with 1 tablespoon olive oil. Season with salt and pepper. Roast the potatoes for 25 minutes, shaking twice. Potatoes will be tender and lightly golden.

2. While the potatoes are roasting, add peppers and green onions in a bowl. In a separate bowl, whisk olive oil, lemon juice, and mustard. When the potatoes are done, transfer them to a large bowl. Pour the mustard dressing over and toss to coat. Serve sprinkled with rosemary.

Simple Taro Fries

Servings: 2
Cooking Time: 20 Minutes
Ingredients:
- 8 small taro, peel and cut into fries shape
- 1 tbsp olive oil
- 1/2 tsp salt

Directions:
1. Add taro slice in a bowl and toss well with olive oil and salt.
2. Transfer taro slices into the air fryer basket.
3. Cook at 360ºF for 20 minutes. Toss halfway through.
4. Serve and enjoy.

Avocado Fries

Servings: 6
Cooking Time: 8 Minutes
Ingredients:
- Olive oil
- 4 slightly under-ripe avocados, cut in half, pits removed
- 1½ cups whole-wheat panko bread crumbs
- ¾ teaspoon freshly ground black pepper
- 1½ teaspoons paprika
- ¾ teaspoon salt
- 3 eggs

Directions:
1. Spray a fryer basket lightly with olive oil.
2. Carefully remove the skin from the avocado leaving the flesh intact. Cut each avocado half lengthwise into 5 to 6 slices. Set aside.
3. In a small bowl, mix together the panko bread crumbs, black pepper, paprika, and salt.
4. In a separate small bowl, whisk the eggs.
5. Coat each avocado slice in the egg and then in the panko mixture, pressing the panko mixture gently into the avocado so it sticks.
6. Place the avocado slices in the fryer basket in a single layer. Lightly spray with olive oil. You may need to cook them in batches.
7. Air fry for 3 to 4 minutes. Turn the slices over and spray lightly with olive oil.
8. Air fry until light brown and crispy, 3 to 4 more minutes.

Rich Spinach Chips

Servings: 4
Cooking Time: 20 Minutes
Ingredients:
- 10 oz spinach
- 2 tbsp lemon juice
- 2 tbsp olive oil
- Salt and pepper to taste
- ½ tsp garlic powder
- ½ tsp onion powder

Directions:
1. Preheat air fryer to 350°F. Place the spinach in a bowl, and drizzle with lemon juice and olive oil and massage with your hands. Scatter with salt, pepper, garlic, and onion and gently toss to coat well. Arrange the leaves in a single layer and Bake for 3 minutes. Shake and Bake for another 1-3 minutes until brown. Let cool completely.

Air Fried Bell Peppers With Onion

Servings: 3
Cooking Time: 15 Minutes
Ingredients:
- 6 bell pepper, sliced
- 1 tablespoon Italian seasoning
- 1 tablespoon olive oil
- 1 onion, sliced

Directions:
1. Add all the recipe ingredients into the suitable mixing bowl and toss well.
2. At 320 degrees F/ 160 degrees C, preheat your air fryer.
3. Transfer bell pepper and onion mixture into the air fryer basket and cook for almost 15 minutes.
4. Toss well and cook for almost 10 minutes more.
5. Serve and enjoy.

Buttery Stuffed Tomatoes

Servings: 6
Cooking Time: 15 Minutes
Ingredients:
- 3 8-ounce round tomatoes
- ½ cup plus 1 tablespoon Plain panko bread crumbs (gluten-free, if a concern)
- 3 tablespoons (about ½ ounce) Finely grated Parmesan cheese
- 3 tablespoons Butter, melted and cooled
- 4 teaspoons Stemmed and chopped fresh parsley leaves
- 1 teaspoon Minced garlic
- ¼ teaspoon Table salt
- Up to ¼ teaspoon Red pepper flakes
- Olive oil spray

Directions:
1. Preheat the air fryer to 375°F.
2. Cut the tomatoes in half through their "equators" (that is, not through the stem ends). One at a time, gently squeeze the tomato halves over a trash can, using a clean finger to gently force out the seeds and most of the juice

inside, working carefully so that the tomato doesn't lose its round shape or get crushed.
3. Stir the bread crumbs, cheese, butter, parsley, garlic, salt, and red pepper flakes in a bowl until the bread crumbs are moistened and the parsley is uniform throughout the mixture. Pile this mixture into the spaces left in the tomato halves. Press gently to compact the filling. Coat the tops of the tomatoes with olive oil spray.
4. Place the tomatoes cut side up in the basket. They may touch each other. Air-fry for 15 minutes, or until the filling is lightly browned and crunchy.
5. Use nonstick-safe spatula and kitchen tongs for balance to gently transfer the stuffed tomatoes to a platter or a cutting board. Cool for a couple of minutes before serving.

Yellow Squash

Servings: 4
Cooking Time: 10 Minutes
Ingredients:
- 1 large yellow squash
- 2 eggs
- ¼ cup buttermilk
- 1 cup panko breadcrumbs
- ¼ cup white cornmeal
- ½ teaspoon salt
- oil for misting or cooking spray

Directions:
1. Preheat air fryer to 390°F.
2. Cut the squash into ¼-inch slices.
3. In a shallow dish, beat together eggs and buttermilk.
4. In sealable plastic bag or container with lid, combine ¼ cup panko crumbs, white cornmeal, and salt. Shake to mix well.
5. Place the remaining ¾ cup panko crumbs in a separate shallow dish.
6. Dump all the squash slices into the egg/buttermilk mixture. Stir to coat.
7. Remove squash from buttermilk mixture with a slotted spoon, letting excess drip off, and transfer to the panko/cornmeal mixture. Close bag or container and shake well to coat.
8. Remove squash from crumb mixture, letting excess fall off. Return squash to egg/buttermilk mixture, stirring gently to coat. If you need more liquid to coat all the squash, add a little more buttermilk.
9. Remove each squash slice from egg wash and dip in a dish of ¾ cup panko crumbs.
10. Mist squash slices with oil or cooking spray and place in air fryer basket. Squash should be in a single layer, but it's okay if the slices crowd together and overlap a little.
11. Cook at 390°F for 5minutes. Shake basket to break up any that have stuck together. Mist again with oil or spray.
12. Cook 5minutes longer and check. If necessary, mist again with oil and cook an additional two minutes, until squash slices are golden brown and crisp.

Fingerling Potatoes

Servings: 4
Cooking Time: 15 Minutes
Ingredients:
- 1 pound fingerling potatoes
- 1 tablespoon light olive oil
- ½ teaspoon dried parsley
- ½ teaspoon lemon juice
- coarsely ground sea salt

Directions:
1. Cut potatoes in half lengthwise.
2. In a large bowl, combine potatoes, oil, parsley, and lemon juice. Stir well to coat potatoes.
3. Place potatoes in air fryer basket and cook at 360°F for 15 minutes or until lightly browned and tender inside.
4. Sprinkle with sea salt before serving.

Spicy Corn On The Cob

Servings:4
Cooking Time: 16 Minutes
Ingredients:
- Olive oil
- 2 tablespoons grated Parmesan cheese
- 1 teaspoon chili powder
- 1 teaspoon garlic powder
- 1 teaspoon ground cumin
- 1 teaspoon paprika
- 1 teaspoon salt
- ¼ teaspoon cayenne pepper, optional
- 4 ears fresh corn, shucked

Directions:
1. Spray a fryer basket lightly with olive oil.
2. In a small bowl, mix together the Parmesan cheese, chili powder, garlic powder, cumin, paprika, salt, and cayenne pepper.
3. Lightly spray the ears of corn with olive oil. Sprinkle them with the seasoning mixture.
4. Place the ears of corn in the fryer basket in a single layer. You may need to cook them in more than one batch.
5. Air fry for 7 minutes. Turn the corn over and air fry until lightly browned, 7 to 9 more minutes.

Air-fried Potato Salad

Servings: 4
Cooking Time: 15 Minutes
Ingredients:
- 1⅓ pounds Yellow potatoes, such as Yukon Golds, cut into ½-inch chunks
- 1 large Sweet white onion(s), such as Vidalia, chopped into ½-inch pieces
- 1 tablespoon plus 2 teaspoons Olive oil

- ¾ cup Thinly sliced celery
- 6 tablespoons Regular or low-fat mayonnaise (gluten-free, if a concern)
- 2½ tablespoons Apple cider vinegar
- 1½ teaspoons Dijon mustard (gluten-free, if a concern)
- ¾ teaspoon Table salt
- ¼ teaspoon Ground black pepper

Directions:
1. Preheat the air fryer to 400°F.
2. Toss the potatoes, onion(s), and oil in a large bowl until the vegetables are glistening with oil.
3. When the machine is at temperature, transfer the vegetables to the basket, spreading them out into as even a layer as you can. Air-fry for 15 minutes, tossing and rearranging the vegetables every 3 minutes so that all surfaces get exposed to the air currents, until the vegetables are tender and even browned at the edges.
4. Pour the contents of the basket into a serving bowl. Cool for at least 5 minutes or up to 30 minutes. Add the celery, mayonnaise, vinegar, mustard, salt, and pepper. Stir well to coat. The potato salad can be made in advance; cover and refrigerate for up to 4 days.

Rosemary Roasted Potatoes With Lemon

Servings: 4
Cooking Time: 12 Minutes
Ingredients:
- 1 pound small red-skinned potatoes, halved or cut into bite-sized chunks
- 1 tablespoon olive oil
- 1 teaspoon finely chopped fresh rosemary
- ¼ teaspoon salt
- freshly ground black pepper
- 1 tablespoon lemon zest

Directions:
1. Preheat the air fryer to 400°F.
2. Toss the potatoes with the olive oil, rosemary, salt and freshly ground black pepper.
3. Air-fry for 12 minutes, tossing the potatoes a few times throughout the cooking process.
4. As soon as the potatoes are tender to a knifepoint, toss them with the lemon zest and more salt if desired.

Pancetta Mushroom & Onion Sautée

Servings: 4
Cooking Time: 20 Minutes
Ingredients:
- 16 oz white button mushrooms, stems trimmed, halved
- 1 onion, cut into half-moons
- 4 pancetta slices, diced
- 1 clove garlic, minced

Directions:
1. Preheat air fryer to 350°F. Add all ingredients, except for the garlic, to the frying basket and Air Fry for 8 minutes, tossing once. Stir in the garlic and cook for 1 more minute. Serve right away.

Chapter 6: Vegetarians Recipes

Crispy Wings With Lemony Old Bay Spice

Servings: 4
Cooking Time: 25 Minutes
Ingredients:
- ½ cup butter
- ¾ cup almond flour
- 1 tablespoon old bay spices
- 1 teaspoon lemon juice, freshly squeezed
- 3 pounds chicken wings
- Salt and pepper to taste

Directions:
1. Preheat the air fryer for 5 minutes.
2. In a mixing bowl, combine all ingredients except for the butter.
3. Place in the air fryer basket.
4. Cook for 25 minutes at 350°F.
5. Halfway through the cooking time, shake the fryer basket for even cooking.
6. Once cooked, drizzle with melted butter.

Vegan Buddha Bowls(2)

Servings: 4
Cooking Time: 20 Minutes
Ingredients:
- 1 carrot, peeled and julienned
- ½ onion, sliced into half-moons
- ¼ cup apple cider vinegar
- ½ tsp ground ginger
- ⅛ tsp cayenne pepper
- 1 parsnip, diced
- 1 tsp avocado oil
- 4 oz extra-firm tofu, cubed
- ½ tsp five-spice powder
- ½ tsp chili powder
- 2 tsp fresh lime zest
- 1 cup fresh arugula
- ½ cup cooked quinoa
- 2 tbsp canned kidney beans
- 2 tbsp canned sweetcorn
- 1 avocado, diced
- 2 tbsp pine nuts

Directions:
1. Preheat air fryer to 350°F. Combine carrot, vinegar, ginger, and cayenne in a bowl. In another bowl, combine onion, parsnip, and avocado oil. In a third bowl, mix the tofu, five-spice powder, and chili powder.
2. Place the onion mixture in the greased basket. Air Fry for 6 minutes. Stir in tofu mixture and cook for 8 more minutes. Mix in lime zest. Divide arugula, cooked quinoa, kidney beans, sweetcorn, drained carrots, avocado, pine nuts, and tofu mixture between 2 bowls. Serve.

Veggie Burgers

Servings: 4
Cooking Time: 15 Minutes
Ingredients:
- 2 cans black beans, rinsed and drained
- ½ cup cooked quinoa
- ½ cup shredded raw sweet potato
- ¼ cup diced red onion
- 2 teaspoons ground cumin
- 1 teaspoon coriander powder
- ½ teaspoon salt
- oil for misting or cooking spray
- 8 slices bread
- suggested toppings: lettuce, tomato, red onion, Pepper Jack cheese, guacamole

Directions:
1. In a medium bowl, mash the beans with a fork.
2. Add the quinoa, sweet potato, onion, cumin, coriander, and salt and mix well with the fork.
3. Shape into 4 patties, each ¾-inch thick.
4. Mist both sides with oil or cooking spray and also mist the basket.
5. Cook at 390°F for 15 minutes.
6. Follow the recipe for Toast, Plain & Simple.
7. Pop the veggie burgers back in the air fryer for a minute or two to reheat if necessary.
8. Serve on the toast with your favorite burger toppings.

Pizza Portobello Mushrooms

Servings: 2
Cooking Time: 18 Minutes
Ingredients:
- 2 portobello mushroom caps, gills removed (see Figure 13-1)
- 1 teaspoon extra-virgin olive oil
- ¼ cup diced onion
- 1 teaspoon minced garlic
- 1 medium zucchini, shredded
- 1 teaspoon dried oregano
- ½ teaspoon black pepper
- ¼ teaspoon salt
- ⅓ cup marinara sauce
- ¼ cup shredded part-skim mozzarella cheese
- ¼ teaspoon red pepper flakes
- 2 tablespoons Parmesan cheese
- 2 tablespoons chopped basil

Directions:
1. Preheat the air fryer to 370°F.
2. Lightly spray the mushrooms with an olive oil mist and place into the air fryer to cook for 10 minutes, cap side up.
3. Add the olive oil to a pan and sauté the onion and garlic together for about 2 to 4 minutes. Stir in the zucchini, oregano, pepper, and salt, and continue to cook.

Quick & Simple Tower Dual Basket Air Fryer Cookbook

When the zucchini has cooked down (usually about 4 to 6 minutes), add in the marinara sauce. Remove from the heat and stir in the mozzarella cheese.
4. Remove the mushrooms from the air fryer basket when cooking completes. Reset the temperature to 350°F.
5. Using a spoon, carefully stuff the mushrooms with the zucchini marinara mixture.
6. Return the stuffed mushrooms to the air fryer basket and cook for 5 to 8 minutes, or until the cheese is lightly browned. You should be able to easily insert a fork into the mushrooms when they're cooked.
7. Remove the mushrooms and sprinkle the red pepper flakes, Parmesan cheese, and fresh basil over the top.
8. Serve warm.

Corn On The Cob

Servings: 2–4 Servings
Cooking Time: 20 Minutes
Ingredients:
- 2–4 ears of cleaned fresh corn
- 2 tablespoons of butter
- Pinch of salt and black pepper, to taste

Directions:
1. Preheat your air fryer to 370°F. Spray some oil inside the air fryer basket.
2. Wash the corn and dry them with a paper towel. Cut the corn in half to fit the size of the air fryer basket.
3. Grease all sides of corn with the melted butter. Season generously with pepper and salt around all sides of the corn.
4. Put in the air fryer and cook at 370°F for 12–16 minutes*, flipping halfway, until lightly browned and tender.
5. Top with grated Parmesan cheese and nutritional yeast for extra flavor.
6. Serve warm and enjoy your Corn on the Cob!

Nutrition:
- al yeast, grated Parmesan cheese, for serving

Lentil Fritters

Servings: 9
Cooking Time: 12 Minutes
Ingredients:
- 1 cup cooked red lentils
- 1 cup riced cauliflower
- ½ medium zucchini, shredded (about 1 cup)
- ¼ cup finely chopped onion
- ¼ teaspoon salt
- ¼ teaspoon black pepper
- ½ teaspoon garlic powder
- ¼ teaspoon paprika
- 1 large egg
- ⅓ cup quinoa flour

Directions:
1. Preheat the air fryer to 370°F.
2. In a large bowl, mix the lentils, cauliflower, zucchini, onion, salt, pepper, garlic powder, and paprika. Mix in the egg and flour until a thick dough forms.
3. Using a large spoon, form the dough into 9 large fritters.
4. Liberally spray the air fryer basket with olive oil. Place the fritters into the basket, leaving space around each fritter so you can flip them.
5. Cook for 6 minutes, flip, and cook another 6 minutes.
6. Remove from the air fryer and repeat with the remaining fritters. Serve warm with desired sauce and sides.

Spinach And Artichoke-stuffed Peppers

Servings: 4
Cooking Time: 15 Minutes
Ingredients:
- 2 ounces cream cheese, softened
- ½ cup shredded mozzarella cheese
- ½ cup chopped fresh spinach leaves
- ¼ cup chopped canned artichoke hearts
- 2 medium green bell peppers, halved and seeded

Directions:
1. In a medium bowl, mix cream cheese, mozzarella, spinach, and artichokes. Spoon ¼ cheese mixture into each pepper half.
2. Place peppers into ungreased air fryer basket. Adjust the temperature to 320°F and set the timer for 15 minutes. Peppers will be tender and cheese will be bubbling and brown when done. Serve warm.

Falafels

Servings: 12
Cooking Time: 10 Minutes
Ingredients:
- 1 pouch falafel mix
- 2–3 tablespoons plain breadcrumbs
- oil for misting or cooking spray

Directions:
1. Prepare falafel mix according to package directions.
2. Preheat air fryer to 390°F.
3. Place breadcrumbs in shallow dish or on wax paper.
4. Shape falafel mixture into 12 balls and flatten slightly. Roll in breadcrumbs to coat all sides and mist with oil or cooking spray.
5. Place falafels in air fryer basket in single layer and cook for 5 minutes. Shake basket, and continue cooking for 5 minutes, until they brown and are crispy.

Italian Seasoned Easy Pasta Chips

Servings: 2
Cooking Time: 10 Minutes
Ingredients:
- ½ teaspoon salt
- 1 ½ teaspoon Italian seasoning blend

- 1 tablespoon nutritional yeast
- 1 tablespoon olive oil
- 2 cups whole wheat bowtie pasta

Directions:
1. Place the baking dish accessory in the air fryer.
2. Give a good stir.
3. Close the air fryer and cook for 10 minutes at 390°F.

Asparagus, Mushroom And Cheese Soufflés

Servings: 3
Cooking Time: 21 Minutes
Ingredients:
- butter
- grated Parmesan cheese
- 3 button mushrooms, thinly sliced
- 8 spears asparagus, sliced ½-inch long
- 1 teaspoon olive oil
- 1 tablespoon butter
- 4½ teaspoons flour
- pinch paprika
- pinch ground nutmeg
- salt and freshly ground black pepper
- ½ cup milk
- ½ cup grated Gruyère cheese or other Swiss cheese (about 2 ounces)
- 2 eggs, separated

Directions:
1. Butter three 6-ounce ramekins and dust with grated Parmesan cheese. (Butter the ramekins and then coat the butter with Parmesan by shaking it around in the ramekin and dumping out any excess.)
2. Preheat the air fryer to 400°F.
3. Toss the mushrooms and asparagus in a bowl with the olive oil. Transfer the vegetables to the air fryer and air-fry for 7 minutes, shaking the basket once or twice to redistribute the Ingredients while they cook.
4. While the vegetables are cooking, make the soufflé base. Melt the butter in a saucepan on the stovetop over medium heat. Add the flour, stir and cook for a minute or two. Add the paprika, nutmeg, salt and pepper. Whisk in the milk and bring the mixture to a simmer to thicken. Remove the pan from the heat and add the cheese, stirring to melt. Let the mixture cool for just a few minutes and then whisk the egg yolks in, one at a time. Stir in the cooked mushrooms and asparagus. Let this soufflé base cool.
5. In a separate bowl, whisk the egg whites to soft peak stage (the point at which the whites can almost stand up on the end of your whisk). Fold the whipped egg whites into the soufflé base, adding a little at a time.
6. Preheat the air fryer to 330°F.
7. Transfer the batter carefully to the buttered ramekins, leaving about ½-inch at the top. Place the ramekins into the air fryer basket and air-fry for 14 minutes. The soufflés should have risen nicely and be brown on top. Serve immediately.

Curried Cauliflower

Servings: 2
Cooking Time: 30 Minutes
Ingredients:
- 1 cup canned diced tomatoes
- 2 cups milk
- 2 tbsp lime juice
- 1 tbsp allspice
- 1 tbsp curry powder
- 1 tsp ground ginger
- ½ tsp ground cumin
- 12 oz frozen cauliflower
- 16 oz cheddar cheese, cubed
- ¼ cup chopped cilantro

Directions:
1. Preheat air fryer to 375°F. Combine the tomatoes and their juices, milk, lime juice, allspice, curry powder, ginger, and cumin in a baking pan. Toss in cauliflower and cheddar cheese until coated. Roast for 15 minutes, stir and Roast for another 10 minutes until bubbly. Scatter with cilantro before serving.

Vegetarian Eggplant "pizzas"

Servings: 4
Cooking Time: 25 Minutes
Ingredients:
- ½ cup diced baby bella mushrooms
- 3 tbsp olive oil
- ¼ cup diced onions
- ½ cup pizza sauce
- 1 eggplant, sliced
- 1 tsp salt
- 1 cup shredded mozzarella
- ¼ cup chopped oregano

Directions:
1. Warm 2 tsp of olive oil in a skillet over medium heat. Add in onion and mushrooms and stir-fry for 4 minutes until tender. Stir in pizza sauce. Turn the heat off.
2. Preheat air fryer to 375°F. Brush the eggplant slices with the remaining olive oil on both sides. Lay out slices on a large plate and season with salt. Then, top with the sauce mixture and shredded mozzarella. Place the eggplant pizzas in the frying basket and Air Fry for 5 minutes. Garnish with oregano to serve.

Sweet Corn Bread

Servings: 6
Cooking Time: 35 Minutes
Ingredients:
- 2 eggs, beaten
- ½ cup cornmeal
- ½ cup pastry flour
- 1/3 cup sugar

- 1 tsp lemon zest
- ½ tbsp baking powder
- ¼ tsp salt
- ¼ tsp baking soda
- ½ tbsp lemon juice
- ½ cup milk
- ¼ cup sunflower oil

Directions:
1. Preheat air fryer to 350°F. Add the cornmeal, flour, sugar, lemon zest, baking powder, salt, and baking soda in a bowl. Stir with a whisk until combined. Add the eggs, lemon juice, milk, and oil to another bowl and stir well. Add the wet mixture to the dry mixture and stir gently until combined. Spray a baking pan with oil. Pour the batter in and Bake in the fryer for 25 minutes or until golden and a knife inserted in the center comes out clean. Cut into wedges and serve.

Broccoli & Parmesan Dish

Servings: 4
Cooking Time: 25 Minutes
Ingredients:
- 1 tbsp olive oil
- 1 lemon, Juiced
- Salt and pepper to taste
- 1-ounce Parmesan cheese, grated

Directions:
1. In a bowl, mix all ingredients. Add the mixture to your air fryer and cook for 20 minutes at 360°F. Serve.

Cheesy Enchilada Stuffed Baked Potatoes

Servings: 4
Cooking Time: 37 Minutes
Ingredients:
- 2 medium russet potatoes, washed
- One 15-ounce can mild red enchilada sauce
- One 15-ounce can low-sodium black beans, rinsed and drained
- 1 teaspoon taco seasoning
- ½ cup shredded cheddar cheese
- 1 medium avocado, halved
- ½ teaspoon garlic powder
- ¼ teaspoon black pepper
- ¼ teaspoon salt
- 2 teaspoons fresh lime juice
- 2 tablespoon chopped red onion
- ¼ cup chopped cilantro

Directions:
1. Preheat the air fryer to 390°F.
2. Puncture the outer surface of the potatoes with a fork.
3. Set the potatoes inside the air fryer basket and cook for 20 minutes, rotate, and cook another 10 minutes.
4. In a large bowl, mix the enchilada sauce, black beans, and taco seasoning.
5. When the potatoes have finished cooking, carefully remove them from the air fryer basket and let cool for 5 minutes.
6. Using a pair of tongs to hold the potato if it's still too hot to touch, slice the potato in half lengthwise. Use a spoon to scoop out the potato flesh and add it into the bowl with the enchilada sauce. Mash the potatoes with the enchilada sauce mixture, creating a uniform stuffing.
7. Place the potato skins into an air-fryer-safe pan and stuff the halves with the enchilada stuffing. Sprinkle the cheese over the top of each potato.
8. Set the air fryer temperature to 350°F, return the pan to the air fryer basket, and cook for another 5 to 7 minutes to heat the potatoes and melt the cheese.
9. While the potatoes are cooking, take the avocado and scoop out the flesh into a small bowl. Mash it with the back of a fork; then mix in the garlic powder, pepper, salt, lime juice, and onion. Set aside.
10. When the potatoes have finished cooking, remove the pan from the air fryer and place the potato halves on a plate. Top with avocado mash and fresh cilantro. Serve immediately.

Sesame Orange Tofu With Snow Peas

Servings: 4
Cooking Time: 40 Minutes
Ingredients:
- 14 oz tofu, cubed
- 1 tbsp tamari
- 1 tsp olive oil
- 1 tsp sesame oil
- 1 ½ tbsp cornstarch, divided
- ½ tsp salt
- ¼ tsp garlic powder
- 1 cup snow peas
- ½ cup orange juice
- ¼ cup vegetable broth
- 1 orange, zested
- 1 garlic clove, minced
- ¼ tsp ground ginger
- 2 scallions, chopped
- 1 tbsp sesame seeds
- 2 cups cooked jasmine rice
- 2 tbsp chopped parsley

Directions:
1. Preheat air fryer to 400°F. Combine tofu, tamari, olive oil, and sesame oil in a large bowl until tofu is coated. Add in 1 tablespoon cornstarch, salt, and garlic powder and toss. Arrange the tofu on the frying basket. Air Fry for 5 minutes, then shake the basket. Add snow peas and Air Fry for 5 minutes. Place tofu mixture in a bowl.
2. Bring the orange juice, vegetable broth, orange zest, garlic, and ginger to a boil over medium heat in a small saucepan. Whisk the rest of the cornstarch and 1 tablespoon water in a small bowl to make a slurry. Pour

the slurry into the saucepan and constantly stir for 2 minutes until the sauce has thickened. Let off the heat for 2 minutes. Pour the orange sauce, scallions, and sesame seeds in the bowl with the tofu and stir to coat. Serve with jasmine rice sprinkled with parsley. Enjoy!

Ricotta Veggie Potpie

Servings: 4
Cooking Time: 30 Minutes
Ingredients:
- 1 ¼ cup flour
- ¾ cup ricotta cheese
- 1 tbsp olive oil
- 1 potato, peeled and diced
- ¼ cup diced mushrooms
- ¼ cup diced carrots
- ¼ cup diced celery
- ¼ cup diced yellow onion
- 1 garlic clove, minced
- 1 tbsp unsalted butter
- 1 cup milk
- ½ tsp ground black pepper
- 1 tsp dried thyme
- 2 tbsp dill, chopped

Directions:
1. Preheat air fryer to 350°F. Combine 1 cup flour and ricotta cheese in a medium bowl and stir until the dough comes together. Heat oil over medium heat in a small skillet. Stir in potato, mushroom, carrots, dill, thyme, celery, onion, and garlic. Cook for 4-5 minutes, often stirring, until the onions are soft and translucent.
2. Add butter and melt, then stir in the rest of the flour. Slowly pour in the milk and keep stirring. Simmer for 5 minutes until the sauce has thickened, then stir in pepper and thyme. Spoon the vegetable mixture into four 6-ounce ramekins. Cut the dough into 4 equal sections and work it into rounds that fit over the size of the ramekins. Top the ramekins with the dough, then place the ramekins in the frying basket. Bake for 10 minutes until the crust is golden. Serve hot and enjoy.

Mexican Twice Air-fried Sweet Potatoes

Servings: 2
Cooking Time: 42 Minutes
Ingredients:
- 2 large sweet potatoes
- olive oil
- salt and freshly ground black pepper
- ⅓ cup diced red onion
- ⅓ cup diced red bell pepper
- ½ cup canned black beans, drained and rinsed
- ½ cup corn kernels, fresh or frozen
- ½ teaspoon chili powder
- 1½ cups grated pepper jack cheese, divided
- Jalapeño peppers, sliced

Directions:
1. Preheat the air fryer to 400°F.
2. Rub the outside of the sweet potatoes with olive oil and season with salt and freshly ground black pepper. Transfer the potatoes into the air fryer basket and air-fry at 400°F for 30 minutes, rotating the potatoes a few times during the cooking process.
3. While the potatoes are air-frying, start the potato filling. Preheat a large sauté pan over medium heat on the stovetop. Add the onion and pepper and sauté for a few minutes, until the vegetables start to soften. Add the black beans, corn, and chili powder and sauté for another 3 minutes. Set the mixture aside.
4. Remove the sweet potatoes from the air fryer and let them rest for 5 minutes. Slice off one inch of the flattest side of both potatoes. Scrape the potato flesh out of the potatoes, leaving half an inch of potato flesh around the edge of the potato. Place all the potato flesh into a large bowl and mash it with a fork. Add the black bean mixture and 1 cup of the pepper jack cheese to the mashed sweet potatoes. Season with salt and freshly ground black pepper and mix well. Stuff the hollowed out potato shells with the black bean and sweet potato mixture, mounding the filling high in the potatoes.
5. Transfer the stuffed potatoes back into the air fryer basket and air-fry at 370°F for 10 minutes. Sprinkle the remaining cheese on top of each stuffed potato, lower the heat to 340°F and air-fry for an additional 2 minutes to melt the cheese. Top with a couple slices of Jalapeño pepper and serve warm with a green salad.

Caramelized Carrots

Servings:3
Cooking Time:15 Minutes
Ingredients:
- 1 small bag baby carrots
- ½ cup butter, melted
- ½ cup brown sugar

Directions:
1. Preheat the Air fryer to 400°F and grease an Air fryer basket.
2. Mix the butter and brown sugar in a bowl.
3. Add the carrots and toss to coat well.
4. Arrange the carrots in the Air fryer basket and cook for about 15 minutes.
5. Dish out and serve warm.

Breaded Avocado Tacos

Servings: 3
Cooking Time: 20 Minutes
Ingredients:
- 2 tomatoes, diced
- ¼ cup diced red onion
- 1 jalapeño, finely diced
- 1 tbsp lime juice
- 1 tsp lime zest
- ¼ cup chopped cilantro

- 1 tsp salt
- 1 egg
- 2 tbsp milk
- 1 cup crumbs
- ¼ cup of almond flour
- 1 avocado, sliced into fries
- 6 flour tortillas
- 1 cup coleslaw mix

Directions:
1. In a bowl, combine the tomatoes, jalapeño, red onion, lime juice, lime zest, cilantro, and salt. Let chill the pico de gallo covered in the fridge until ready to use.
2. Preheat air fryer at 375°F. In a small bowl, beat egg and milk. In another bowl, add breadcrumbs. Dip avocado slices in the egg mixture, then dredge them in the mixed almond flour and breadcrumbs. Place avocado slices in the greased frying basket and Air Fry for 5 minutes. Add 2 avocado fries to each tortilla. Top each with coleslaw mix. Serve immediately.

Bell Pepper & Lentil Tacos

Servings: 2
Cooking Time: 40 Minutes
Ingredients:
- 2 corn tortilla shells
- ½ cup cooked lentils
- ½ white onion, sliced
- ½ red pepper, sliced
- ½ green pepper, sliced
- ½ yellow pepper, sliced
- ½ cup shredded mozzarella
- ½ tsp Tabasco sauce

Directions:
1. Preheat air fryer to 320°F. Sprinkle half of the mozzarella cheese over one of the tortillas, then top with lentils, Tabasco sauce, onion, and peppers. Scatter the remaining mozzarella cheese, cover with the other tortilla and place in the frying basket. Bake for 6 minutes, flipping halfway through cooking. Serve and enjoy!

Golden Fried Tofu

Servings: 4
Cooking Time: 20 Minutes
Ingredients:
- ¼ cup flour
- ¼ cup cornstarch
- 1 tsp garlic powder
- ¼ tsp onion powder
- Salt and pepper to taste
- 1 firm tofu, cubed
- 2 tbsp cilantro, chopped

Directions:
1. Preheat air fryer to 390°F. Combine the flour, cornstarch, salt, garlic, onion powder, and black pepper in a bowl. Stir well. Place the tofu cubes in the flour mix. Toss to coat. Spray the tofu with oil and place them in a single layer in the greased frying basket. Air Fry for 14-16 minutes, flipping the pieces once until golden and crunchy. Top with freshly chopped cilantro and serve immediately.

Easy Glazed Carrots

Servings: 4
Cooking Time: 12 Minutes
Ingredients:
- 3 cups carrots, peeled and cut into large chunks
- 1 tablespoon olive oil
- 1 tablespoon honey
- Salt and black pepper, to taste

Directions:
1. Preheat the Air fryer to 390°F and grease an Air fryer basket.
2. Mix all the ingredients in a bowl and toss to coat well.
3. Transfer into the Air fryer basket and cook for about 12 minutes.
4. Dish out and serve hot.

Buttered Broccoli

Servings: 4
Cooking Time: 7 Minutes
Ingredients:
- 4 cups fresh broccoli florets
- 2 tablespoons butter, melted
- ¼ cup water
- Salt and black pepper, to taste

Directions:
1. Preheat the Air fryer to 400°F and grease an Air fryer basket.
2. Mix broccoli, butter, salt, and black pepper in a bowl and toss to coat well.
3. Place water at the bottom of Air fryer pan and arrange the broccoli florets into the Air fryer basket.
4. Cook for about 7 minutes and dish out in a bowl to serve hot.

Spicy Celery Sticks

Servings: 4
Cooking Time: 20 Minutes
Ingredients:
- 1 pound celery, cut into matchsticks
- 2 tablespoons peanut oil
- 1 jalapeño, seeded and minced
- 1/4 teaspoon dill
- 1/2 teaspoon basil
- Salt and white pepper to taste

Directions:
1. Start by preheating your Air Fryer to 380°F.
2. Toss all ingredients together and place them in the Air Fryer basket.
3. Cook for 15 minutes, shaking the basket halfway through the cooking time. Transfer to a serving platter and enjoy!

Tacos

Servings: 24
Cooking Time: 8 Minutes Per Batch
Ingredients:
- 1 24-count package 4-inch corn tortillas
- 1½ cups refried beans
- 4 ounces sharp Cheddar cheese, grated
- ½ cup salsa
- oil for misting or cooking spray

Directions:
1. Preheat air fryer to 390°F.
2. Wrap refrigerated tortillas in damp paper towels and microwave for 30 to 60 seconds to warm. If necessary, rewarm tortillas as you go to keep them soft enough to fold without breaking.
3. Working with one tortilla at a time, top with 1 tablespoon of beans, 1 tablespoon of grated cheese, and 1 teaspoon of salsa. Fold over and press down very gently on the center. Press edges firmly all around to seal. Spray both sides with oil or cooking spray.
4. Cooking in two batches, place half the tacos in the air fryer basket. To cook 12 at a time, you may need to stand them upright and lean some against the sides of basket. It's okay if they're crowded as long as you leave a little room for air to circulate around them.
5. Cook for 8 minutes or until golden brown and crispy.
6. Repeat steps 4 and 5 to cook remaining tacos.

Two-cheese Grilled Sandwiches

Servings: 2
Cooking Time: 30 Minutes
Ingredients:
- 4 sourdough bread slices
- 2 cheddar cheese slices
- 2 Swiss cheese slices
- 1 tbsp butter
- 2 dill pickles, sliced

Directions:
1. Preheat air fryer to 360°F. Smear both sides of the sourdough bread with butter and place them in the frying basket. Toast the bread for 6 minutes, flipping once.
2. Divide the cheddar cheese between 2 of the bread slices. Cover the remaining 2 bread slices with Swiss cheese slices. Bake for 10 more minutes until the cheeses have melted and lightly bubbled and the bread has golden brown. Set the cheddar-covered bread slices on a serving plate, cover with pickles, and top each with the Swiss-covered slices. Serve and enjoy!

Basil Tomatoes

Servings: 2
Cooking Time: 10 Minutes
Ingredients:
- 2 tomatoes, halved
- 1 tablespoon fresh basil, chopped
- Olive oil cooking spray
- Salt and black pepper, as required

Directions:
1. Preheat the Air fryer to 320°F and grease an Air fryer basket.
2. Spray the tomato halves evenly with olive oil cooking spray and season with salt, black pepper and basil.
3. Arrange the tomato halves into the Air fryer basket, cut sides up.
4. Cook for about 10 minutes and dish out onto serving plates.

Thyme Lentil Patties

Servings: 2
Cooking Time: 35 Minutes
Ingredients:
- ½ cup grated American cheese
- 1 cup cooked lentils
- ¼ tsp dried thyme
- 2 eggs, beaten
- Salt and pepper to taste
- 1 cup bread crumbs

Directions:
1. Preheat air fryer to 350°F. Put the eggs, lentils, and cheese in a bowl and mix to combine. Stir in half the bread crumbs, thyme, salt, and pepper. Form the mixture into 2 patties and coat them in the remaining bread crumbs. Transfer to the greased frying basket. Air Fry for 14-16 minutes until brown, flipping once. Serve.

Kale & Lentils With Crispy Onions

Servings: 4
Cooking Time: 40 Minutes
Ingredients:
- 2 cups cooked red lentils
- 1 onion, cut into rings
- ½ cup kale, steamed
- 3 garlic cloves, minced
- ½ lemon, juiced and zested
- 2 tsp cornstarch
- 1 tsp dried oregano
- Salt and pepper to taste

Directions:
1. Preheat air fryer to 390°F. Put the onion rings in the greased frying basket; do not overlap. Spray with oil and season with salt. Air Fry for 14-16 minutes, stirring twice until crispy and crunchy. Place the kale and lentils into a pan over medium heat and stir until heated through. Remove and add the garlic, lemon juice, cornstarch, salt, zest, oregano and black pepper. Stir well and pour in bowls. Top with the crisp onion rings and serve.

Chapter 7: Poultry Recipes

Crispy Duck With Cherry Sauce

Servings: 2
Cooking Time: 33 Minutes
Ingredients:
- 1 whole duck (up to 5 pounds), split in half, back and rib bones removed
- 1 teaspoon olive oil
- salt and freshly ground black pepper
- Cherry Sauce:
- 1 tablespoon butter
- 1 shallot, minced
- ½ cup sherry
- ¾ cup cherry preserves 1 cup chicken stock
- 1 teaspoon white wine vinegar
- 1 teaspoon fresh thyme leaves
- salt and freshly ground black pepper

Directions:
1. Preheat the air fryer to 400°F.
2. Trim some of the fat from the duck. Rub olive oil on the duck and season with salt and pepper. Place the duck halves in the air fryer basket, breast side up and facing the center of the basket.
3. Air-fry the duck for 20 minutes. Turn the duck over and air-fry for another 6 minutes.
4. While duck is air-frying, make the cherry sauce. Melt the butter in a large sauté pan. Add the shallot and sauté until it is just starting to brown – about 2 to 3 minutes. Add the sherry and deglaze the pan by scraping up any brown bits from the bottom of the pan. Simmer the liquid for a few minutes, until it has reduced by half. Add the cherry preserves, chicken stock and white wine vinegar. Whisk well to combine all the ingredients. Simmer the sauce until it thickens and coats the back of a spoon – about 5 to 7 minutes. Season with salt and pepper and stir in the fresh thyme leaves.
5. When the air fryer timer goes off, spoon some cherry sauce over the duck and continue to air-fry at 400°F for 4 more minutes. Then, turn the duck halves back over so that the breast side is facing up. Spoon more cherry sauce over the top of the duck, covering the skin completely. Air-fry for 3 more minutes and then remove the duck to a plate to rest for a few minutes.
6. Serve the duck in halves, or cut each piece in half again for a smaller serving. Spoon any additional sauce over the duck or serve it on the side.

Mediterranean Stuffed Chicken Breasts

Servings: 4
Cooking Time: 24 Minutes
Ingredients:
- 4 boneless, skinless chicken breasts
- ½ teaspoon salt
- ½ teaspoon black pepper
- ½ teaspoon garlic powder
- ½ teaspoon paprika
- ½ cup canned artichoke hearts, chopped
- 4 ounces cream cheese
- ¼ cup grated Parmesan cheese

Directions:
1. Pat the chicken breasts with a paper towel. Using a sharp knife, cut a pouch in the side of each chicken breast for filling.
2. In a small bowl, mix the salt, pepper, garlic powder, and paprika. Season the chicken breasts with this mixture.
3. In a medium bowl, mix together the artichokes, cream cheese, and grated Parmesan cheese. Divide the filling between the 4 breasts, stuffing it inside the pouches. Use toothpicks to close the pouches and secure the filling.
4. Preheat the air fryer to 360°F.
5. Spray the air fryer basket liberally with cooking spray, add the stuffed chicken breasts to the basket, and spray liberally with cooking spray again. Cook for 14 minutes, carefully turn over the chicken breasts, and cook another 10 minutes. Check the temperature at 20 minutes cooking. Chicken breasts are fully cooked when the center measures 165°F. Cook in batches, if needed.

Fried Herbed Chicken Wings

Servings: 4
Cooking Time: 11 Minutes
Ingredients:
- 1 tablespoon Emperor herbs chicken spices
- 8 chicken wings
- Cooking spray

Directions:
1. Generously sprinkle the chicken wings with Emperor herbs chicken spices and place in the preheated to 400°F air fryer. Cook the chicken wings for 6 minutes from each side.

Chicken Strips

Servings: 4
Cooking Time: 8 Minutes
Ingredients:
- 1 pound chicken tenders
- Marinade
- ¼ cup olive oil
- 2 tablespoons water
- 2 tablespoons honey
- 2 tablespoons white vinegar
- ½ teaspoon salt
- ½ teaspoon crushed red pepper
- 1 teaspoon garlic powder
- 1 teaspoon onion powder
- ½ teaspoon paprika

Directions:
1. Combine all marinade ingredients and mix well.

2. Add chicken and stir to coat. Cover tightly and let marinate in refrigerator for 30minutes.
3. Remove tenders from marinade and place them in a single layer in the air fryer basket.
4. Cook at 390°F for 3minutes. Turn tenders over and cook for 5 minutes longer or until chicken is done and juices run clear.
5. Repeat step 4 to cook remaining tenders.

Barbecued Chicken Thighs

Servings:4
Cooking Time: 15 To 18 Minutes
Ingredients:
- 6 boneless, skinless chicken thighs
- ¼ cup store-bought gluten-free barbecue sauce
- 2 cloves garlic, minced
- 2 tablespoons lemon juice

Directions:
1. In a medium bowl, combine the chicken, barbecue sauce, cloves, and lemon juice, and mix well. Let marinate for 10 minutes.
2. Remove the chicken thighs from the bowl and shake off excess sauce. Put the chicken pieces in the air fryer, leaving a bit of space between each one.
3. Grill for 15 to 18 minutes or until the chicken is 165°F on an instant-read meat thermometer.

Simple Chicken Shawarma

Servings:4
Cooking Time: 15 Minutes
Ingredients:
- Shawarma Spice:
- 2 teaspoons dried oregano
- 1 teaspoon ground cinnamon
- 1 teaspoon ground cumin
- 1 teaspoon ground coriander
- 1 teaspoon kosher salt
- ½ teaspoon ground allspice
- ½ teaspoon cayenne pepper
- Chicken:
- 1 pound (454 g) boneless, skinless chicken thighs, cut into large bite-size chunks
- 2 tablespoons vegetable oil
- For Serving:
- Tzatziki
- Pita bread

Directions:
1. For the shawarma spice: In a small bowl, combine the oregano, cayenne, cumin, coriander, salt, cinnamon, and allspice.
2. For the chicken: In a large bowl, toss together the chicken, vegetable oil, and shawarma spice to coat. Marinate at room temperature for 30 minutes or cover and refrigerate for up to 24 hours.

3. Preheat the air fryer to 350°F (177°C). Place the chicken in the air fryer basket. Air fry for 15 minutes, or until the chicken reaches an internal temperature of 165°F (74°C).
4. Transfer the chicken to a serving platter. Serve with tzatziki and pita bread.

Turkey & Rice Frittata

Servings: 4
Cooking Time: 30 Minutes
Ingredients:
- 6 large eggs
- ½ tsp dried thyme
- ½ cup rice, cooked
- ½ cup pulled turkey, cooked
- ½ cup fresh baby spinach
- 1 red bell pepper, chopped
- 2 tsp Parmesan cheese, grated

Directions:
1. Preheat air fryer to 320°F. Put the rice, turkey, spinach, and red bell pepper in a greased pan. Whisk the eggs, and thyme, then pour over the rice mix. Top with Parmesan cheese and Bake for 15 minutes, until the frittata is puffy and golden. Serve hot and enjoy!

Chicken & Fruit Biryani

Servings: 4
Cooking Time: 30 Minutes
Ingredients:
- 3 chicken breasts, cubed
- 2 tsp olive oil
- 2 tbsp cornstarch
- 1 tbsp curry powder
- 1 apple, chopped
- ½ cup chicken broth
- 1/3 cup dried cranberries
- 1 cooked basmati rice

Directions:
1. Preheat air fryer to 380°F. Combine the chicken and olive oil, then add some corn starch and curry powder. Mix to coat, then add the apple and pour the mix in a baking pan. Put the pan in the air fryer and Bake for 8 minutes, stirring once. Add the chicken broth, cranberries, and 2 tbsp of water and continue baking for 10 minutes, letting the sauce thicken. The chicken should be lightly charred and cooked through. Serve warm with basmati rice.

Nashville Hot Chicken

Servings: 4
Cooking Time: 27 Minutes
Ingredients:
- 1 (4-pound) chicken, cut into 6 pieces (2 breasts, 2 thighs and 2 drumsticks)
- 2 eggs
- 1 cup buttermilk

- 2 cups all-purpose flour
- 2 tablespoons paprika
- 1 teaspoon garlic powder
- 1 teaspoon onion powder
- 2 teaspoons salt
- 1 teaspoon freshly ground black pepper
- vegetable oil, in a spray bottle
- Nashville Hot Sauce:
- 1 tablespoon cayenne pepper
- 1 teaspoon salt
- ¼ cup vegetable oil
- 4 slices white bread
- dill pickle slices

Directions:
1. Cut the chicken breasts into 2 pieces so that you have a total of 8 pieces of chicken.
2. Set up a two-stage dredging station. Whisk the eggs and buttermilk together in a bowl. Combine the flour, paprika, garlic powder, onion powder, salt and black pepper in a zipper-sealable plastic bag. Dip the chicken pieces into the egg-buttermilk mixture, then toss them in the seasoned flour, coating all sides. Repeat this procedure (egg mixture and then flour mixture) one more time. This can be a little messy, but make sure all sides of the chicken are completely covered. Spray the chicken with vegetable oil and set aside.
3. Preheat the air fryer to 370°F. Spray or brush the bottom of the air-fryer basket with a little vegetable oil.
4. Air-fry the chicken in two batches at 370°F for 20 minutes, flipping the pieces over halfway through the cooking process. Transfer the chicken to a plate, but do not cover. Repeat with the second batch of chicken.
5. Lower the temperature on the air fryer to 340°F. Flip the chicken back over and place the first batch of chicken on top of the second batch already in the basket. Air-fry for another 7 minutes.
6. While the chicken is air-frying, combine the cayenne pepper and salt in a bowl. Heat the vegetable oil in a small saucepan and when it is very hot, add it to the spice mix, whisking until smooth. It will sizzle briefly when you add it to the spices. Place the fried chicken on top of the white bread slices and brush the hot sauce all over chicken. Top with the pickle slices and serve warm. Enjoy the heat and the flavor!

Paprika Duck
Servings: 6
Cooking Time: 28 Minutes
Ingredients:
- 10 oz duck skin
- 1 teaspoon sunflower oil
- ½ teaspoon salt
- ½ teaspoon ground paprika

Directions:
1. Preheat the air fryer to 375°F. Then sprinkle the duck skin with sunflower oil, salt, and ground paprika. Put the duck skin in the air fryer and cook it for 18 minutes. Then flip it on another side and cook for 10 minutes more or until it is crunchy from both sides.

Spice Chicken Pieces
Servings: 6
Cooking Time: 20 Minutes
Ingredients:
- 3 pounds' chicken, cut into eight pieces
- ¼ teaspoon cayenne
- 1 teaspoon paprika
- 2 teaspoons onion powder
- 1 ½ teaspoons garlic powder
- 1 ½ teaspoons dried oregano
- ½ tablespoon dried thyme
- Black pepper
- Salt

Directions:
1. Season chicken with black pepper and salt.
2. In a suitable bowl, mix together spices and herbs and rub spice mixture over chicken pieces.
3. Spray its air fryer basket with cooking spray.
4. Place prepared chicken in air fryer basket and cook at 350 degrees F/ 175 degrees C for almost 20 minutes, turning halfway through.
5. Serve and enjoy.

Breaded Chicken Patties
Servings: 4
Cooking Time: 15 Minutes
Ingredients:
- 1 pound ground chicken breast
- 1 cup shredded sharp Cheddar cheese
- ½ cup plain bread crumbs
- 1 teaspoon salt
- ½ teaspoon ground black pepper
- 2 tablespoons mayonnaise
- 1 cup panko bread crumbs
- Cooking spray

Directions:
1. Preheat the air fryer to 400°F.
2. In a large bowl, mix chicken, Cheddar, plain bread crumbs, salt, and pepper until well combined. Separate into four portions and form into patties ½" thick.
3. Brush each patty with mayonnaise, then press into panko bread crumbs to fully coat. Spritz with cooking spray.
4. Place in the air fryer basket and cook 15 minutes, turning halfway through cooking time, until patties are golden brown and internal temperature reaches at least 165°F. Serve warm.

Crispy Chicken Cordon Bleu

Servings: 4
Cooking Time: 13 To 15 Minutes
Ingredients:
- 4 chicken breast fillets
- ¼ cup chopped ham
- ⅓ cup grated Swiss or Gruyère cheese
- ¼ cup flour
- Pinch salt
- Freshly ground black pepper, to taste
- ½ teaspoon dried marjoram
- 1 egg
- 1 cup panko bread crumbs
- Olive oil for misting

Directions:
1. Preheat the air fryer to 380ºF (193ºC).
2. Put the chicken breast fillets on a work surface and gently press them with the palm of your hand to make them a bit thinner. Don't tear the meat.
3. In a small bowl, combine the ham and cheese. Divide this mixture among the chicken fillets. Wrap the chicken around the filling to enclose it, using toothpicks to hold the chicken together.
4. In a shallow bowl, mix the flour, salt, pepper, and marjoram. In another bowl, beat the egg. Spread the bread crumbs out on a plate.
5. Dip the chicken into the flour mixture, then into the egg, then into the bread crumbs to coat thoroughly.
6. Put the chicken in the air fryer basket and mist with olive oil.
7. Bake for 13 to 15 minutes or until the chicken is thoroughly cooked to 165ºF (74ºC). Carefully remove the toothpicks and serve.

Chicken Tenderloins With Parmesan Cheese

Servings: 6
Cooking Time: 12 Minutes
Ingredients:
- 1 lime
- 2 pounds' chicken tenderloins cut up
- 1 cup cornflakes, crushed
- ½ cup Parmesan cheese, grated
- 1 tablespoon olive oil
- Salt and black pepper, to taste
- 1 teaspoon cayenne pepper
- ⅓ teaspoon ground cumin
- 1 teaspoon chili powder
- 1 egg

Directions:
1. Squeeze and rub the lime juice all over the chicken.
2. Spritz the cooking basket with a nonstick cooking spray.
3. In a suitable mixing bowl, thoroughly combine the cornflakes, Parmesan, olive oil, salt, black pepper, cayenne pepper, cumin, and chili powder.
4. In a suitable shallow bowl, whisk the egg until well beaten.
5. Dip the chicken tenders in the egg, then in cornflakes mixture.
6. Transfer the coated chicken to the prepared cooking basket.
7. Cook in the preheated Air Fryer at about 380 degrees F/ 195 degrees C for 12 minutes almost.
8. Flip them halfway through the cooking time.
9. Serve immediately.

Perfect Grill Chicken Breast

Servings: 2
Cooking Time: 12 Minutes
Ingredients:
- 2 chicken breast, skinless and boneless
- 2 tsp olive oil
- Pepper
- Salt

Directions:
1. Remove air fryer basket and replace it with air fryer grill pan.
2. Place chicken breast to the grill pan. Season chicken with pepper and salt. Drizzle with oil.
3. Cook chicken for 375°F for 12 minutes.
4. Serve and enjoy.

Herb-roasted Turkey Breast

Servings: 6
Cooking Time: 45 Minutes
Ingredients:
- 1 tablespoon olive oil, plus more for spraying
- 2 garlic cloves, minced
- 2 teaspoons Dijon mustard
- 1½ teaspoons rosemary
- 1½ teaspoons sage
- 1½ teaspoons thyme
- 1 teaspoon salt
- ½ teaspoon freshly ground black pepper
- 3 pounds turkey breast, thawed if frozen

Directions:
1. Spray a fryer basket lightly with olive oil.
2. In a small bowl, mix together the garlic, olive oil, Dijon mustard, rosemary, sage, thyme, salt, and pepper to make a paste. Smear the paste all over the turkey breast.
3. Place the turkey breast in the fryer basket.
4. Air fry for 20 minutes. Flip turkey breast over and baste it with any drippings that have collected in the bottom drawer of the air fryer. Air fry until the internal temperature of the meat reaches at least 170°F, 20 more minutes.
5. If desired, increase the temperature to 400°F, flip the turkey breast over one last time, and air fry for up to 5 minutes to get a crispy exterior.
6. Let the turkey rest for 10 minutes before slicing and serving.

Indian-style Chicken With Raita

Servings: 2
Cooking Time: 12 Minutes
Ingredients:
- 2 chicken fillets
- Sea salt and ground black pepper, to taste
- 2 teaspoons garam masala
- 1 teaspoon ground turmeric
- ½ cup plain yogurt
- 1 English cucumber, shredded and drained
- 1 tablespoon fresh cilantro, coarsely chopped
- ½ red onion, chopped
- A pinch of grated nutmeg
- A pinch of ground cinnamon

Directions:
1. Before cooking, heat your air fryer to 380 degrees F/ 195 degrees C.
2. Rub pepper, garam masala, ground turmeric, and salt over the chicken fillets until well coated.
3. Cook in your air fryer for 12 minutes. Flip once or twice halfway through cooking.
4. To make additional raita, mix all the rest of the ingredients in a mixing bowl.
5. Serve the chicken with raita sauce.

Flavorful Spiced Chicken Pieces

Servings: 10
Cooking Time: 20 Minutes
Ingredients:
- 5 pounds' chicken, about 10 pieces
- 1 tablespoon coconut oil
- 2 ½ teaspoon white black pepper
- 1 teaspoon ground ginger
- 1 ½ teaspoon garlic salt
- 1 tablespoon paprika
- 1 teaspoon dried mustard
- 1 teaspoon black pepper
- 1 teaspoon celery salt
- ⅓ teaspoon oregano
- ½ teaspoon basil
- ½ teaspoon thyme
- 2 cups pork rinds, crushed
- 1 tablespoon vinegar
- 1 cup unsweetened almond milk
- ½ teaspoon salt

Directions:
1. Add chicken in a suitable mixing bowl.
2. Add milk and vinegar over chicken and place in the refrigerator for 2 hours.
3. In a shallow dish, mix together pork rinds, white black pepper, ginger, garlic salt, paprika, mustard, black pepper, celery salt, oregano, basil, thyme, and salt.
4. Coat air fryer basket with coconut oil.
5. Coat each chicken piece with pork rind mixture and place on a plate.
6. Place ½ coated chicken in the air fryer basket.
7. Cook chicken at 360 degrees F/ 180 degrees C for almost 10 minutes then turn chicken and continue cooking for almost 10 minutes more or until internal temperature reaches at 165 F.
8. Cook remaining chicken using the same method.
9. Serve and enjoy.

Chicken Fajita Poppers

Servings: 18
Cooking Time: 20 Minutes
Ingredients:
- 1 pound ground chicken thighs
- ½ medium green bell pepper, seeded and finely chopped
- ¼ medium yellow onion, peeled and finely chopped
- ½ cup shredded pepper jack cheese
- 1 packet gluten-free fajita seasoning

Directions:
1. In a large bowl, combine all ingredients. Form mixture into eighteen 2" balls and place in a single layer into ungreased air fryer basket, working in batches if needed.
2. Adjust the temperature to 350°F and set the timer for 20 minutes. Carefully use tongs to turn poppers halfway through cooking. When 5 minutes remain on timer, increase temperature to 400°F to give the poppers a dark golden-brown color. Shake air fryer basket once more when 2 minutes remain on timer. Serve warm.

German Chicken Frikadellen

Servings: 6
Cooking Time: 20 Minutes
Ingredients:
- 1 lb ground chicken
- 1 egg
- 3/4 cup bread crumbs
- ¼ cup diced onions
- 1 grated carrot
- 1 tsp yellow mustard
- Salt and pepper to taste
- ¼ cup chopped parsley

Directions:
1. Preheat air fryer at 350ºF. In a bowl, combine the ground chicken, egg, crumbs, onions, carrot, parsley, salt, and pepper. Mix well with your hands. Form mixture into meatballs. Place them in the frying basket and Air Fry for 8-10 minutes, tossing once until golden. Serve right away.

Curried Chicken With Fruit

Servings: 4
Cooking Time: 18 Minutes
Ingredients:
- 3 (5-ounce) low-sodium boneless skinless chicken breasts, cut into 1½-inch cubes (see Tip)
- 2 teaspoons olive oil

- 2 tablespoons cornstarch
- 1 tablespoon curry powder
- 1 tart apple, chopped
- ½ cup low-sodium chicken broth
- ⅓ cup dried cranberries
- 2 tablespoons freshly squeezed orange juice
- Brown rice, cooked (optional)

Directions:
1. In a medium bowl, mix the chicken and olive oil. Sprinkle with the cornstarch and curry powder. Toss to coat. Stir in the apple and transfer to a 6-by-2-inch metal pan. Bake in the air fryer for 8 minutes, stirring once during cooking.
2. Add the chicken broth, cranberries, and orange juice. Bake for about 10 minutes more, or until the sauce is slightly thickened and the chicken reaches an internal temperature of 165°F on a meat thermometer. Serve over hot cooked brown rice, if desired.

Cal-mex Turkey Patties

Servings: 4
Cooking Time: 30 Minutes
Ingredients:
- 1/3 cup crushed corn tortilla chips
- 1/3 cup grated American cheese
- 1 egg, beaten
- ¼ cup salsa
- Salt and pepper to taste
- 1 lb ground turkey
- 1 tbsp olive oil
- 1 tsp chili powder

Directions:
1. Preheat air fryer to 330°F. Mix together egg, tortilla chips, salsa, cheese, salt, and pepper in a bowl. Using your hands, add the ground turkey and mix gently until just combined. Divide the meat into 4 equal portions and shape into patties about ½ inch thick. Brush the patties with olive oil and sprinkle with chili powder. Air Fry the patties for 14-16 minutes, flipping once until cooked through and golden. Serve and enjoy!

Mediterranean Fried Chicken

Servings: 2
Cooking Time: 21 Minutes
Ingredients:
- 2 (6-ounce) boneless skinless chicken breast halves
- 3 tablespoons olive oil
- 6 pitted Greek or ripe olives, sliced
- 2 tablespoons. capers, drained
- ½-pint grape tomatoes
- ¼ teaspoon salt
- ¼ teaspoon. pepper

Directions:
1. Before cooking, heat your air fryer to 390 degrees F/ 200 degrees C.
2. Using the cooking spray, gently grease a baking pan that fits in your air fryer.
3. To season, add salt and pepper, as well as the chicken inside the baking pan and toss well.
4. Brown in the preheated air fryer for 6 minutes, flipping to the other side halfway through cooking.
5. Add olives, oil, capers, and tomatoes in the baking pan and stir to combine.
6. Cook in your air fryer at 330 degrees F/ 165 degrees C for 15 minutes.
7. When cooked, remove from the air fryer and serve.

Chicken & Pepperoni Pizza

Servings: 6
Cooking Time: 20 Minutes
Ingredients:
- 2 cups cooked chicken, cubed
- 20 slices pepperoni
- 1 cup sugar-free pizza sauce
- 1 cup mozzarella cheese, shredded
- ¼ cup parmesan cheese, grated

Directions:
1. Place the chicken into the base of a four-cup baking dish and add the pepperoni and pizza sauce on top. Mix well so as to completely coat the meat with the sauce.
2. Add the parmesan and mozzarella on top of the chicken, then place the baking dish into your fryer.
3. Cook for 15 minutes at 375°F.
4. When everything is bubbling and melted, remove from the fryer. Serve hot.

Lemon Parmesan Chicken

Servings:4
Cooking Time: 20 Minutes
Ingredients:
- 1 egg
- 2 tablespoons lemon juice
- 2 teaspoons minced garlic
- ½ teaspoon salt
- ½ teaspoon freshly ground black pepper
- 4 boneless, skinless chicken breasts, thin cut
- Olive oil spray
- ½ cup whole-wheat bread crumbs
- ¼ cup grated Parmesan cheese

Directions:
1. In a medium bowl, whisk together the egg, lemon juice, garlic, salt, and pepper. Add the chicken breasts, cover, and refrigerate for up to 1 hour.
2. In a shallow bowl, combine the bread crumbs and Parmesan cheese.
3. Preheat the air fryer to 360ºF (182ºC). Spray the air fryer basket lightly with olive oil spray.
4. Remove the chicken breasts from the egg mixture, then dredge them in the bread crumb mixture, and place in the air fryer basket in a single layer. Lightly spray the

chicken breasts with olive oil spray. You may need to cook the chicken in batches.
5. Air fry for 8 minutes. Flip the chicken over, lightly spray with olive oil spray, and air fry until the chicken reaches an internal temperature of 165°F (74°C), for an additional 7 to 12 minutes.
6. Serve warm.

Parmesan Crusted Chicken Cordon Bleu

Servings: 2
Cooking Time: 14 Minutes
Ingredients:
- 2 (6-ounce) boneless, skinless chicken breasts
- salt and freshly ground black pepper
- 1 tablespoon Dijon mustard
- 4 slices Swiss cheese
- 4 slices deli-sliced ham
- ¼ cup all-purpose flour*
- 1 egg, beaten
- ¾ cup panko breadcrumbs*
- ⅓ cup grated Parmesan cheese
- olive oil, in a spray bottle

Directions:
1. Butterfly the chicken breasts. Place the chicken breast on a cutting board and press down on the breast with the palm of your hand. Slice into the long side of the chicken breast, parallel to the cutting board, but not all the way through to the other side. Open the chicken breast like a "book". Place a piece of plastic wrap over the chicken breast and gently pound it with a meat mallet to make it evenly thick.
2. Season the chicken with salt and pepper. Spread the Dijon mustard on the inside of each chicken breast. Layer one slice of cheese on top of the mustard, then top with the 2 slices of ham and the other slice of cheese.
3. Starting with the long edge of the chicken breast, roll the chicken up to the other side. Secure it shut with 1 or 2 toothpicks.
4. Preheat the air fryer to 350°F.
5. Set up a dredging station with three shallow dishes. Place the flour in the first dish. Place the beaten egg in the second shallow dish. Combine the panko breadcrumbs and Parmesan cheese together in the third shallow dish. Dip the stuffed and rolled chicken breasts in the flour, then the beaten egg and then roll in the breadcrumb-cheese mixture to cover on all sides. Press the crumbs onto the chicken breasts with your hands to make sure they are well adhered. Spray the chicken breasts with olive oil and transfer to the air fryer basket.
6. Air-fry at 350°F for 14 minutes, flipping the breasts over halfway through the cooking time. Let the chicken rest for a few minutes before removing the toothpicks, slicing and serving.

Duck Breast With Figs

Servings: 2 Servings
Cooking Time: 40 Minutes
Ingredients:
- 1 pound of boneless duck breast
- 6 halved fresh figs
- 2 cups of pomegranate juice
- 3 tablespoons of brown sugar
- 2 tablespoons of lemon juice
- Pinch of black pepper and salt, to taste

Directions:
1. Add juice, sugar, and lemon to a saucepan. Bring it to a boil, then lower to low heat and simmer for about 25 minutes until thick consistency.
2. Preheat your air fryer to 400°F. Spray the air fryer basket with some oil.
3. Dry the duck breast with a paper towel. Make 4 slits across the skin diagonally with a knife, then make another 4 slits in the opposite diagonal direction. Rub both sides generously with salt and black pepper.
4. Put the prepared duck breast skin-side down in the preheated air fryer basket and cook at 400°F for 8 minutes. Flip it and continue cooking for 5 minutes. Flip it again and cook for 1 minute to make crispy skin. Remove from the air fryer.
5. Drizzle the fig halves with oil, season them with black pepper and salt. Put the figs into the air fryer and cook for 5 minutes.
6. Meanwhile, cut the cooked duck breast into slices, pour over pomegranate sauce, and add some roasted figs on the top.
7. Serve warm and enjoy your Duck Breast with Figs!

Chicken Salad With White Dressing

Servings: 2
Cooking Time: 20 Minutes
Ingredients:
- 2 chicken breasts, cut into strips
- ¼ cup diced peeled red onion
- ½ peeled English cucumber, diced
- 1 tbsp crushed red pepper flakes
- 1 cup Greek yogurt
- 3 tbsp light mayonnaise
- 1 tbsp mustard
- 1 tsp chopped dill
- 1 tsp chopped mint
- 1 tsp lemon juice
- 2 cloves garlic, minced
- Salt and pepper to taste
- 3 cups mixed greens
- 10 Kalamata olives, halved
- 1 tomato, diced
- ¼ cup feta cheese crumbles

Directions:

1. Preheat air fryer at 350ºF. In a small bowl, whisk the Greek yogurt, mayonnaise, mustard, cucumber, dill, mint, salt, lemon juice, and garlic, and let chill the resulting dressing covered in the fridge until ready to use. Sprinkle the chicken strips with salt and pepper. Place them in the frying basket and Air Fry for 10 minutes, tossing once. Place the mixed greens and pepper flakes in a salad bowl. Top each with red onion, olives, tomato, feta cheese, and grilled chicken. Drizzle with the dressing and serve.

Parmesan Chicken Meatloaf

Servings: 4
Cooking Time: 45 Minutes
Ingredients:
- 1 ½ tsp evaporated cane sugar
- 1 lb ground chicken
- 4 garlic cloves, minced
- 2 tbsp grated Parmesan
- ¼ cup heavy cream
- ¼ cup minced onion
- 2 tbsp chopped basil
- 2 tbsp chopped parsley
- Salt and pepper to taste
- ½ tsp onion powder
- ½ cup bread crumbs
- ¼ tsp red pepper flakes
- 1 egg
- 1 cup tomato sauce
- ½ tsp garlic powder
- ½ tsp dried thyme
- ½ tsp dried oregano
- 1 tbsp coconut aminos

Directions:
1. Preheat air fryer to 400°F. Combine chicken, garlic, minced onion, oregano, thyme, basil, salt, pepper, onion powder, Parmesan cheese, red pepper flakes, bread crumbs, egg, and cream in a large bowl. Transfer the chicken mixture to a prepared baking dish. Stir together tomato sauce, garlic powder, coconut aminos, and sugar in a small bowl. Spread over the meatloaf. Loosely cover with foil. Place the pan in the frying basket and bake for 15 minutes. Take the foil off and bake for another 15 minutes. Allow resting for 10 minutes before slicing. Serve sprinkled with parsley.

Honey Rosemary Chicken

Servings:4
Cooking Time: 20 Minutes
Ingredients:
- ¼ cup balsamic vinegar
- ¼ cup honey
- 2 tablespoons olive oil
- 1 tablespoon dried rosemary leaves
- 1 teaspoon salt
- ½ teaspoon freshly ground black pepper
- 2 whole boneless, skinless chicken breasts (about 1 pound / 454 g each), halved
- Cooking spray

Directions:
1. In a large resealable bag, combine the vinegar, honey, olive oil, rosemary, salt, and pepper. Add the chicken pieces, seal the bag, and refrigerate to marinate for at least 2 hours.
2. Preheat the air fryer to 325ºF (163ºC). Line the air fryer basket with parchment paper.
3. Remove the chicken from the marinade and place it on the parchment. Spritz with cooking spray.
4. Bake for 10 minutes. Flip the chicken, spritz it with cooking spray, and bake for 10 minutes more until the internal temperature reaches 165ºF (74ºC) and the chicken is no longer pink inside. Let sit for 5 minutes before serving.

Parmesan Chicken Fingers

Servings: 2
Cooking Time: 19 Minutes
Ingredients:
- ½ cup flour
- 1 teaspoon salt
- freshly ground black pepper
- 2 eggs, beaten
- ¾ cup seasoned panko breadcrumbs
- ¾ cup grated Parmesan cheese
- 8 chicken tenders (about 1 pound)
- OR
- 2 to 3 boneless, skinless chicken breasts, cut into strips
- vegetable oil
- marinara sauce

Directions:
1. Set up a dredging station. Combine the flour, salt and pepper in a shallow dish. Place the beaten eggs in second shallow dish, and combine the panko breadcrumbs and Parmesan cheese in a third shallow dish.
2. Dredge the chicken tenders in the flour mixture. Then dip them into the egg, and finally place the chicken in the breadcrumb mixture. Press the coating onto both sides of the chicken tenders. Place the coated chicken tenders on a baking sheet until they are all coated. Spray both sides of the chicken fingers with vegetable oil.
3. Preheat the air fryer to 360°F.
4. Air-fry the chicken fingers in two batches. Transfer half the chicken fingers to the air fryer basket and air-fry for 9 minutes, turning the chicken over halfway through the cooking time. When the second batch of chicken fingers has finished cooking, return the first batch to the air fryer with the second batch and air-fry for one minute to heat everything through.
5. Serve immediately with marinara sauce, honey-mustard, ketchup or your favorite dipping sauce.

Chicken Wings With Bbq Sauce

Servings: 4
Cooking Time: 12 Minutes
Ingredients:
- 1 ½ pounds chicken wings
- 2 tablespoons unsweetened BBQ sauce
- 1 teaspoon paprika
- 1 tablespoon olive oil
- 1 teaspoon garlic powder
- Black pepper
- Salt

Directions:
1. In a suitable bowl, toss chicken wings with garlic powder, oil, paprika, black pepper, and salt.
2. At 360 degrees F/ 180 degrees C, preheat your Air fryer.
3. Add chicken wings in air fryer basket and cook for 12 minutes.
4. Turn chicken wings to another side and cook for 5 minutes more.
5. Remove chicken wings from air fryer and toss with BBQ sauce.
6. Return chicken wings in air fryer basket and cook for 2 minutes more.
7. Serve and enjoy.

Chicken Fajitas

Servings: 4
Cooking Time:10 To 15 Minutes
Ingredients:
- 4 (5-ounce) low-sodium boneless skinless chicken breasts, cut into 4-by-½-inch strips
- 1 tablespoon freshly squeezed lemon juice
- 2 teaspoons olive oil
- 2 teaspoons chili powder
- 2 red bell peppers, sliced (see Tip)
- 4 low-sodium whole-wheat tortillas
- ⅓ cup nonfat sour cream
- 1 cup grape tomatoes, sliced (see Tip)

Directions:
1. In a large bowl, mix the chicken, lemon juice, olive oil, and chili powder. Toss to coat. Transfer the chicken to the air fryer basket. Add the red bell peppers. Grill for 10 to 15 minutes, or until the chicken reaches an internal temperature of 165°F on a meat thermometer.
2. Assemble the fajitas with the tortillas, chicken, bell peppers, sour cream, and tomatoes. Serve immediately.

Crispy Chicken Parmesan

Servings: 4
Cooking Time: 12 Minutes
Ingredients:
- 4 skinless, boneless chicken breasts, pounded thin to ¼-inch thickness
- 1 teaspoon salt, divided
- ½ teaspoon black pepper, divided
- 1 cup flour
- 2 eggs
- 1 cup panko breadcrumbs
- ½ teaspoon dried oregano
- ½ cup grated Parmesan cheese

Directions:
1. Pat the chicken breasts with a paper towel. Season the chicken with ½ teaspoon of the salt and ¼ teaspoon of the pepper.
2. In a medium bowl, place the flour.
3. In a second bowl, whisk the eggs.
4. In a third bowl, place the breadcrumbs, oregano, cheese, and the remaining ½ teaspoon of salt and ¼ teaspoon of pepper.
5. Dredge the chicken in the flour and shake off the excess. Dip the chicken into the eggs and then into the breadcrumbs. Set the chicken on a plate and repeat with the remaining chicken pieces.
6. Preheat the air fryer to 360°F.
7. Place the chicken in the air fryer basket and spray liberally with cooking spray. Cook for 8 minutes, turn the chicken breasts over, and cook another 4 minutes. When golden brown, check for an internal temperature of 165°F.

Cheese Turkey Meatloaf

Servings: 6
Cooking Time: 47 Minutes
Ingredients:
- 2 pounds' turkey mince
- ½ cup scallions, chopped
- 2 garlic cloves, finely minced
- 1 teaspoon dried thyme
- ½ teaspoon dried basil
- ¾ cup Colby cheese, shredded
- 1 tablespoon tamari sauce
- Black pepper and salt, to your liking
- ¼ cup roasted red pepper tomato sauce
- ¾ tablespoons. olive oil
- 1 medium-sized egg, well beaten

Directions:
1. In a nonstick skillet, that is preheated over a moderate heat, sauté the turkey mince, scallions, garlic, thyme, and basil until just tender and fragrant.
2. Then set your Air Fryer to cook at almost 360 degrees F/ 180 degrees C.
3. Combine sautéed mixture with the cheese and tamari sauce; then form the mixture into a loaf shape.
4. Mix the remaining items and pour them over the meatloaf.
5. Cook in the preheated air fryer basket for 45 to 47 minutes.
6. Serve warm.

Quick & Simple Tower Dual Basket Air Fryer Cookbook

Chipotle Drumsticks

Servings: 4
Cooking Time: 25 Minutes
Ingredients:
- 1 tablespoon tomato paste
- ½ teaspoon chipotle powder
- ¼ teaspoon apple cider vinegar
- ¼ teaspoon garlic powder
- 8 chicken drumsticks
- ½ teaspoon salt
- ⅛ teaspoon ground black pepper

Directions:
1. In a small bowl, combine tomato paste, chipotle powder, vinegar, and garlic powder.
2. Sprinkle drumsticks with salt and pepper, then place into a large bowl and pour in tomato paste mixture. Toss or stir to evenly coat all drumsticks in mixture.
3. Place drumsticks into ungreased air fryer basket. Adjust the temperature to 400°F and set the timer for 25 minutes, turning drumsticks halfway through cooking. Drumsticks will be dark red with an internal temperature of at least 165°F when done. Serve warm.

Vip´s Club Sandwiches

Servings: 4
Cooking Time: 50 Minutes
Ingredients:
- 1 cup buttermilk
- 1 egg
- 1 cup bread crumbs
- 1 tsp garlic powder
- Salt and pepper to taste
- 4 chicken cutlets
- 3 tbsp butter, melted
- 4 hamburger buns
- 4 tbsp mayonnaise
- 4 tsp yellow mustard
- 8 dill pickle chips
- 4 pieces iceberg lettuce
- ½ sliced avocado
- 4 slices cooked bacon
- 8 vine-ripe tomato slices
- 1 tsp chia seeds

Directions:
1. Preheat air fryer at 400°F. Beat the buttermilk and egg in a bowl. In another bowl, combine breadcrumbs, garlic powder, salt, and black pepper. Dip chicken cutlets in the egg mixture, then dredge them in the breadcrumbs mixture. Brush chicken cutlets lightly with melted butter on both sides, place them in the greased frying basket, and Air Fry for 18-20 minutes. Spread the mayonnaise on the top buns and mustard on the bottom buns. Add chicken onto bottom buns and top with pickles, lettuce, chia seeds, avocado, bacon, and tomato. Cover with the top buns. Serve and enjoy!

Orange Curried Chicken Stir-fry

Servings: 4
Cooking Time: 16 To 19 Minutes
Ingredients:
- ¾ pound boneless, skinless chicken thighs, cut into 1-inch pieces
- 1 yellow bell pepper, cut into 1½-inch pieces
- 1 small red onion, sliced
- Olive oil for misting
- ¼ cup chicken stock
- 2 tablespoons honey
- ¼ cup orange juice
- 1 tablespoon cornstarch
- 2 to 3 teaspoons curry powder

Directions:
1. Put the chicken thighs, pepper, and red onion in the air fryer basket and mist with olive oil.
2. Cook for 12 to 14 minutes or until the chicken is cooked to 165°F, shaking the basket halfway through cooking time.
3. Remove the chicken and vegetables from the air fryer basket and set aside.
4. In a 6-inch metal bowl, combine the stock, honey, orange juice, cornstarch, and curry powder, and mix well. Add the chicken and vegetables, stir, and put the bowl in the basket.
5. Return the basket to the air fryer and cook for 2 minutes. Remove and stir, then cook for 2 to 3 minutes or until the sauce is thickened and bubbly.
6. Did You Know? Curry powder isn't one single spice, but a combination of many spices. In India, each family makes their own unique blend.

Sesame Chicken Tenders

Servings: 4
Cooking Time: 15 Minutes
Ingredients:
- Olive oil
- ¼ cup soy sauce
- 2 tablespoons white vinegar
- 1 tablespoon honey
- 1 tablespoon toasted sesame oil
- 1 tablespoon lime juice
- 1 teaspoon ground ginger
- 1 pound boneless skinless, chicken tenderloins
- 2 teaspoon toasted sesame seeds

Directions:
1. Spray a fryer basket lightly with olive oil.
2. In a large zip-top plastic bag, combine the soy sauce, white vinegar, honey, sesame oil, lime juice, and ginger to make a marinade.

3. Add the chicken tenderloins to the bag, seal, and marinate the chicken in the refrigerator for at least 2 hours or overnight.
4. If using wooden skewers, soak them in water for at least 30 minutes before using.
5. Thread 1 chicken tenderloin onto each skewer. Sprinkle with sesame seeds. Reserve the marinade.
6. Place the skewers in the fryer basket in a single layer. You may need to cook the chicken in batches.
7. Air fry for 6 minutes. Flip the chicken over, baste with more marinade, and cook until crispy, an additional 5 to 8 minutes.

Fiesta Chicken Plate

Servings: 4
Cooking Time: 15 Minutes
Ingredients:
- 1 pound boneless, skinless chicken breasts (2 large breasts)
- 2 tablespoons lime juice
- 1 teaspoon cumin
- ½ teaspoon salt
- ½ cup grated Pepper Jack cheese
- 1 16-ounce can refried beans
- ½ cup salsa
- 2 cups shredded lettuce
- 1 medium tomato, chopped
- 2 avocados, peeled and sliced
- 1 small onion, sliced into thin rings
- sour cream
- tortilla chips (optional)

Directions:
1. Split each chicken breast in half lengthwise.
2. Mix lime juice, cumin, and salt together and brush on all surfaces of chicken breasts.
3. Place in air fryer basket and cook at 390°F for 15 minutes, until well done.
4. Divide the cheese evenly over chicken breasts and cook for an additional minute to melt cheese.
5. While chicken is cooking, heat refried beans on stovetop or in microwave.
6. When ready to serve, divide beans among 4 plates. Place chicken breasts on top of beans and spoon salsa over. Arrange the lettuce, tomatoes, and avocados artfully on each plate and scatter with the onion rings.
7. Pass sour cream at the table and serve with tortilla chips if desired.

Celery Chicken Mix

Servings: 4
Cooking Time: 9 Minutes
Ingredients:
- 1 teaspoon fennel seeds
- ½ teaspoon ground celery
- ½ teaspoon salt
- 1 tablespoon olive oil
- 12 oz chicken fillet

Directions:
1. Cut the chicken fillets on 4 chicken chops. In the shallow bowl mix up fennel seeds and olive oil. Rub the chicken chops with salt and ground celery. Preheat the air fryer to 365°F. Brush the chicken chops with the fennel oil and place it in the air fryer basket. Cook them for 9 minutes.

Buffalo Chicken Taquitos

Servings:6
Cooking Time: 10 Minutes
Ingredients:
- Olive oil
- 8 ounces fat-free cream cheese, softened
- ⅛ cup Buffalo sauce
- 2 cups shredded cooked chicken
- 12 (7-inch) low-carb flour tortillas

Directions:
1. Spray a fryer basket lightly with olive oil.
2. In a large bowl, mix together the cream cheese and Buffalo sauce until well-combined. Add the chicken and stir until combined.
3. Place the tortillas on a clean workspace. Spoon 2 to 3 tablespoons of the chicken mixture in a thin line down the center of each tortilla. Roll up the tortillas.
4. Place the tortillas in the fryer basket, seam side down. Spray each tortilla lightly with olive oil. You may need to cook the taquitos in batches.
5. Air fry until golden brown, 5 to 10 minutes.

Turkey And Cranberry Quesadillas

Servings:4
Cooking Time: 4 To 8 Minutes
Ingredients:
- 6 low-sodium whole-wheat tortillas
- ⅓ cup shredded low-sodium low-fat Swiss cheese
- ¾ cup shredded cooked low-sodium turkey breast
- 2 tablespoons cranberry sauce
- 2 tablespoons dried cranberries
- ½ teaspoon dried basil
- Olive oil spray, for spraying the tortillas

Directions:
1. Preheat the air fryer to 400°F (204°C).
2. Put 3 tortillas on a work surface.
3. Evenly divide the Swiss cheese, turkey, cranberry sauce, and dried cranberries among the tortillas. Sprinkle with the basil and top with the remaining tortillas.
4. Spray the outsides of the tortillas with olive oil spray.
5. One at a time, air fry the quesadillas in the air fryer for 4 to 8 minutes, or until crisp and the cheese is melted. Cut into quarters and serve.

Lemon-pepper Chicken Wings

Servings: 4
Cooking Time: 20 Minute
Ingredients:
- 8 whole chicken wings
- Juice of ½ lemon
- ½ teaspoon garlic powder
- 1 teaspoon onion powder
- Salt
- Pepper
- ¼ cup low-fat buttermilk
- ½ cup all-purpose flour
- Cooking oil

Directions:
1. Place the wings in a sealable plastic bag. Drizzle the wings with the lemon juice. Season the wings with the garlic powder, onion powder, and salt and pepper to taste.
2. Seal the bag. Shake thoroughly to combine the seasonings and coat the wings.
3. Pour the buttermilk and the flour into separate bowls large enough to dip the wings.
4. Spray the air fryer basket with cooking oil.
5. One at a time, dip the wings in the buttermilk and then the flour.
6. Place the wings in the air fryer basket. It is okay to stack them on top of each other. Spray the wings with cooking oil, being sure to spray the bottom layer. Cook for 5 minutes.
7. Remove the basket and shake it to ensure all of the pieces will cook fully.
8. Return the basket to the air fryer and continue to cook the chicken. Repeat shaking every 5 minutes until a total of 20 minutes has passed.
9. Cool before serving.

Chicken Burgers With Blue Cheese Sauce

Servings: 4
Cooking Time: 40 Minutes
Ingredients:
- ¼ cup crumbled blue cheese
- ¼ cup sour cream
- 2 tbsp mayonnaise
- 1 tbsp red hot sauce
- Salt to taste
- 3 tbsp buffalo wing sauce
- 1 lb ground chicken
- 2 tbsp grated carrot
- 2 tbsp diced celery
- 1 egg white

Directions:
1. Whisk the blue cheese, sour cream, mayonnaise, red hot sauce, salt, and 1 tbsp of buffalo sauce in a bowl. Let sit covered in the fridge until ready to use.
2. Preheat air fryer at 350ºF. In another bowl, combine the remaining ingredients. Form mixture into 4 patties, making a slight indentation in the middle of each. Place patties in the greased frying basket and Air Fry for 13 minutes until you reach your desired doneness, flipping once. Serve with the blue cheese sauce.

Gluten-free Nutty Chicken Fingers

Servings: 4
Cooking Time: 10 Minutes
Ingredients:
- ½ cup gluten-free flour
- ½ teaspoon garlic powder
- ¼ teaspoon onion powder
- ¼ teaspoon black pepper
- ¼ teaspoon salt
- 1 cup walnuts, pulsed into coarse flour
- ½ cup gluten-free breadcrumbs
- 2 large eggs
- 1 pound boneless, skinless chicken tenders

Directions:
1. Preheat the air fryer to 400°F.
2. In a medium bowl, mix the flour, garlic, onion, pepper, and salt. Set aside.
3. In a separate bowl, mix the walnut flour and breadcrumbs.
4. In a third bowl, whisk the eggs.
5. Liberally spray the air fryer basket with olive oil spray.
6. Pat the chicken tenders dry with a paper towel. Dredge the tenders one at a time in the flour, then dip them in the egg, and toss them in the breadcrumb coating. Repeat until all tenders are coated.
7. Set each tender in the air fryer, leaving room on each side of the tender to allow for flipping.
8. When the basket is full, cook 5 minutes, flip, and cook another 5 minutes. Check the internal temperature after cooking completes; it should read 165°F. If it does not, cook another 2 to 4 minutes.
9. Remove the tenders and let cool 5 minutes before serving. Repeat until all the tenders are cooked.

Cinnamon Chicken Thighs

Servings: 4
Cooking Time: 30 Minutes
Ingredients:
- 2 pounds chicken thighs
- A pinch of salt and black pepper
- 2 tablespoons olive oil
- ½ teaspoon cinnamon, ground

Directions:
1. Season the chicken thighs with salt and pepper, and rub with the rest of the ingredients. Put the chicken thighs in air fryer's basket, cook at 360°F for 15 minutes on each side, divide between plates and serve.

Crispy Chicken Strips

Servings: 4
Cooking Time: 20 Minutes
Ingredients:
- 1 tablespoon olive oil
- 1 pound (454 g) boneless, skinless chicken tenderloins
- 1 teaspoon salt
- ½ teaspoon freshly ground black pepper
- ½ teaspoon paprika
- ½ teaspoon garlic powder
- ½ cup whole-wheat seasoned bread crumbs
- 1 teaspoon dried parsley
- Cooking spray

Directions:
1. Preheat the air fryer to 370°F (188°C). Spray the air fryer basket lightly with cooking spray.
2. In a medium bowl, toss the chicken with the salt, pepper, paprika, and garlic powder until evenly coated.
3. Add the olive oil and toss to coat the chicken evenly.
4. In a separate, shallow bowl, mix together the bread crumbs and parsley.
5. Coat each piece of chicken evenly in the bread crumb mixture.
6. Place the chicken in the air fryer basket in a single layer and spray it lightly with cooking spray. You may need to cook them in batches.
7. Air fry for 10 minutes. Flip the chicken over, lightly spray it with cooking spray, and air fry for an additional 8 to 10 minutes, until golden brown. Serve.

Katsu Chicken Thighs

Servings: 4
Cooking Time: 35 Minutes
Ingredients:
- 1 ½ lb boneless, skinless chicken thighs
- 3 tbsp tamari sauce
- 3 tbsp lemon juice
- ½ tsp ground ginger
- Black pepper to taste
- 6 tbsp cornstarch
- 1 cup chicken stock
- 2 tbsp hoisin sauce
- 2 tbsp light brown sugar
- 2 tbsp sesame seeds

Directions:
1. Preheat the air fryer to 400°F. After cubing the chicken thighs, put them in a cake pan. Add a tbsp of tamari sauce, a tbsp of lemon juice, ginger, and black pepper. Mix and let marinate for 10 minutes. Remove the chicken and coat it in 4 tbsp of cornstarch; set aside. Add the rest of the marinade to the pan and add the stock, hoisin sauce, brown sugar, and the remaining tamari sauce, lemon juice, and cornstarch. Mix well. Put the pan in the frying basket and Air Fry for 5-8 minutes or until bubbling and thick, stirring once. Remove and set aside. Put the chicken in the frying basket and Fry for 15-18 minutes, shaking the basket once. Remove the chicken to the sauce in the pan and return to the fryer to reheat for 2 minutes. Sprinkle with the sesame seeds and serve.

Korean-style Chicken Bulgogi

Servings: 4
Cooking Time: 30 Minutes
Ingredients:
- 6 boneless, skinless chicken thighs, cubed
- 3 scallions, sliced, whites and green separated
- 2 carrots, grated
- ½ cup rice vinegar
- 2 tsp granulated sugar
- Salt to taste
- 2 tbsp tamari
- 2 tsp sesame oil
- 1 tbsp light brown sugar
- 1 tbsp lime juice
- 1 tbsp soy sauce
- 2 cloves garlic, minced
- ½ Asian pear
- 2 tsp minced ginger
- 4 cups cooked white rice
- 2 tsp sesame seeds

Directions:
1. In a bowl, combine the carrots, half of the rice vinegar, sugar, and salt. Let chill covered in the fridge until ready to use. Mix the tamari, sesame oil, soy sauce, brown sugar, remaining rice vinegar, lime juice, garlic, Asian pear, ginger, and scallion whites in a bowl. Toss in chicken thighs and let marinate for 10 minutes.
2. Preheat air fryer at 350°F. Using a slotted spoon, transfer chicken thighs to the frying basket, reserve marinade, and Air Fry for 10-12 minutes, shaking once. Place chicken over a rice bed on serving plates and scatter with scallion greens and sesame seeds. Serve with pickled carrots.

Chapter 8: Beef, pork & Lamb Recipes

Tasty Pork Chops

Servings: 4
Cooking Time: 9 Minutes
Ingredients:
- 4 pork chops, boneless
- 1 teaspoon onion powder
- 1 teaspoon smoked paprika
- ½ cup parmesan cheese, grated
- 2 tablespoons olive oil
- ½ teaspoon black pepper
- 1 teaspoon kosher salt

Directions:
1. Brush pork chops with olive oil.
2. In a suitable bowl, mix together parmesan cheese and spices.
3. Grease its air fryer basket with cooking spray.
4. Coat pork chops with parmesan cheese mixture and place in the air fryer basket.
5. Cook pork chops at 375 degrees F/ 190 degrees C for 9 minutes. Turn halfway through the cooking time.
6. Serve and enjoy.

Marinated Beef And Vegetable Stir Fry

Servings: 4
Cooking Time: 35 Minutes
Ingredients:
- 2 lbs. top round, cut into bite-sized strips
- 2 garlic cloves, sliced
- 1 teaspoon dried marjoram
- ¼ cup red wine
- 1 tablespoon tamari sauce
- Salt and black pepper, to taste
- ½ tablespoon olive oil
- 1 red onion, sliced
- 2 bell peppers, sliced
- 1 carrot, sliced

Directions:
1. In a suitable bowl, add the top round, marjoram, red wine, garlic, tamari sauce, salt, and pepper in a bowl; cover and marinate for 1 hour.
2. Oil the cooking tray of your air fryer.
3. Take the marinated beef out of the marinade and arrange to the tray.
4. Cook at 390 degrees F/200 degrees C for 15 minutes.
5. After that, add the garlic, onion, peppers and carrot, cook for 15 minutes more or until tender.
6. Open the Air Fryer every 5 minutes and baste the meat with the remaining marinade.
7. When done, serve and enjoy.

Breaded Italian Pork Chops

Servings:4
Cooking Time: 15 Minutes
Ingredients:
- Olive oil
- 2 eggs, beaten
- ¼ cup whole-wheat bread crumbs
- 1 envelope zesty Italian dressing mix
- 4 thin boneless pork chops, trimmed of excess fat
- Salt
- Freshly ground black pepper

Directions:
1. Spray a fryer basket lightly with olive oil.
2. Place the eggs in a shallow bowl.
3. In a separate shallow bowl, mix together the bread crumbs and Italian dressing mix.
4. Season the pork chops with salt and pepper. Coat the pork chops in the egg, shaking off any excess. Dredge them in the bread crumb mixture.
5. Place the pork chops in the fryer basket in a single layer and spray lightly with olive oil. You may need to cook them in batches.
6. Air fry for 7 minutes. Flip the pork chops over, lightly spray with olive oil, and cook until they reach an internal temperature of at least 145°F, an additional 5 to 8 minutes.

Sweet And Spicy Pork Ribs

Servings:4
Cooking Time: 20 Minutes Per Batch
Ingredients:
- 1 rack pork spareribs, white membrane removed
- ¼ cup brown sugar
- 2 teaspoons salt
- 2 teaspoons ground black pepper
- 1 tablespoon chili powder
- 1 teaspoon garlic powder
- ½ teaspoon cayenne pepper

Directions:
1. Preheat the air fryer to 400°F.
2. Place ribs on a work surface and cut the rack into two pieces to fit in the air fryer basket.
3. In a medium bowl, whisk together brown sugar, salt, black pepper, chili powder, garlic powder, and cayenne to make a dry rub.
4. Massage dry rub onto both sides of ribs until well coated. Place a portion of ribs in the air fryer basket, working in batches as necessary.
5. Cook 20 minutes until internal temperature reaches at least 190°F and no pink remains. Let rest 5 minutes before cutting and serving.

Sweet And Sour Pork

Servings: 2
Cooking Time: 11 Minutes
Ingredients:
- ⅓ cup all-purpose flour
- ⅓ cup cornstarch

- 2 teaspoons Chinese 5-spice powder
- 1 teaspoon salt
- freshly ground black pepper
- 1 egg
- 2 tablespoons milk
- ¾ pound boneless pork, cut into 1-inch cubes
- vegetable or canola oil, in a spray bottle
- 1½ cups large chunks of red and green peppers
- ½ cup ketchup
- 2 tablespoons rice wine vinegar or apple cider vinegar
- 2 tablespoons brown sugar
- ¼ cup orange juice
- 1 tablespoon soy sauce
- 1 clove garlic, minced
- 1 cup cubed pineapple
- chopped scallions

Directions:
1. Set up a dredging station with two bowls. Combine the flour, cornstarch, Chinese 5-spice powder, salt and pepper in one large bowl. Whisk the egg and milk together in a second bowl. Dredge the pork cubes in the flour mixture first, then dip them into the egg and then back into the flour to coat on all sides. Spray the coated pork cubes with vegetable or canola oil.
2. Preheat the air fryer to 400°F.
3. Toss the pepper chunks with a little oil and air-fry at 400°F for 5 minutes, shaking the basket halfway through the cooking time.
4. While the peppers are cooking, start making the sauce. Combine the ketchup, rice wine vinegar, brown sugar, orange juice, soy sauce, and garlic in a medium saucepan and bring the mixture to a boil on the stovetop. Reduce the heat and simmer for 5 minutes. When the peppers have finished air-frying, add them to the saucepan along with the pineapple chunks. Simmer the peppers and pineapple in the sauce for an additional 2 minutes. Set aside and keep warm.
5. Add the dredged pork cubes to the air fryer basket and air-fry at 400°F for 6 minutes, shaking the basket to turn the cubes over for the last minute of the cooking process.
6. When ready to serve, toss the cooked pork with the pineapple, peppers and sauce. Serve over white rice and garnish with chopped scallions.

Garlic Steak With Cheese Butter

Servings: 2
Cooking Time: 10 Minutes
Ingredients:
- 2 rib-eye steaks
- 2 teaspoons garlic powder
- 2 ½ tablespoons blue cheese butter
- 1 teaspoon black pepper
- 2 teaspoons kosher salt

Directions:
1. At 400 degrees F/ 205 degrees C, preheat your air fryer.
2. Mix together garlic powder, black pepper, and salt and rub over the steaks.
3. Grease its air fryer basket with cooking spray.
4. Place trimmed steak in the air fryer basket and cook for 4-5 minutes on each side.
5. Top with blue butter cheese.
6. Serve and enjoy.

Bbq Pork Chops With Vegetables

Servings: 5-6
Cooking Time: 20 Minutes
Ingredients:
- 6 pork chops
- 1 teaspoon onion powder
- ½ teaspoon garlic powder
- Ground black pepper and salt as needed
- ½ teaspoon cayenne pepper
- 1 teaspoon brown sugar
- ⅓ cup all-purpose flour

Directions:
1. To marinate, prepare a Ziploc bag, add the ingredients, seal and shake well.
2. Coat the cooking basket of your air fryer with cooking oil or spray.
3. Place the chops on the basket and then arrange the basket to the air fryer.
4. Cook the chops at 375 degrees F/ 190 degrees C for 20 minutes.
5. When done, serve warm with sautéed vegetables!

Tender Pork Ribs With Bbq Sauce

Servings: 4
Cooking Time: 25 Minutes
Ingredients:
- 1 lb. baby back ribs
- 3 tablespoons olive oil
- ½ teaspoon pepper
- ½ teaspoon smoked salt
- 1 tablespoon Dijon mustard
- ⅓ cup soy sauce
- 2 cloves garlic, minced
- ½ cup BBQ sauce

Directions:
1. Cut the ribs in half after removing their back membrane.
2. To marinate the ribs completely, prepare a large dish, add the olive oil, pepper, salt, Dijon mustard, soy sauce, garlic and ribs, then cover and refrigerate for 2 hours.
3. When ready, cook the pork ribs in your air fryer at 370 degrees F/ 185 degrees C for 25 minutes.
4. With the BBQ sauce on the top, serve and enjoy!

Parmesan-crusted Pork Chops

Servings: 4
Cooking Time: 12 Minutes
Ingredients:
- 1 large egg
- ½ cup grated Parmesan cheese
- 4 boneless pork chops
- ½ teaspoon salt
- ¼ teaspoon ground black pepper

Directions:
1. Whisk egg in a medium bowl and place Parmesan in a separate medium bowl.
2. Sprinkle pork chops on both sides with salt and pepper. Dip each pork chop into egg, then press both sides into Parmesan.
3. Place pork chops into ungreased air fryer basket. Adjust the temperature to 400°F and set the timer for 12 minutes, turning chops halfway through cooking. Pork chops will be golden and have an internal temperature of at least 145°F when done. Serve warm.

Potato And Prosciutto Salad

Servings: 8
Cooking Time: 7 Minutes
Ingredients:
- Salad:
- 4 pounds (1.8 kg) potatoes, boiled and cubed
- 15 slices prosciutto, diced
- 2 cups shredded Cheddar cheese
- Dressing:
- 15 ounces (425 g) sour cream
- 2 tablespoons mayonnaise
- 1 teaspoon salt
- 1 teaspoon black pepper
- 1 teaspoon dried basil

Directions:
1. Preheat the air fryer to 350°F (177°C).
2. Put the potatoes, prosciutto, and Cheddar in a baking dish. Put it in the air fryer and air fry for 7 minutes.
3. In a separate bowl, mix the sour cream, mayonnaise, salt, pepper, and basil using a whisk.
4. Coat the salad with the dressing and serve.

Beef And Pork Sausage Meatloaf

Servings: 4
Cooking Time: 25 Minutes
Ingredients:
- ¾ pound (340 g) ground chuck
- 4 ounces (113 g) ground pork sausage
- 1 cup shallots, finely chopped
- 2 eggs, well beaten
- 3 tablespoons plain milk
- 1 tablespoon oyster sauce
- 1 teaspoon porcini mushrooms
- ½ teaspoon cumin powder
- 1 teaspoon garlic paste
- 1 tablespoon fresh parsley
- Salt and crushed red pepper flakes, to taste
- 1 cup crushed saltines
- Cooking spray

Directions:
1. Preheat the air fryer to 360°F (182°C). Sprtiz a baking dish with cooking spray.
2. Mix all the ingredients in a large bowl, combining everything well.
3. Transfer to the baking dish and bake in the air fryer for 25 minutes.
4. Serve hot.

Spiced Pork Chops

Servings: 2
Cooking Time: 20 Minutes
Ingredients:
- 1 tablespoon olive oil
- ½ lb. pork chops
- ½ teaspoon dried oregano
- ¼ teaspoon red pepper flakes
- 1 teaspoon dried thyme
- ½ teaspoon salt
- ½ teaspoon pepper
- 6 large mushrooms, cleaned and sliced
- 1 large yellow onion, chopped
- 1 ½ tablespoons soy sauce
- 2 tablespoons fresh parsley, finely chopped

Directions:
1. Mix the pork chops with the onion, mushrooms, pepper, red pepper flakes, thyme, oregano, olive oil, soy sauce, and olive oil in a large bowl.
2. When coated, cook the pork chops and clean mushrooms in your air fryer at 390 degrees F/ 200 degrees C for 20 minutes.
3. Sprinkle with the fresh parsley, serve and enjoy!

Mexican-style Shredded Beef

Servings: 6
Cooking Time: 35 Minutes
Ingredients:
- 1 beef chuck roast, cut into 2" cubes
- 1 teaspoon salt
- ½ teaspoon ground black pepper
- ½ cup no-sugar-added chipotle sauce

Directions:
1. In a large bowl, sprinkle beef cubes with salt and pepper and toss to coat. Place beef into ungreased air fryer basket. Adjust the temperature to 400°F and set the timer for 30 minutes, shaking the basket halfway through cooking. Beef will be done when internal temperature is at least 160°F.
2. Place cooked beef into a large bowl and shred with two forks. Pour in chipotle sauce and toss to coat.
3. Return beef to air fryer basket for an additional 5 minutes at 400°F to crisp with sauce. Serve warm.

Barbecued Baby Back Ribs

Servings: 4
Cooking Time: 30 Minutes
Ingredients:
- 1 rack baby back ribs
- 1 teaspoon onion powder
- 1 teaspoon garlic powder
- 1 teaspoon brown sugar
- 1 teaspoon dried oregano
- Salt
- Pepper
- ½ cup barbecue sauce

Directions:
1. Use a sharp knife to remove the thin membrane from the back of the ribs. Cut the rack in half or as needed so that the ribs are able to fit in the air fryer.
2. In a small bowl, combine the onion powder, garlic powder, brown sugar, oregano, and salt and pepper to taste. Rub the seasoning onto the front and back of the ribs.
3. Cover the ribs with plastic wrap or foil and allow them to sit at room temperature for 30 minutes.
4. Place the ribs in the air fryer. It is okay to stack them. Cook for 15 minutes.
5. Open the air fryer. Flip the ribs. Cook for an additional 15 minutes.
6. Transfer the ribs to a serving dish. Drizzle the ribs with the barbecue sauce and serve.

Cinnamon-stick Kofta Skewers

Servings: 8
Cooking Time: 15 Minutes
Ingredients:
- 1 pound Lean ground beef
- ½ teaspoon Ground cumin
- ½ teaspoon Onion powder
- ½ teaspoon Ground dried turmeric
- ½ teaspoon Ground cinnamon
- ½ teaspoon Table salt
- Up to a ⅛ teaspoon Cayenne
- 8 3½- to 4-inch-long cinnamon sticks (see the headnote)
- Vegetable oil spray

Directions:
1. Preheat the air fryer to 375°F.
2. Gently mix the ground beef, cumin, onion powder, turmeric, cinnamon, salt, and cayenne in a bowl until the meat is evenly mixed with the spices. (Clean, dry hands work best!) Divide this mixture into 2-ounce portions, each about the size of a golf ball.
3. Wrap one portion of the meat mixture around a cinnamon stick, using about three-quarters of the length of the stick, covering one end but leaving a little "handle" of cinnamon stick protruding from the other end. Set aside and continue making more kofta skewers.
4. Generously coat the formed kofta skewers on all sides with vegetable oil spray. Set them in the basket with as much air space between them as possible. Air-fry undisturbed for 13 minutes, or until browned and cooked through. If the machine is at 360°F, you may need to add 2 minutes to the cooking time.
5. Use a nonstick-safe spatula, and perhaps kitchen tongs for balance, to gently transfer the kofta skewers to a wire rack. Cool for at least 5 minutes or up to 20 minutes before serving.

Korean Short Ribs

Servings: 4
Cooking Time: 10 Minutes
Ingredients:
- 8 (8-ounce) bone-in short ribs
- ½ cup soy sauce
- ¼ cup rice wine vinegar (see Substitution tip)
- ½ cup chopped onion
- 2 garlic cloves, minced
- 1 tablespoon sesame oil
- 1 teaspoon Sriracha
- 4 scallions, green parts (white parts optional), thinly sliced, divided
- Salt
- Pepper

Directions:
1. Place the short ribs in a sealable plastic bag. Add the soy sauce, rice wine vinegar, onion, garlic, sesame oil, Sriracha, and half of the scallions. Season with salt and pepper to taste.
2. Seal the bag and place it in the refrigerator to marinate for at least 1 hour; overnight is optimal.
3. Place the short ribs in the air fryer. Do not overfill. You may have to cook in two batches. Cook for 4 minutes.
4. Open the air fryer and flip the ribs. Cook for an additional 4 minutes.
5. If necessary, remove the cooked short ribs from the air fryer, then repeat steps 3 and 4 for the remaining ribs.
6. Sprinkle the short ribs with the remaining scallions, and serve.

Crispy Steak Subs

Servings: 2
Cooking Time: 30 Minutes
Ingredients:
- 1 hoagie bun baguette, halved
- 6 oz flank steak, sliced
- ½ white onion, sliced
- ½ red pepper, sliced
- 2 mozzarella cheese slices

Directions:
1. Preheat air fryer to 320°F. Place the flank steak slices, onion, and red pepper on one side of the frying

basket. Add the hoagie bun halves, crusty side up, to the other half of the air fryer. Bake for 10 minutes. Flip the hoagie buns. Cover both sides with one slice of mozzarella cheese. Gently stir the steak, onions, and peppers. Cook for 6 more minutes until the cheese is melted and the steak is juicy on the inside and crispy on the outside.

2. Remove the cheesy hoagie halves to a serving plate. Cover one side with the steak, and top with the onions and peppers. Close with the other cheesy hoagie half, slice into two pieces, and enjoy!

Steak Fajitas With Vegetables

Servings: 6
Cooking Time: 15 Minutes
Ingredients:
- 1-pound steak, sliced
- 1 tablespoon olive oil
- 1 tablespoon fajita seasoning, gluten-free
- ½ cup onion, sliced
- 3 bell peppers, sliced

Directions:
1. Line air fryer basket with aluminum foil.
2. Add all the recipe ingredients suitable bowl and toss until well coated.
3. Transfer fajita mixture into the air fryer basket and cook at almost 390 degrees F/ 200 degrees C for 5 minutes.
4. Toss well and cook for 5-10 minutes more.
5. Serve and enjoy.

Better-than-chinese-take-out Pork Ribs

Servings: 3
Cooking Time: 35 Minutes
Ingredients:
- 1½ tablespoons Hoisin sauce (see here; gluten-free, if a concern)
- 1½ tablespoons Regular or low-sodium soy sauce or gluten-free tamari sauce
- 1½ tablespoons Shaoxing (Chinese cooking rice wine), dry sherry, or white grape juice
- 1½ teaspoons Minced garlic
- ¾ teaspoon Ground dried ginger
- ¾ teaspoon Ground white pepper
- 1½ pounds Pork baby back rib rack(s), cut into 2-bone pieces

Directions:
1. Mix the hoisin sauce, soy or tamari sauce, Shaoxing or its substitute, garlic, ginger, and white pepper in a large bowl. Add the rib sections and stir well to coat. Cover and refrigerate for at least 2 hours or up to 24 hours, stirring the rib sections in the marinade occasionally.

2. Preheat the air fryer to 350°F. Set the ribs in their bowl on the counter as the machine heats.
3. When the machine is at temperature, set the rib pieces on their sides in a single layer in the basket with as much air space between them as possible. Air-fry for 35 minutes, turning and rearranging the pieces once, until deeply browned and sizzling.
4. Use kitchen tongs to transfer the rib pieces to a large serving bowl or platter. Wait a minute or two before serving them so the meat can reabsorb some of its own juices.

Country-style Pork Ribs

Servings: 4
Cooking Time: 40 Minutes
Ingredients:
- 1 teaspoon salt
- 1 teaspoon cayenne pepper
- ½-teaspoon ground black pepper
- 1 teaspoon raw honey
- 2 garlic cloves, minced
- 1 (1-inch) piece ginger, peeled and grated
- ½-teaspoon onion powder
- ½-teaspoon porcini powder
- 1 teaspoon mustard seeds
- 1 tablespoon sweet chili sauce
- 1 tablespoon balsamic vinegar
- 1 ½ lbs. pork country-style ribs

Directions:
1. Thoroughly mix up the cayenne pepper, honey, garlic, ginger, onion powder, porcini powder, mustard seeds, sweet chili sauce, balsamic vinegar, salt and black pepper in a suitable bowl.
2. Rub the pork ribs with the spice mixture.
3. Cook the ribs in your air fryer at 360 degrees F/ 180 degrees C for 15 minutes.
4. After 15 minutes, flip the ribs and cook for 20 minutes more or until they are tender inside and crisp outside.
5. Garnished with fresh chives if desired.
6. Serve and enjoy.

Easy Tex-mex Chimichangas

Servings: 2
Cooking Time: 8 Minutes
Ingredients:
- ¼ pound Thinly sliced deli roast beef, chopped
- ½ cup (about 2 ounces) Shredded Cheddar cheese or shredded Tex-Mex cheese blend
- ¼ cup Jarred salsa verde or salsa rojo
- ½ teaspoon Ground cumin
- ½ teaspoon Dried oregano
- 2 Burrito-size (12-inch) flour tortilla(s), not corn tortillas (gluten-free, if a concern)
- ⅔ cup Canned refried beans

- Vegetable oil spray

Directions:
1. Preheat the air fryer to 375°F.
2. Stir the roast beef, cheese, salsa, cumin, and oregano in a bowl until well mixed.
3. Lay a tortilla on a clean, dry work surface. Spread ⅓ cup of the refried beans in the center lower third of the tortilla(s), leaving an inch on either side of the spread beans.
4. For one chimichanga, spread all of the roast beef mixture on top of the beans. For two, spread half of the roast beef mixture on each tortilla.
5. At either "end" of the filling mixture, fold the sides of the tortilla up and over the filling, partially covering it. Starting with the unfolded side of the tortilla just below the filling, roll the tortilla closed. Fold and roll the second filled tortilla, as necessary.
6. Coat the exterior of the tortilla(s) with vegetable oil spray. Set the chimichanga(s) seam side down in the basket, with at least ½ inch air space between them if you're working with two. Air-fry undisturbed for 8 minutes, or until the tortilla is lightly browned and crisp.
7. Use kitchen tongs to gently transfer the chimichanga(s) to a wire rack. Cool for at last 5 minutes or up to 20 minutes before serving.

Grilled Steak With Salsa

Servings: 4
Cooking Time: 10 Minutes
Ingredients:
- 2 tablespoons salsa
- 1 tablespoon minced chipotle pepper
- ⅛ teaspoon black pepper
- 1 tablespoon apple cider vinegar
- 1 teaspoon ground cumin
- ⅛ teaspoon red pepper flakes
- ¾ pound sirloin tip steak, diced

Directions:
1. In a suitable bowl, thoroughly mix the salsa, chipotle pepper, cider vinegar, cumin, black pepper, and red pepper flakes.
2. Rub this mixture into per side of each steak piece.
3. Let stand for almost 15 minutes at room temperature.
4. Cook the steaks in the air fryer, 2 at a time, for 6 to 9 minutes.
5. Slice and serve

Simple Rib-eye Steak

Servings: 2
Cooking Time: 14 Minutes
Ingredients:
- 2 medium-sized rib eye steaks
- Salt & freshly ground black pepper, to taste

Directions:
1. Use the kitchen towels to pat dry the steaks.
2. Season the rib eye steaks with salt and pepper well on both sides.
3. Cook the steaks at 400 degrees F/ 205 degrees C for 14 minutes, flipping halfway through.
4. Let the steaks cool for 5 minutes before serving.

Albóndigas

Servings: 4
Cooking Time: 15 Minutes
Ingredients:
- 1 pound Lean ground pork
- 3 tablespoons Very finely chopped trimmed scallions
- 3 tablespoons Finely chopped fresh cilantro leaves
- 3 tablespoons Plain panko bread crumbs (gluten-free, if a concern)
- 3 tablespoons Dry white wine, dry sherry, or unsweetened apple juice
- 1½ teaspoons Minced garlic
- 1¼ teaspoons Mild smoked paprika
- ¾ teaspoon Dried oregano
- ¾ teaspoon Table salt
- ¼ teaspoon Ground black pepper
- Olive oil spray

Directions:
1. Preheat the air fryer to 400°F.
2. Mix the ground pork, scallions, cilantro, bread crumbs, wine or its substitute, garlic, smoked paprika, oregano, salt, and pepper in a bowl until the herbs and spices are evenly distributed in the mixture.
3. Lightly coat your clean hands with olive oil spray, then form the ground pork mixture into balls, using 2 tablespoons for each one. Spray your hands frequently so that the meat mixture doesn't stick.
4. Set the balls in the basket so that they're not touching, even if they're close together. Air-fry undisturbed for 15 minutes, or until well browned and an instant-read meat thermometer inserted into one or two balls registers 165°F.
5. Use a nonstick-safe spatula and kitchen tongs for balance to gently transfer the fragile balls to a wire rack to cool for 5 minutes before serving.

Marinated Rib-eye Steak With Herb Roasted Mushrooms

Servings: 2
Cooking Time: 10-15 Minutes
Ingredients:
- 2 tablespoons Worcestershire sauce
- ¼ cup red wine
- 2 (8-ounce) boneless rib-eye steaks
- coarsely ground black pepper
- 8 ounces baby bella (cremini) mushrooms, stems trimmed and caps halved
- 2 tablespoons olive oil

- 1 teaspoon dried parsley
- 1 teaspoon fresh thyme leaves
- salt and freshly ground black pepper
- chopped fresh chives or parsley

Directions:
1. Combine the Worcestershire sauce and red wine in a shallow baking dish. Add the steaks to the marinade, pierce them several times with the tines of a fork or a meat tenderizer and season them generously with the coarsely ground black pepper. Flip the steaks over and pierce the other side in a similar fashion, seasoning again with the coarsely ground black pepper. Marinate the steaks for 2 hours.
2. Preheat the air fryer to 400°F.
3. Toss the mushrooms in a bowl with the olive oil, dried parsley, thyme, salt and freshly ground black pepper. Transfer the steaks from the marinade to the air fryer basket, season with salt and scatter the mushrooms on top.
4. Air-fry the steaks for 10 minutes for medium-rare, 12 minutes for medium, or 15 minutes for well-done, flipping the steaks once halfway through the cooking time.
5. Serve the steaks and mushrooms together with the chives or parsley sprinkled on top. A good steak sauce or some horseradish would be a nice accompaniment.

Salty Lamb Chops

Servings: 4
Cooking Time: 8 Minutes
Ingredients:
- 1-pound lamb chops
- 1 egg, beaten
- ½ teaspoon salt
- ½ cup coconut flour
- Cooking spray

Directions:
1. Chop the lamb chops into small pieces (popcorn) and sprinkle with salt. Then add a beaten egg and stir the meat well. After this, add coconut flour and shake the lamb popcorn until all meat pieces are coated. Preheat the air fryer to 380°F. Put the lamb popcorn in the air fryer and spray it with cooking spray. Cook the lamb popcorn for 4 minutes. Then shake the meat well and cook it for 4 minutes more.

Original Köttbullar

Servings: 4
Cooking Time: 30 Minutes
Ingredients:
- 1 lb ground beef
- 1 small onion, chopped
- 1 clove garlic, minced
- 1/3 cup bread crumbs
- 1 egg, beaten
- Salt and pepper to taste
- 1 cup beef broth
- 1/3 cup heavy cream
- 2 tbsp flour

Directions:
1. Preheat air fryer to 370°F. Combine beef, onion, garlic, crumbs, egg, salt and pepper in a bowl. Scoop 2 tbsp of mixture and form meatballs with hands. Place the meatballs in the greased frying basket. Bake for 14 minutes.
2. Meanwhile, stir-fry beef broth and heavy cream in a saucepan over medium heat for 2 minutes; stir in flour. Cover and simmer for 4 minutes or until the sauce thicken. Transfer meatballs to a serving dish and drizzle with sauce. Serve and enjoy!

Rice And Meatball Stuffed Bell Peppers

Servings:4
Cooking Time: 11 To 17 Minutes
Ingredients:
- 4 bell peppers
- 1 tablespoon olive oil
- 1 small onion, chopped
- 2 cloves garlic, minced
- 1 cup frozen cooked rice, thawed
- 16 to 20 small frozen precooked meatballs, thawed
- ½ cup tomato sauce
- 2 tablespoons Dijon mustard

Directions:
1. To prepare the peppers, cut off about ½ inch of the tops. Carefully remove the membranes and seeds from inside the peppers. Set aside.
2. In a 6-by-6-by-2-inch pan, combine the olive oil, onion, and garlic. Bake in the air fryer for 2 to 4 minutes or until crisp and tender. Remove the vegetable mixture from the pan and set aside in a medium bowl.
3. Add the rice, meatballs, tomato sauce, and mustard to the vegetable mixture and stir to combine.
4. Stuff the peppers with the meat-vegetable mixture.
5. Place the peppers in the air fryer basket and bake for 9 to 13 minutes or until the filling is hot and the peppers are tender.

Honey Pork Links

Servings:4
Cooking Time: 20 Minutes
Ingredients:
- 12 oz ground mild pork sausage, removed from casings
- 1 tsp rubbed sage
- 2 tbsp honey
- ⅛ tsp cayenne pepper
- ⅛ tsp paprika
- Salt and pepper to taste

Directions:
1. Preheat air fryer to 400°F. Remove the sausage from the casings. Transfer to a bowl and add the remaining ingredients. Mix well. Make 8 links out of the mixture. Add the links to the frying basket and Air Fry for 8-10 minutes, flipping once. Serve right away.

Avocado Buttered Flank Steak

Servings:1
Cooking Time: 12 Minutes
Ingredients:
- 1 flank steak
- Salt and ground black pepper, to taste
- 2 avocados
- 2 tablespoons butter, melted
- ½ cup chimichurri sauce

Directions:
1. Rub the flank steak with salt and pepper to taste and leave to sit for 20 minutes.
2. Preheat the air fryer to 400°F (204°C) and place a rack inside.
3. Halve the avocados and take out the pits. Spoon the flesh into a bowl and mash with a fork. Mix in the melted butter and chimichurri sauce, making sure everything is well combined.
4. Put the steak in the air fryer and air fry for 6 minutes. Flip over and allow to air fry for another 6 minutes.
5. Serve the steak with the avocado butter.

Bacon Wrapped Pork With Apple Gravy

Servings:4
Cooking Time: 25 Minutes
Ingredients:
- Pork:
- 1 tablespoons Dijon mustard
- 1 pork tenderloin
- 3 strips bacon
- Apple Gravy:
- 3 tablespoons ghee, divided
- 1 small shallot, chopped
- 2 apples
- 1 tablespoon almond flour
- 1 cup vegetable broth
- ½ teaspoon Dijon mustard

Directions:
1. Preheat the air fryer to 360°F (182°C).
2. Spread Dijon mustard all over tenderloin and wrap with strips of bacon.
3. Put into air fryer and air fry for 12 minutes. Use a meat thermometer to check for doneness.
4. To make sauce, heat 1 tablespoons of ghee in a pan and add shallots. Cook for 1 minute.
5. Then add apples, cooking for 4 minutes until softened.
6. Add flour and 2 tablespoons of ghee to make a roux. Add broth and mustard, stirring well to combine.
7. When sauce starts to bubble, add 1 cup of sautéed apples, cooking until sauce thickens.
8. Once pork tenderloin is cooked, allow to sit 8 minutes to rest before slicing.
9. Serve topped with apple gravy.

Fajita Flank Steak Rolls

Servings:4
Cooking Time: 12 Minutes
Ingredients:
- 1 pound flank steak
- 4 slices pepper jack cheese
- 1 medium green bell pepper, seeded and chopped
- ½ medium red bell pepper, seeded and chopped
- ¼ cup finely chopped yellow onion
- 1 teaspoon salt
- ½ teaspoon ground black pepper
- Cooking spray

Directions:
1. Preheat the air fryer to 400°F.
2. Carefully butterfly steak, leaving the two halves connected. Place slices of cheese on top of steak. Scatter bell peppers and onion over cheese in an even layer.
3. Place steak so that the grain runs horizontally. Tightly roll up steak and secure it with eight evenly spaced toothpicks or eight sections of butcher's twine.
4. Slice steak into four even rolls. Spritz with cooking spray, then sprinkle with salt and black pepper. Place in the air fryer basket and cook 12 minutes until steak is brown on the edges and internal temperature reaches at least 160°F for well-done. Serve.

Crispy Lamb Shoulder Chops

Servings: 3
Cooking Time: 28 Minutes
Ingredients:
- ¾ cup All-purpose flour or gluten-free all-purpose flour
- 2 teaspoons Mild paprika
- 2 teaspoons Table salt
- 1½ teaspoons Garlic powder
- 1½ teaspoons Dried sage leaves
- 3 6-ounce bone-in lamb shoulder chops, any excess fat trimmed
- Olive oil spray

Directions:
1. Whisk the flour, paprika, salt, garlic powder, and sage in a large bowl until the mixture is of a uniform color. Add the chops and toss well to coat. Transfer them to a cutting board.
2. Preheat the air fryer to 375°F.
3. When the machine is at temperature, again dredge the chops one by one in the flour mixture. Lightly coat

both sides of each chop with olive oil spray before putting it in the basket. Continue on with the remaining chop(s), leaving air space between them in the basket.
4. Air-fry, turning once, for 25 minutes, or until the chops are well browned and tender when pierced with the point of a paring knife. If the machine is at 360°F, you may need to add up to 3 minutes to the cooking time.
5. Use kitchen tongs to transfer the chops to a wire rack. Cool for 5 minutes before serving.

Beef Kebabs

Servings: 4 Servings
Cooking Time: 40 Minutes
Ingredients:
- 1 pound of 1-inch steak cubes
- 1 large sliced bell pepper
- 1 large sliced onion
- 2 minced garlic cloves
- 4 tablespoons of olive oil
- ½ teaspoon of cumin
- ½ teaspoon of chili powder
- 1 tablespoon of lemon juice
- Pinch of salt and black pepper, to taste

Directions:
1. Mix beef, olive oil, garlic, lemon juice, chili, cumin, salt, and pepper in a large bowl until well combined. Keep it in a fridge for 30 minutes or up to 24 hours.
2. Preheat your air fryer to 400°F.
3. Thread the beef cubes, bell pepper, and onion slices onto skewers. Put the prepared skewers in the air fryer basket and cook at 400°F for 8–10 minutes, flipping halfway until charred outside and tendered inside.
4. Serve warm and enjoy your Beef Kebabs!

Pork Meatballs

Servings: 18
Cooking Time: 12 Minutes
Ingredients:
- 1 pound ground pork
- 1 large egg, whisked
- ½ teaspoon garlic powder
- ½ teaspoon salt
- ½ teaspoon ground ginger
- ¼ teaspoon crushed red pepper flakes
- 1 medium scallion, trimmed and sliced

Directions:
1. Combine all ingredients in a large bowl. Spoon out 2 tablespoons mixture and roll into a ball. Repeat to form eighteen meatballs total.
2. Place meatballs into ungreased air fryer basket. Adjust the temperature to 400°F and set the timer for 12 minutes, shaking the basket three times throughout cooking. Meatballs will be browned and have an internal temperature of at least 145°F when done. Serve warm.

Flank Steak With Tamari Sauce

Servings: 2
Cooking Time: 30 Minutes
Ingredients:
- olive oil spray
- 2 pounds flank steak, cut into 6 pieces
- kosher salt and black pepper
- 2 cloves of minced garlic
- 4 cups asparagus
- half cup tamari sauce
- 3 bell peppers: sliced thinly
- beef broth: ⅓ cup
- 1 tbsp. of unsalted butter
- ¼ cup balsamic vinegar

Directions:
1. Rub the steak pieces with salt and pepper.
2. In a zip-lock bag, toss the steak pieces well with Tamari sauce and garlic, seal the bag and let the steak pieces marinate for overnight.
3. Top the steak pieces with the bell peppers and asparagus.
4. Roll the steak piece around the vegetables and secure with toothpick. Deal the remaining pieces with the same steps.
5. Transfer the processed steak rolls to the oiled cooking basket and cook at 400 degrees F/ 205 degrees C for 15 minutes.
6. When the time is up, remove the rolls from the air fryer and set aside for 5 minutes.
7. Meanwhile, stir fry the balsamic vinegar, butter, and broth over medium flame.
8. Mix well and reduce it by half. Add salt and pepper to taste.
9. Pour over steaks, serve and enjoy.

Cheeseburgers

Servings: 4
Cooking Time: 10 Hours
Ingredients:
- 1 pound 70/30 ground beef
- ½ teaspoon salt
- ¼ teaspoon ground black pepper
- 4 slices American cheese
- 4 hamburger buns

Directions:
1. Preheat the air fryer to 360°F.
2. Separate beef into four equal portions and form into patties.
3. Sprinkle both sides of patties with salt and pepper. Place in the air fryer basket and cook 10 minutes, turning halfway through cooking time, until internal temperature reaches at least 160°F.
4. For each burger, place a slice of cheese on a patty and place on a hamburger bun. Serve warm.

Lamb Meatballs

Servings: 4
Cooking Time: 8 Minutes
Ingredients:
- Meatballs:
- ½ small onion, finely diced
- 1 clove garlic, minced
- 1 pound (454 g) ground lamb
- 2 tablespoons fresh parsley, finely chopped (plus more for garnish)
- 2 teaspoons fresh oregano, finely chopped
- 2 tablespoons milk
- 1 egg yolk
- Salt and freshly ground black pepper, to taste
- ½ cup crumbled feta cheese, for garnish
- Tomato Sauce:
- 2 tablespoons butter
- 1 clove garlic, smashed
- Pinch crushed red pepper flakes
- ¼ teaspoon ground cinnamon
- 1 (28-ounce / 794-g) can crushed tomatoes
- Salt, to taste
- Olive oil, for greasing

Directions:
1. Combine all ingredients for the meatballs in a large bowl and mix just until everything is combined. Shape the mixture into 1½-inch balls or shape the meat between two spoons to make quenelles.
2. Preheat the air fryer to 400ºF (204ºC).
3. While the air fryer is preheating, start the quick tomato sauce. Put the butter, garlic and red pepper flakes in a sauté pan and heat over medium heat on the stovetop. Let the garlic sizzle a little, but before the butter browns, add the cinnamon and tomatoes. Bring to a simmer and simmer for 15 minutes. Season with salt.
4. Grease the bottom of the air fryer basket with olive oil and transfer the meatballs to the air fryer basket in one layer, air frying in batches if necessary.
5. Air fry for 8 minutes, giving the basket a shake once during the cooking process to turn the meatballs over.
6. To serve, spoon a pool of the tomato sauce onto plates and add the meatballs. Sprinkle the feta cheese on top and garnish with more fresh parsley. Serve immediately.

Garlic And Oregano Lamb Chops

Servings: 4
Cooking Time: 17 Minutes
Ingredients:
- 1½ tablespoons Olive oil
- 1 tablespoon Minced garlic
- 1 teaspoon Dried oregano
- 1 teaspoon Finely minced orange zest
- ¾ teaspoon Fennel seeds
- ¾ teaspoon Table salt
- ¾ teaspoon Ground black pepper
- 6 4-ounce, 1-inch-thick lamb loin chops

Directions:
1. Mix the olive oil, garlic, oregano, orange zest, fennel seeds, salt, and pepper in a large bowl. Add the chops and toss well to coat. Set aside as the air fryer heats, tossing one more time.
2. Preheat the air fryer to 400°F.
3. Set the chops bone side down in the basket with as much air space between them as possible. Air-fry undisturbed for 14 minutes for medium-rare, or until an instant-read meat thermometer inserted into the thickest part of a chop registers 132°F. Or air-fry undisturbed for 17 minutes for well done, or until an instant-read meat thermometer registers 145°F.
4. Use kitchen tongs to transfer the chops to a wire rack. Cool for 5 minutes before serving.

Juicy Beef Kabobs With Sour Cream

Servings: 4
Cooking Time: 10 Minutes
Ingredients:
- 1-pound beef, cut into chunks
- 1 bell pepper, cut into 1-inch pieces
- 2 tablespoons soy sauce
- ⅓ cup sour cream
- ½ onion, cut into 1-inch pieces

Directions:
1. In a suitable bowl, mix together soy sauce and sour cream.
2. Add beef into the bowl and coat well and place in the refrigerator for overnight.
3. Thread marinated beef, bell peppers, and onions onto the soaked wooden skewers.
4. Place in your air fryer basket and cook at almost 400 degrees F/ 205 degrees C for almost 10 minutes. Turn halfway through the cooking time.
5. Serve and enjoy.

Steak Bites And Spicy Dipping Sauce

Servings: 4
Cooking Time: 8 Minutes
Ingredients:
- 2 pounds sirloin steak, cut into 2" cubes
- 2 teaspoons salt
- 1 teaspoon ground black pepper
- 1 teaspoon garlic powder
- ½ cup mayonnaise
- 2 tablespoons sriracha

Directions:
1. Preheat the air fryer to 400°F.
2. Sprinkle steak with salt, pepper, and garlic powder.
3. Place steak in the air fryer basket and cook 8 minutes, shaking the basket twice during cooking, until internal temperature reaches at least 160°F.
4. In a small bowl, combine mayonnaise and sriracha. Serve with steak bites for dipping.

Bacon With Shallot And Greens

Servings: 2
Cooking Time: 10 Minutes
Ingredients:
- 7 ounces mixed greens
- 8 thick slices pork bacon
- 2 shallots, peeled and diced
- Nonstick cooking spray

Directions:
1. Begin by preheating the air fryer to 345°F.
2. Now, add the shallot and bacon to the Air Fryer cooking basket; set the timer for 2 minutes. Spritz with a nonstick cooking spray.
3. After that, pause the Air Fryer; throw in the mixed greens; give it a good stir and cook an additional 5 minutes. Serve warm.

Air Fried London Broil

Servings: 8
Cooking Time: 25 Minutes
Ingredients:
- 2 pounds (907 g) London broil
- 3 large garlic cloves, minced
- 3 tablespoons balsamic vinegar
- 3 tablespoons whole-grain mustard
- 2 tablespoons olive oil
- Sea salt and ground black pepper, to taste
- ½ teaspoons dried hot red pepper flakes

Directions:
1. Wash and dry the London broil. Score its sides with a knife.
2. Mix the remaining ingredients. Rub this mixture into the broil, coating it well. Allow to marinate for a minimum of 3 hours.
3. Preheat the air fryer to 400°F (204°C).
4. Air fry the meat for 15 minutes. Turn it over and air fry for an additional 10 minutes before serving.

Sweet-and-sour Polish Sausage

Servings: 4
Cooking Time: 10 To 15 Minutes
Ingredients:
- ¾ pound Polish sausage
- 1 red bell pepper, cut into 1-inch strips
- ½ cup minced onion
- 3 tablespoons brown sugar
- ⅓ cup ketchup
- 2 tablespoons mustard
- 2 tablespoons apple cider vinegar
- ½ cup chicken broth

Directions:
1. Cut the sausage into 1½-inch pieces and put into a 6-inch metal bowl. Add the pepper and minced onion.
2. In a small bowl, combine the brown sugar, ketchup, mustard, apple cider vinegar, and chicken broth, and mix well. Pour into the bowl.
3. Roast for 10 to 15 minutes or until the sausage is hot, the vegetables tender, and the sauce bubbling and slightly thickened.
4. Did You Know? Polish sausage is almost always fully cooked when it is sold; read the label carefully to make sure you buy a fully cooked type for this recipe. Uncooked sausages are too fatty and release too much grease to cook in this appliance.

Creole Pork Chops

Servings: 4
Cooking Time: 12 Minutes
Ingredients:
- 1 ½ lbs. pork chops, boneless
- 1 teaspoon garlic powder
- 5-tablespoon parmesan cheese, grated
- ⅓ cup almond flour
- 1 ½-teaspoon paprika
- 1 teaspoon Creole seasoning

Directions:
1. Heat the air fryer to 360 degrees F/ 180 degrees C in advance.
2. In a zip-lock bag, in addition to the pork chops, mix the other ingredients well.
3. Add pork chops into the bag and coat it with the mixture well by shaking the bag.
4. Coat the basket of your air fryer with cooking spray.
5. Place pork chops into the air fryer basket and cook for 12 minutes at 360 degrees F/ 180 degrees C.
6. Serve and enjoy.

Bourbon-bbq Sauce Marinated Beef Bbq

Servings: 4
Cooking Time: 60 Minutes
Ingredients:
- ¼ cup bourbon
- ¼ cup barbecue sauce
- 1 tablespoon Worcestershire sauce
- 2 pounds beef steak, pounded
- Salt and pepper to taste

Directions:
1. Place all ingredients in a Ziploc bag and allow to marinate in the fridge for at least 2 hours.
2. Preheat the air fryer to 390°F.
3. Place the grill pan accessory in the air fryer.
4. Place on the grill pan and cook for 20 minutes per batch.
5. Halfway through the cooking time, give a stir to cook evenly.
6. Meanwhile, pour the marinade on a saucepan and allow to simmer until the sauce thickens.
7. Serve beef with the bourbon sauce.

Mini Meatloaves With Pancetta

Servings: 4
Cooking Time: 40 Minutes
Ingredients:

Quick & Simple Tower Dual Basket Air Fryer Cookbook

- ¼ cup grated Parmesan
- 1/3 cup quick-cooking oats
- 2 tbsp milk
- 3 tbsp ketchup
- 3 tbsp Dijon mustard
- 1 egg
- 1 tsp dried oregano
- Salt and pepper to taste
- 1 lb lean ground beef
- 4 pancetta slices, uncooked

Directions:
1. Preheat the air fryer to 375°F. Combine the oats, milk, 1 tbsp of ketchup, 1 tbsp of mustard, the egg, oregano, Parmesan cheese, salt, and pepper, and mix. Add the beef and mix with your hands, then form 4 mini loaves. Wrap each mini loaf with pancetta, covering the meat.
2. Combine the remaining ketchup and mustard and set aside. Line the frying basket with foil and poke holes in it, then set the loaves in the basket. Brush with the ketchup/mustard mix. Bake for 17-22 minutes or until cooked and golden. Serve and enjoy!

Beef Taco Chimichangas

Servings: 4
Cooking Time: 20 Minutes
Ingredients:
- Cooking oil
- ½ cup chopped onion
- 2 garlic cloves, minced
- 1 pound 93% lean ground beef
- 2 tablespoons taco seasoning
- Salt
- Pepper
- 1 (15-ounce) can diced tomatoes with chiles
- 4 medium (8-inch) flour tortillas
- 1 cup shredded Cheddar cheese (a blend of ½ cup shredded Cheddar and ½ cup shredded Monterey Jack works great, too)

Directions:
1. Spray a skillet with cooking oil and place over medium-high heat. Add the chopped onion and garlic. Cook for 2 to 3 minutes, until fragrant.
2. Add the ground beef, taco seasoning, and salt and pepper to taste. Use a large spoon or spatula to break up the beef. Cook for 2 to 4 minutes, until browned.
3. Add the diced tomatoes with chiles. Stir to combine.
4. Mound ½ cup of the ground beef mixture on each of the tortillas.
5. To form the chimichangas, fold the sides of the tortilla in toward the middle and then roll up from the bottom. You can secure the chimichanga with a toothpick. Or you can moisten the upper edge of the tortilla with a small amount of water before sealing. I prefer to use a cooking brush, but you can dab with your fingers.
6. Spray the chimichangas with cooking oil.
7. Place the chimichangas in the air fryer. Do not stack. Cook in batches. Cook for 8 minutes.
8. Remove the cooked chimichangas from the air fryer and top them with the shredded cheese. The heat from the chimichangas will melt the cheese.
9. Repeat steps 7 and 8 for the remaining chimichangas, and serve.

Homemade Pork Gyoza

Servings: 4
Cooking Time: 50 Minutes
Ingredients:
- 8 wonton wrappers
- 4 oz ground pork, browned
- 1 green apple
- 1 tsp rice vinegar
- 1 tbsp vegetable oil
- ½ tbsp oyster sauce
- 1 tbsp soy sauce
- A pinch of white pepper

Directions:
1. Preheat air fryer to 350°F. Combine the oyster sauce, soy sauce, rice vinegar, and white pepper in a small bowl. Add in the pork and stir thoroughly. Peel and core the apple, and slice into small cubes. Add the apples to the meat mixture, and combine thoroughly. Divide the filling between the wonton wrappers. Wrap the wontons into triangles and seal with a bit of water. Brush the wrappers with vegetable oil. Place them in the greased frying basket. Bake for 25 minutes until crispy golden brown on the outside and juicy and delicious on the inside. Serve.

Tender Country Ribs

Servings: 4
Cooking Time: 20 To 25 Minutes
Ingredients:
- 12 country-style pork ribs, trimmed of excess fat
- 2 tablespoons cornstarch
- 2 tablespoons olive oil
- 1 teaspoon dry mustard
- ½ teaspoon thyme
- ½ teaspoon garlic powder
- 1 teaspoon dried marjoram
- Pinch salt
- Freshly ground black pepper

Directions:
1. Place the ribs on a clean work surface.
2. In a small bowl, combine the cornstarch, olive oil, mustard, thyme, garlic powder, marjoram, salt, and pepper, and rub into the ribs.
3. Place the ribs in the air fryer basket and roast for 10 minutes.
4. Carefully turn the ribs using tongs and roast for 10 to 15 minutes or until the ribs are crisp and register an internal temperature of at least 150°F.

Chapter 9: Fish And Seafood Recipes

Southwestern Prawns With Asparagus

Servings: 3
Cooking Time: 5 Minutes
Ingredients:
- 1-pound prawns, deveined
- ½ pound asparagus spears, cut into 1-inch chinks
- 1 teaspoon butter, melted
- ¼ teaspoon oregano
- ½ teaspoon mixed peppercorns, crushed
- Salt, to taste
- 1 ripe avocado
- 1 lemon, sliced
- ½ cup chunky-style salsa

Directions:
1. Toss your prawns and asparagus with melted butter, oregano, salt and mixed peppercorns.
2. Cook the prawns and asparagus at 400 degrees F/ 205 degrees C for 5 minutes, shaking the air fryer basket halfway through the cooking time.
3. Divide the prawns and asparagus between serving plates and garnish with avocado and lemon slices. Serve with the salsa on the side. Bon appétit!

Mustard-crusted Fish Fillets

Servings: 4
Cooking Time: 8 To 11 Minutes
Ingredients:
- 5 teaspoons low-sodium yellow mustard (see Tip)
- 1 tablespoon freshly squeezed lemon juice
- 4 (3.5-ounce) sole fillets
- ½ teaspoon dried thyme
- ½ teaspoon dried marjoram
- ⅛ teaspoon freshly ground black pepper
- 1 slice low-sodium whole-wheat bread, crumbled
- 2 teaspoons olive oil

Directions:
1. In a small bowl, mix the mustard and lemon juice. Spread this evenly over the fillets. Place them in the air fryer basket.
2. In another small bowl, mix the thyme, marjoram, pepper, bread crumbs, and olive oil. Mix until combined.
3. Gently but firmly press the spice mixture onto the top of each fish fillet.
4. Bake for 8 to 11 minutes, or until the fish reaches an internal temperature of at least 145°F on a meat thermometer and the topping is browned and crisp. Serve immediately.

Ham Tilapia

Servings: 4
Cooking Time: 10 Minutes
Ingredients:
- 16 oz tilapia fillet
- 4 ham slices
- 1 teaspoon sunflower oil
- ½ teaspoon salt
- 1 teaspoon dried rosemary

Directions:
1. Cut the tilapia on 4 servings. Sprinkle every fish serving with salt, dried rosemary, and sunflower oil. Then carefully wrap the fish fillets in the ham slices and secure with toothpicks. Preheat the air fryer to 400°F. Put the wrapped tilapia in the air fryer basket in one layer and cook them for 10 minutes. Gently flip the fish on another side after 5 minutes of cooking.

Air Fried Mussels With Parsley

Servings: 5
Cooking Time: 12 Minutes
Ingredients:
- 1 ⅔ pound mussels
- 1 garlic clove
- 1 teaspoon oil
- Black pepper to taste
- Parsley Taste

Directions:
1. Clean and scrape the mold cover and remove the byssus.
2. Pour the oil, clean the mussels and the crushed garlic in the air fryer basket.
3. At 425 degrees F/ 220 degrees C, preheat your air fryer and air fry for 12 minutes.
4. Towards the end of cooking, add black pepper and chopped parsley.
5. Finally, distribute the mussel juice well at the bottom of the basket, stirring the basket.

Fish Nuggets With Broccoli Dip

Servings: 4
Cooking Time: 40 Minutes
Ingredients:
- 1 lb cod fillets, cut into chunks
- 1 ½ cups broccoli florets
- ¼ cup grated Parmesan
- 3 garlic cloves, peeled
- 3 tbsp sour cream
- 2 tbsp lemon juice
- 2 tbsp olive oil
- 2 egg whites
- 1 cup panko bread crumbs
- 1 tsp dried dill
- Salt and pepper to taste

Directions:
1. Preheat the air fryer to 400°F. Put the broccoli and garlic in the greased frying basket and Air Fry for 5-7 minutes or until tender. Remove to a blender and add sour cream, lemon juice, olive oil, and ½ tsp of salt and process until smooth. Set the sauce aside. Beat the egg

whites until frothy in a shallow bowl. On a plate, combine the panko, Parmesan, dill, pepper, and the remaining ½ tsp of salt. Dip the cod fillets in the egg whites, then the breadcrumbs, pressing to coat. Put half the cubes in the frying basket and spray with cooking oil. Air Fry for 6-8 minutes or until the fish is cooked through. Serve the fish with the sauce and enjoy!

Potato Chip-crusted Cod

Servings: 2
Cooking Time: 20 Minutes
Ingredients:
- ½ cup crushed potato chips
- 1 tsp chopped tarragon
- 1/8 tsp salt
- 1 tsp cayenne powder
- 1 tbsp Dijon mustard
- ¼ cup buttermilk
- 1 tsp lemon juice
- 1 tbsp butter, melted
- 2 cod fillets

Directions:
1. Preheat air fryer at 350°F. Mix all ingredients in a bowl. Press potato chip mixture evenly across tops of cod. Place cod fillets in the greased frying basket and Air Fry for 10 minutes until the fish is opaque and flakes easily with a fork. Serve immediately.

Lime Bay Scallops

Servings: 4
Cooking Time: 10 Minutes
Ingredients:
- 2 tbsp butter, melted
- 1 lime, juiced
- ¼ tsp salt
- 1 lb bay scallops
- 2 tbsp chopped cilantro

Directions:
1. Preheat air fryer to 350°F. Combine all ingredients in a bowl, except for the cilantro. Place scallops in the frying basket and Air Fry for 5 minutes, tossing once. Serve immediately topped with cilantro.

Easy Scallops With Lemon Butter

Servings: 3
Cooking Time: 4 Minutes
Ingredients:
- 1 tablespoon Olive oil
- 2 teaspoons Minced garlic
- 1 teaspoon Finely grated lemon zest
- ½ teaspoon Red pepper flakes
- ¼ teaspoon Table salt
- 1 pound Sea scallops
- 3 tablespoons Butter, melted
- 1½ tablespoons Lemon juice

Directions:
1. Preheat the air fryer to 400°F.
2. Gently stir the olive oil, garlic, lemon zest, red pepper flakes, and salt in a bowl. Add the scallops and stir very gently until they are evenly and well coated.
3. When the machine is at temperature, arrange the scallops in a single layer in the basket. Some may touch. Air-fry undisturbed for 4 minutes, or until the scallops are opaque and firm.
4. While the scallops cook, stir the melted butter and lemon juice in a serving bowl. When the scallops are ready, pour them from the basket into this bowl. Toss well before serving.

Cilantro Sea Bass

Servings: 2
Cooking Time: 15 Minutes
Ingredients:
- Salt and pepper to taste
- 1 tsp olive oil
- 2 sea bass fillets
- ½ tsp berbere seasoning
- 2 tsp chopped cilantro
- 1 tsp dried thyme
- ½ tsp garlic powder
- 4 lemon quarters

Directions:
1. Preheat air fryer at 375°F. Rub sea bass fillets with olive oil, thyme, garlic powder, salt and black pepper. Season with berbere seasoning. Place fillets in the greased frying basket and Air Fry for 6-8 minutes. Let rest for 5 minutes on a serving plate. Scatter with cilantro and serve with lemon quarters on the side.

Seafood Spring Rolls

Servings: 4
Cooking Time: 22 Minutes
Ingredients:
- Olive oil
- 2 teaspoon minced garlic
- 2 cups finely sliced cabbage
- 1 cup matchstick cut carrots
- 2 (4-ounce) cans tiny shrimp, drained
- 4 teaspoons soy sauce
- Salt
- Freshly ground black pepper
- 16 square spring roll wrappers

Directions:
1. Spray a fryer basket lightly with olive oil. Spray a medium sauté pan with olive oil.
2. Add the garlic to the sauté pan and cook over medium heat until fragrant, 30 to 45 seconds. Add the cabbage and carrots and sauté until the vegetables are slightly tender, about 5 minutes.

3. Add the shrimp and soy sauce and season with salt and pepper, then stir to combine. Sauté until the moisture has evaporated, 2 more minutes. Set aside to cool.
4. Place a spring roll wrapper on a work surface so it looks like a diamond. Place 1 tablespoon of the shrimp mixture on the lower end of the wrapper.
5. Roll the wrapper away from you halfway, then fold in the right and left sides, like an envelope. Continue to roll to the very end, using a little water to seal the edge. Repeat with the remaining wrappers and filling.
6. Place the spring rolls in the fryer basket in a single layer, leaving room between each roll. Lightly spray with olive oil. You may need to cook them in batches.
7. Air fry for 5 minutes. Turn the rolls over, lightly spray with olive oil, and cook until heated through and the rolls start to brown, 5 to 10 more minutes.

Tortilla-crusted With Lemon Filets

Servings: 4
Cooking Time: 15 Minutes
Ingredients:
- 1 cup tortilla chips, pulverized
- 1 egg, beaten
- 1 tablespoon lemon juice
- 4 fillets of white fish fillet
- Salt and pepper to taste

Directions:
1. Preheat the air fryer to 390°F.
2. Place a grill pan in the air fryer.
3. Season the fish fillet with salt, pepper, and lemon juice.
4. Soak in beaten eggs and dredge in tortilla chips.
5. Place on the grill pan.
6. Cook for 15 minutes.
7. Make sure to flip the fish halfway through the cooking time.

Blackened Red Snapper

Servings: 4
Cooking Time: 8 Minutes
Ingredients:
- 1½ teaspoons black pepper
- ¼ teaspoon thyme
- ¼ teaspoon garlic powder
- ⅛ teaspoon cayenne pepper
- 1 teaspoon olive oil
- 4 4-ounce red snapper fillet portions, skin on
- 4 thin slices lemon
- cooking spray

Directions:
1. Mix the spices and oil together to make a paste. Rub into both sides of the fish.
2. Spray air fryer basket with nonstick cooking spray and lay snapper steaks in basket, skin-side down.
3. Place a lemon slice on each piece of fish.
4. Cook at 390°F for 8 minutes. The fish will not flake when done, but it should be white through the center.

Thyme Scallops

Servings: 1
Cooking Time: 12 Minutes
Ingredients:
- 1 lb. scallops
- Salt and pepper
- ½ tbsp. butter
- ½ cup thyme, chopped

Directions:
1. Wash the scallops and dry them completely. Season with pepper and salt, then set aside while you prepare the pan.
2. Grease a foil pan in several spots with the butter and cover the bottom with the thyme. Place the scallops on top.
3. Pre-heat the fryer at 400°F and set the rack inside.
4. Place the foil pan on the rack and allow to cook for seven minutes.
5. Take care when removing the pan from the fryer and transfer the scallops to a serving dish. Spoon any remaining butter in the pan over the fish and enjoy.

Mediterranean Sea Scallops

Servings: 2
Cooking Time: 20 Minutes
Ingredients:
- 1 tbsp olive oil
- 1 shallot, minced
- 2 tbsp capers
- 2 cloves garlic, minced
- ½ cup heavy cream
- 3 tbsp butter
- 1 tbsp lemon juice
- Salt and pepper to taste
- ¼ tbsp cumin powder
- ¼ tbsp curry powder
- 1 lb jumbo sea scallops
- 2 tbsp chopped parsley
- 1 tbsp chopped cilantro

Directions:
1. Warm the olive oil in a saucepan over medium heat. Add shallot and stir-fry for 2 minutes until translucent. Stir in capers, cumin, curry, garlic, heavy cream, 1 tbsp of butter, lemon juice, salt, and pepper and cook for 2 minutes until rolling a boil. Low the heat and simmer for 3 minutes until the caper sauce thickens. Turn the heat off.
2. Preheat air fryer at 400°F. In a bowl, add the remaining butter and scallops and toss to coat on all sides. Place scallops in the greased frying basket and Air Fry for 8 minutes, flipping once. Drizzle caper sauce over, scatter with parsley, cilantro and serve.

Caribbean Skewers

Servings: 4
Cooking Time: 25 Minutes
Ingredients:
- 1 ½ lb large shrimp, peeled and deveined
- 1 can pineapple chunks, drained, liquid reserved
- 1 red bell pepper, chopped
- 3 scallions, chopped
- 1 tbsp lemon juice
- 1 tbsp olive oil
- ½ tsp jerk seasoning
- ⅛ tsp cayenne pepper
- 2 tbsp cilantro, chopped

Directions:
1. Preheat the air fryer to 37-°F. Thread the shrimp, pineapple, bell pepper, and scallions onto 8 bamboo skewers. Mix 3 tbsp of pineapple juice with lemon juice, olive oil, jerk seasoning, and cayenne pepper. Brush every bit of the mix over the skewers. Place 4 kebabs in the frying basket, add a rack, and put the rest of the skewers on top. Bake for 6-9 minutes and rearrange at about 4-5 minutes. Cook until the shrimp curl and pinken. Sprinkle with freshly chopped cilantro and serve.

Kid's Flounder Fingers

Servings: 4
Cooking Time: 45 Minutes
Ingredients:
- 1 lb catfish flounder fillets, cut into 1-inch chunks
- ½ cup seasoned fish fry breading mix

Directions:
1. Preheat air fryer to 400°F. In a resealable bag, add flounder and breading mix. Seal bag and shake until the fish is coated. Place the nuggets in the greased frying basket and Air Fry for 18-20 minutes, shaking the basket once until crisp. Serve warm and enjoy!

Cod Nuggets

Servings: 4
Cooking Time: 12 Minutes
Ingredients:
- 2 boneless, skinless cod fillets
- 1 ½ teaspoons salt, divided
- ¾ teaspoon ground black pepper, divided
- 2 large eggs
- 1 cup plain bread crumbs

Directions:
1. Preheat the air fryer to 350°F.
2. Cut cod fillets into sixteen even-sized pieces. In a large bowl, add cod nuggets and sprinkle with 1 teaspoon salt and ½ teaspoon pepper.
3. In a small bowl, whisk eggs. In another small bowl, mix bread crumbs with remaining ½ teaspoon salt and ¼ teaspoon pepper.
4. One by one, dip nuggets in the eggs, shaking off excess before rolling in the bread crumb mixture. Repeat to make sixteen nuggets.
5. Place nuggets in the air fryer basket and spritz with cooking spray. Cook 12 minutes, turning halfway through cooking time. Nuggets will be done when golden brown and have an internal temperature of at least 145°F. Serve warm.

Italian Shrimp

Servings: 4
Cooking Time: 12 Minutes
Ingredients:
- 1 pound shrimp, peeled and deveined
- A pinch of salt and black pepper
- 1 tablespoon sesame seeds, toasted
- ½ teaspoon Italian seasoning
- 1 tablespoon olive oil

Directions:
1. In a bowl, mix the shrimp with the rest of the ingredients and toss well. Put the shrimp in the air fryer's basket, cook at 370°F for 12 minutes, divide into bowls and serve,

Breaded Parmesan Perch

Servings: 5
Cooking Time: 15 Minutes
Ingredients:
- ¼ cup grated Parmesan
- ½ tsp salt
- ¼ tsp paprika
- 1 tbsp chopped dill
- 1 tsp dried thyme
- 2 tsp Dijon mustard
- 2 tbsp bread crumbs
- 4 ocean perch fillets
- 1 lemon, quartered
- 2 tbsp chopped cilantro

Directions:
1. Preheat air fryer to 400°F. Combine salt, paprika, pepper, dill, mustard, thyme, Parmesan, and bread crumbs in a wide bowl. Coat all sides of the fillets in the breading, then transfer to the greased frying basket. Air Fry for 8 minutes until outside is golden and the inside is cooked through. Garnish with lemon wedges and sprinkle with cilantro. Serve and enjoy!

Korean-style Fried Calamari

Servings: 4
Cooking Time: 25 Minutes
Ingredients:
- 2 tbsp tomato paste
- 1 tbsp gochujang
- 1 tbsp lime juice
- 1 tsp lime zest

- 1 tsp smoked paprika
- ½ tsp salt
- 1 cup bread crumbs
- 1/3 lb calamari rings

Directions:
1. Preheat air fryer to 400°F. Whisk tomato paste, gochujang, lime juice and zest, paprika, and salt in a bowl. In another bowl, add in the bread crumbs. Dredge calamari rings in the tomato mixture, shake off excess, then roll through the crumbs. Place calamari rings in the greased frying basket and Air Fry for 4-5 minutes, flipping once. Serve.

Cajun Fish Cakes

Servings: 4
Cooking Time: 30 Minutes
Ingredients:
- 2 catfish fillets
- 1 cup all-purpose flour
- 1 ounce butter
- 1 teaspoon baking powder
- 1 teaspoon baking soda
- ½ cup buttermilk
- 1 teaspoon Cajun seasoning
- 1 cup Swiss cheese, shredded

Directions:
1. Boil a pot of water, the put in the fish fillets and boil for 5 minutes or until it is opaque.
2. When done, flake the fish into small pieces.
3. In a bowl, mix up the other ingredients, then add the fish and mix them well.
4. Form 12 fish patties from the mixture.
5. Place the patties to the cooking pan and arrange the pan to your air fryer.
6. Cook at 380 degrees F/ 195 degrees C for 15 minutes.
7. Working in batches is suggested.
8. Enjoy!

Lemon-dill Salmon With Green Beans

Servings: 4
Cooking Time: 20 Minutes
Ingredients:
- 20 halved cherry tomatoes
- 4 tbsp butter
- 4 garlic cloves, minced
- ¼ cup chopped dill
- Salt and pepper to taste
- 4 wild-caught salmon fillets
- ¼ cup white wine
- 1 lemon, thinly sliced
- 1 lb green beans, trimmed
- 2 tbsp chopped parsley

Directions:
1. Preheat air fryer to 390°F. Combine butter, garlic, dill, wine, salt, and pepper in a small bowl. Spread the seasoned butter over the top of the salmon. Arrange the fish in a single layer in the frying basket. Top with ½ of the lemon slices and surround the fish with green beans and tomatoes. Bake for 12-15 minutes until salmon is cooked and vegetables are tender. Top with parsley and serve with lemon slices on the side.

Sesame-crusted Tuna Steaks

Servings:3
Cooking Time: 10-13 Minutes
Ingredients:
- ½ cup Sesame seeds, preferably a blend of white and black
- 1½ tablespoons Toasted sesame oil
- 3 6-ounce skinless tuna steaks

Directions:
1. Preheat the air fryer to 400°F.
2. Pour the sesame seeds on a dinner plate. Use ½ tablespoon of the sesame oil as a rub on both sides and the edges of a tuna steak. Set it in the sesame seeds, then turn it several times, pressing gently, to create an even coating of the seeds, including around the steak's edge. Set aside and continue coating the remaining steak(s).
3. When the machine is at temperature, set the steaks in the basket with as much air space between them as possible. Air-fry undisturbed for 10 minutes for medium-rare, or 12 to 13 minutes for cooked through.
4. Use a nonstick-safe spatula to transfer the steaks to serving plates. Serve hot.

Tuna Wraps

Servings: 4
Cooking Time:4 To 7 Minutes
Ingredients:
- 1 pound fresh tuna steak, cut into 1-inch cubes
- 1 tablespoon grated fresh ginger
- 2 garlic cloves, minced
- ½ teaspoon toasted sesame oil
- 4 low-sodium whole-wheat tortillas
- ¼ cup low-fat mayonnaise
- 2 cups shredded romaine lettuce (see Tip)
- 1 red bell pepper, thinly sliced

Directions:
1. In a medium bowl, mix the tuna, ginger, garlic, and sesame oil. Let it stand for 10 minutes.
2. Grill the tuna in the air fryer for 4 to 7 minutes, or until done to your liking and lightly browned.
3. Make wraps with the tuna, tortillas, mayonnaise, lettuce, and bell pepper. Serve immediately.

Snow Crab Legs

Servings: 6
Cooking Time: 15 Minutes Per Batch
Ingredients:
- 8 pounds fresh shell-on snow crab legs
- 2 tablespoons olive oil
- 2 teaspoons Old Bay Seasoning
- 4 tablespoons salted butter, melted
- 2 teaspoons lemon juice

Directions:
1. Preheat the air fryer to 400°F.
2. Drizzle crab legs with oil and sprinkle with Old Bay. Place in the air fryer basket, working in batches as necessary. Cook 15 minutes, turning halfway through cooking time, until crab turns a bright red-orange.
3. In a small bowl, whisk together butter and lemon juice. Serve as a dipping sauce with warm crab legs.

Collard Green & Cod Packets

Servings: 4
Cooking Time: 20 Minutes
Ingredients:
- 2 cups collard greens, chopped
- 1 tsp salt
- ½ tsp dried rosemary
- ½ tsp dried thyme
- ½ tsp garlic powder
- 4 cod fillets
- 1 shallot, thinly sliced
- ¼ cup olive oil
- 1 lemon, juiced

Directions:
1. Preheat air fryer to 380°F. Mix together the salt, rosemary, thyme, and garlic powder in a small bowl. Rub the spice mixture onto the cod fillets. Divide the fish fillets among 4 sheets of foil. Top with shallot slices and collard greens. Drizzle with olive oil and lemon juice. Fold and seal the sides of the foil packets and then place them into the frying basket. Steam in the fryer for 11-13 minutes until the cod is cooked through. Serve and enjoy!

Cajun Fish Sticks

Servings: 4
Cooking Time: 10 Minutes
Ingredients:
- 1-pound white fish, cut into pieces
- ¾ teaspoon Cajun seasoning
- 1 ½ cups pork rind, crushed
- 2 tablespoons water
- 2 tablespoons Dijon mustard
- ¼ cup mayonnaise
- Black pepper
- Salt

Directions:
1. Grease its air fryer basket with cooking spray.
2. In a suitable bowl, whisk water, mayonnaise, and mustard.
3. In a shallow bowl, mix black pepper, pork rind, Cajun seasoning, and salt.
4. Dip fish pieces in mayo mixture and coat well with pork rind mixture them set in the air fryer basket evenly.
5. Cook at almost 400 degrees F/ 205 degrees C for 5 minutes.
6. Flip the fish sticks and continue cooking for 5 minutes more.
7. Serve and enjoy.

Creole Tilapia With Garlic Mayo

Servings: 4
Cooking Time: 20 Minutes
Ingredients:
- 4 tilapia fillets
- 2 tbsp olive oil
- 1 tsp paprika
- 1 tsp garlic powder
- 1 tsp dried basil
- ½ tsp Creole seasoning
- ½ tsp chili powder
- 2 garlic cloves, minced
- 1 tbsp mayonnaise
- 1 tsp olive oil
- ½ lemon, juiced
- Salt and pepper to taste

Directions:
1. Preheat air fryer to 400°F. Coat the tilapia with some olive oil, then season with paprika, garlic powder, basil, and Creole seasoning. Bake in the greased frying basket for 15 minutes, flipping once during cooking.
2. While the fish is cooking, whisk together garlic, mayonnaise, olive oil, lemon juice, chili powder, salt and pepper in a bowl. Serve the cooked fish with the aioli.

Tilapia Teriyaki

Servings: 3
Cooking Time: 10 Minutes
Ingredients:
- 4 tablespoons teriyaki sauce
- 1 tablespoon pineapple juice
- 1 pound tilapia fillets
- cooking spray
- 6 ounces frozen mixed peppers with onions, thawed and drained
- 2 cups cooked rice

Directions:
1. Mix the teriyaki sauce and pineapple juice together in a small bowl.
2. Split tilapia fillets down the center lengthwise.
3. Brush all sides of fish with the sauce, spray air fryer basket with nonstick cooking spray, and place fish in the basket.

4. Stir the peppers and onions into the remaining sauce and spoon over the fish. Save any leftover sauce for drizzling over the fish when serving.
5. Cook at 360°F for 10 minutes, until fish flakes easily with a fork and is done in center.
6. Divide into 3 or 4 servings and serve each with approximately ½ cup cooked rice.

Crab Rangoon

Servings: 4
Cooking Time: 5 Minutes
Ingredients:
- ½ cup imitation crabmeat
- 4 ounces full-fat cream cheese, softened
- ¼ teaspoon Worcestershire sauce
- 8 wonton wrappers

Directions:
1. Preheat the air fryer to 400°F.
2. In a medium bowl, mix crabmeat, cream cheese, and Worcestershire until combined.
3. Place wonton wrappers on work surface. For each rangoon, scoop ½ tablespoon crab mixture onto center of a wonton wrapper. Press opposing edges toward the center and pinch to close. Spray with cooking spray to coat well. Repeat with remaining crab mixture and wontons.
4. Place in the air fryer basket and cook 5 minutes until brown at the edges. Serve warm.

Lemon Butter-dill Salmon

Servings: 4
Cooking Time: 10 Minutes
Ingredients:
- 4 skin-on salmon fillets
- ¾ teaspoon salt
- ½ teaspoon ground black pepper
- 1 medium lemon, halved
- 2 tablespoons salted butter, melted
- 1 teaspoon dried dill

Directions:
1. Preheat the air fryer to 375°F.
2. Sprinkle salmon with salt and pepper.
3. Juice half the lemon and slice the other half into ¼"-thick pieces. In a small bowl, combine juice with butter. Brush mixture over salmon.
4. Sprinkle dill evenly over salmon. Place lemon slices on top of salmon.
5. Place salmon in the air fryer basket and cook 10 minutes until salmon flakes easily and internal temperature reaches at least 145°F. Remove lemon slices before serving.

Old Bay Cod Fish Fillets

Servings: 2
Cooking Time: 12 Minutes
Ingredients:
- 2 cod fish fillets
- 1 teaspoon butter, melted
- 1 teaspoon Old Bay seasoning
- 1 egg, beaten
- 2 tablespoons coconut milk, unsweetened
- ⅓ cup coconut flour, unsweetened

Directions:
1. Prepare a Ziploc bag, add the cod fish fillets, butter and Old Bay seasoning, shake to coat the fillets well on all sides.
2. Whisk the egg and coconut milk until frothy in a shallow bowl.
3. In another bowl, place the coconut flour.
4. Coat the fish fillets with the egg mixture and coconut flour in order, pressing to adhere.
5. Cook the fish fillets at 390 degrees F/ 200 degrees C until the fish fillets flake easily when poking it with a fork, for 12 minutes.
6. Flip halfway through.
7. Bon appétit!

Spicy Halibut Steak

Servings: 3
Cooking Time: 10 Minutes
Ingredients:
- 1 pound halibut steak
- 1 teaspoon olive oil
- Sea salt, to taste
- Ground black pepper, to taste
- 7 ounces Cremini mushrooms
- 1 teaspoon butter, melted
- ¼ teaspoon onion powder
- ¼ teaspoon garlic powder
- ½ teaspoon rosemary
- ½ teaspoon basil
- ½ teaspoon oregano

Directions:
1. Combine the halibut steak with olive oil, salt and black pepper and toss well.
2. Transfer the halibut steak to the cooking basket and arrange the basket to the air fryer.
3. Cook the halibut steak at 400 degrees F/ 205 degrees C for 5 minutes, then, turn the halibut steak, put the Cremini mushrooms on the top and cook for an additional 5 minutes or until the mushrooms are fragrant.
4. Once done, serve and enjoy.

Easy Air Fried Salmon

Servings: 2
Cooking Time: 10 Minutes
Ingredients:
- 2 salmon fillets, skinless and boneless
- 1 teaspoon olive oil
- Black pepper
- Salt

Directions:
1. Coat boneless salmon fillets with olive oil and season with black pepper and salt.
2. Place salmon fillets in air fryer basket and Cook at almost 360 degrees F/ 180 degrees C for 8-10 minutes.
3. Serve and enjoy.

Crispy Smelts

Servings: 3
Cooking Time: 20 Minutes
Ingredients:
- 1 pound Cleaned smelts
- 3 tablespoons Tapioca flour
- Vegetable oil spray
- To taste Coarse sea salt or kosher salt

Directions:
1. Preheat the air fryer to 400°F.
2. Toss the smelts and tapioca flour in a large bowl until the little fish are evenly coated.
3. Lay the smelts out on a large cutting board. Lightly coat both sides of each fish with vegetable oil spray.
4. When the machine is at temperature, set the smelts close together in the basket, with a few even overlapping on top. Air-fry undisturbed for 20 minutes, until lightly browned and crisp.
5. Remove the basket from the machine and turn out the fish onto a wire rack. The smelts will most likely come out as one large block, or maybe in a couple of large pieces. Cool for a minute or two, then sprinkle the smelts with salt and break the block(s) into much smaller sections or individual fish to serve.

Maple Butter Salmon

Servings: 4
Cooking Time: 12 Minutes
Ingredients:
- 2 tablespoons salted butter, melted
- 1 teaspoon low-carb maple syrup
- 1 teaspoon yellow mustard
- 4 boneless, skinless salmon fillets
- ½ teaspoon salt

Directions:
1. In a small bowl, whisk together butter, syrup, and mustard. Brush ½ mixture over each fillet on both sides. Sprinkle fillets with salt on both sides.
2. Place salmon into ungreased air fryer basket. Adjust the temperature to 400°F and set the timer for 12 minutes. Halfway through cooking, brush fillets on both sides with remaining syrup mixture. Salmon will easily flake and have an internal temperature of at least 145°F when done. Serve warm.

Trimmed Mackerel With Spring Onions

Servings: 5
Cooking Time: 20 Minutes
Ingredients:
- 1 pound mackerel, trimmed
- 1 tablespoon ground paprika
- 1 green bell pepper
- ½ cup spring onions, chopped
- 1 tablespoon avocado oil
- 1 teaspoon apple cider vinegar
- ½-teaspoon salt

Directions:
1. Sprinkle the clean mackerel with ground paprika.
2. Chop the green bell pepper.
3. Fill the mackerel with bell pepper and spring onion.
4. After this, sprinkle the fish with avocado oil, salt and apple cider vinegar.
5. At 375 degrees F/ 190 degrees C, heat your air fryer in advance.
6. Place the mackerel in the basket and arrange the basket to the air fryer.
7. Cook the mackerel for 20 minutes at 375 degrees F/ 190 degrees C.
8. When cooked, serve and enjoy.

Lobster Tails

Servings: 4
Cooking Time: 10 Minutes
Ingredients:
- 4 lobster tails
- 2 tablespoons salted butter, melted
- 1 tablespoon finely minced garlic
- ¼ teaspoon salt
- ¼ teaspoon ground black pepper
- 2 tablespoons lemon juice

Directions:
1. Preheat the air fryer to 400°F.
2. Carefully cut open lobster tails with kitchen scissors and pull back the shell a little to expose the meat. Drizzle butter over each tail, then sprinkle with garlic, salt, and pepper.
3. Place tails in the air fryer basket and cook 10 minutes until lobster is firm and opaque and internal temperature reaches at least 145°F.
4. Drizzle lemon juice over lobster meat. Serve warm.

Shrimp "scampi"

Servings: 4
Cooking Time: 5 Minutes
Ingredients:
- 1½ pounds Large shrimp, peeled and deveined
- ¼ cup Olive oil
- 2 tablespoons Minced garlic
- 1 teaspoon Dried oregano
- Up to 1 teaspoon Red pepper flakes
- ½ teaspoon Table salt
- 2 tablespoons White balsamic vinegar

Directions:
1. Preheat the air fryer to 400°F.

2. Stir the shrimp, olive oil, garlic, oregano, red pepper flakes, and salt in a large bowl until the shrimp are well coated.
3. When the machine is at temperature, transfer the shrimp to the basket. They will overlap and even sit on top of each other. Air-fry for 5 minutes, tossing and rearranging the shrimp twice to make sure the covered surfaces are exposed, until pink and firm.
4. Pour the contents of the basket into a serving bowl. Pour the vinegar over the shrimp while hot and toss to coat.

Spanish Garlic Shrimp

Servings: 4
Cooking Time: 15 Minutes
Ingredients:
- 2 teaspoons olive oil plus more for spraying
- 2 teaspoons minced garlic
- 2 teaspoons lemon juice
- ½ to 1 teaspoon crushed red pepper
- 12 ounces medium cooked shrimp, thawed, and deveined, with tails on

Directions:
1. Spray a fryer basket lightly with olive oil.
2. In a medium bowl, mix together the garlic, lemon juice, 2 teaspoons of olive oil, and crushed red pepper to make a marinade.
3. Add the shrimp and toss to coat in the marinade. Cover with plastic wrap and place the bowl in the refrigerator for 30 minutes.
4. Place the shrimp in the fryer basket. Air fry for 5 minutes. Shake the basket and cook until the shrimp are cooked through and nicely browned, an additional 5 to 10 minutes.

Lemon Shrimp And Zucchinis

Servings: 4
Cooking Time: 15 Minutes
Ingredients:
- 1 pound shrimp, peeled and deveined
- A pinch of salt and black pepper
- 2 zucchinis, cut into medium cubes
- 1 tablespoon lemon juice
- 1 tablespoon olive oil
- 1 tablespoon garlic, minced

Directions:
1. In a pan that fits the air fryer, combine all the ingredients, toss, put the pan in the machine and cook at 370°F for 15 minutes. Divide between plates and serve right away.

Maryland-style Crab Cakes

Servings: 6
Cooking Time: 15 Minutes
Ingredients:
- 4 (6-ounce) cans lump crab meat, drained
- 1 cup whole-wheat panko bread crumbs
- 1 cup chopped fresh parsley
- 4 cloves garlic, minced
- 4 teaspoons Dijon mustard
- 2 teaspoons Old Bay seasoning
- 2 large eggs, beaten
- Olive oil

Directions:
1. In a large bowl, mix together the crab meat, panko bread crumbs, parsley, garlic, Dijon mustard, and Old Bay seasoning. Add the eggs and stir to combine. Cover the bowl and refrigerate for 30 minutes.
2. Spray a fryer basket lightly with olive oil.
3. Form the mixture into 12 crab cakes.
4. Place the crab cakes in the fryer basket in a single layer. Spray the tops lightly with olive oil. You may need to cook them in batches.
5. Air fry for 6 to 8 minutes. Turn the crab cakes over, spray lightly with olive oil, and cook until golden brown, 4 to 7 more minutes.

Fried Shrimp

Servings: 3
Cooking Time: 7 Minutes
Ingredients:
- 1 Large egg white
- 2 tablespoons Water
- 1 cup Plain dried bread crumbs (gluten-free, if a concern)
- ¼ cup All-purpose flour or almond flour
- ¼ cup Yellow cornmeal
- 1 teaspoon Celery salt
- 1 teaspoon Mild paprika
- Up to ½ teaspoon Cayenne (optional)
- ¾ pound Large shrimp (20–25 per pound), peeled and deveined
- Vegetable oil spray

Directions:
1. Preheat the air fryer to 400°F.
2. Set two medium or large bowls on your counter. In the first, whisk the egg white and water until foamy. In the second, stir the bread crumbs, flour, cornmeal, celery salt, paprika, and cayenne (if using) until well combined.
3. Pour all the shrimp into the egg white mixture and stir gently until all the shrimp are coated. Use kitchen tongs to pick them up one by one and transfer them to the bread-crumb mixture. Turn each in the bread-crumb mixture to coat it evenly and thoroughly on all sides before setting it on a cutting board. When you're done coating the shrimp, coat them all on both sides with the vegetable oil spray.
4. Set the shrimp in as close to one layer in the basket as you can. Some may overlap. Air-fry for 7 minutes, gently rearranging the shrimp at the 4-minute mark to get covered surfaces exposed, until golden brown and firm but not hard.
5. Use kitchen tongs to gently transfer the shrimp to a wire rack. Cool for only a minute or two before serving.

Old Bay Fish 'n' Chips

Servings: 4
Cooking Time: 40 Minutes
Ingredients:
- 2 russet potatoes, peeled
- 2 tbsp olive oil
- 4 tilapia filets
- ¼ cup flour
- Salt and pepper to taste
- 1 tsp Old Bay seasoning
- 1 lemon, zested
- 1 egg, beaten
- 1 cup panko bread crumbs
- 3 tbsp tartar sauce

Directions:
1. Preheat the air fryer to 400°F. Slice the potatoes into ½-inch-thick chips and drizzle with olive oil. Sprinkle with salt. Add the fries to the frying basket and Air Fry for 12-16 minutes, shaking once. Remove the potatoes to a plate. Cover loosely with foil to keep warm. Sprinkle the fish with salt and season with black pepper, lemon zest, and Old Bay seasoning, then lay on a plate. Put the egg in a shallow bowl and spread the panko on a separate plate. Dip the fish in the flour, then the egg, then the panko. Press to coat completely. Add half the fish to the frying basket and spray with cooking oil. Set a raised rack on the frying basket, top with the other half of the fish, and spray with cooking oil. Air Fry for 8-10 minutes until the fish flakes. Serve the fish and chips with tartar sauce.

Fried Catfish Nuggets

Servings: 4
Cooking Time: 40 Minutes
Ingredients:
- 1 pound catfish fillets, cut into 1-inch chunks
- ½ cup seasoned fish fry breading mix (such as Louisiana Fish Fry)
- Cooking oil

Directions:
1. Rinse and thoroughly dry the catfish. Pour the seasoned fish fry breading mix into a sealable plastic bag and add the catfish. (You may need to use two bags depending on the size of your nuggets.) Seal the bag and shake to evenly coat the fish with breading.
2. Spray the air fryer basket with cooking oil.
3. Transfer the catfish nuggets to the air fryer. Do not overcrowd the basket. You may need to cook the nuggets in two batches. Spray the nuggets with cooking oil. Cook for 10 minutes.
4. Open the air fryer and shake the basket. Cook for an additional 8 to 10 minutes, or until the fish is crisp.
5. If necessary, remove the cooked catfish nuggets from the air fryer, then repeat steps 3 and 4 for the remaining fish.
6. Cool before serving.

Chapter 10: Desserts And Sweets Recipes

Cranberries Pudding

Servings: 6
Cooking Time: 20 Minutes
Ingredients:
- 1 cup cauliflower rice
- 2 cups almond milk
- ½ cup cranberries
- 1 teaspoon vanilla extract

Directions:
1. In a pan that fits your air fryer, mix all the ingredients, whisk a bit, put the pan in the fryer and cook at 360°F for 20 minutes. Stir the pudding, divide into bowls and serve cold.

Chocolate Coconut Brownies

Servings: 8
Cooking Time: 15 Minutes
Ingredients:
- ½ cup coconut oil
- 2 ounces (57 g) dark chocolate
- 1 cup sugar
- 2½ tablespoons water
- 4 whisked eggs
- ¼ teaspoon ground cinnamon
- ½ teaspoons ground anise star
- ¼ teaspoon coconut extract
- ½ teaspoons vanilla extract
- 1 tablespoon honey
- ½ cup flour
- ½ cup desiccated coconut
- Sugar, for dusting

Directions:
1. Preheat the air fryer to 355ºF (179ºC).
2. Melt the coconut oil and dark chocolate in the microwave.
3. Combine with the sugar, water, eggs, cinnamon, anise, coconut extract, vanilla, and honey in a large bowl.
4. Stir in the flour and desiccated coconut. Incorporate everything well.
5. Lightly grease a baking dish with butter. Transfer the mixture to the dish.
6. Put the dish in the air fryer and bake for 15 minutes.
7. Remove from the air fryer and allow to cool slightly.
8. Take care when taking it out of the baking dish. Slice it into squares.
9. Dust with sugar before serving.

Toasted Coconut Flakes

Servings: 1
Cooking Time: 5 Minutes
Ingredients:
- 1 cup unsweetened coconut flakes
- 2 tsp. coconut oil, melted
- ¼ cup granular erythritol
- Salt

Directions:
1. In a large bowl, combine the coconut flakes, oil, granular erythritol, and a pinch of salt, ensuring that the flakes are coated completely.
2. Place the coconut flakes in your fryer and cook at 300°F for three minutes, giving the basket a good shake a few times throughout the cooking time. Fry until golden and serve.

Simple & Tasty Brownies

Servings: 2
Cooking Time: 5 Minutes
Ingredients:
- 2 tablespoons of baking chips
- ⅓ cup of almond flour
- 1 egg
- ½ teaspoon of baking powder
- 3 tablespoons of powdered sweetener sugar alternative
- 2 tablespoons of cocoa powder unsweetened
- 2 tablespoons of chopped pecans
- 4 tablespoons of melted butter

Directions:
1. Let the air fryer preheat to 350 degrees F/ 175 degrees C
2. In a suitable bowl, add cocoa powder, almond flour, Swerve sugar substitute, and baking powder, give it a good mix.
3. Add melted butter and crack in the egg in the dry ingredients.
4. Mix well until combined and smooth.
5. Fold in the chopped pecans and baking chips.
6. Take 2 ramekins to grease them well with softened butter. Add the batter to them.
7. Air fry for 10 minutes. Make sure to place them as far from the heat source from the top in the air fryer.
8. Take the brownies out from the air fryer and let them cool for 5 minutes.
9. Serve with your favorite toppings and enjoy.

Giant Vegan Chocolate Chip Cookie

Servings: 4
Cooking Time: 16 Minutes
Ingredients:
- ⅔ cup All-purpose flour
- 5 tablespoons Rolled oats (not quick-cooking or steel-cut oats)
- ¼ teaspoon Baking soda
- ¼ teaspoon Table salt
- 5 tablespoons Granulated white sugar
- ¼ cup Vegetable oil
- 2½ tablespoons Tahini (see here)
- 2½ tablespoons Maple syrup
- 2 teaspoons Vanilla extract

- ⅔ cup Vegan semisweet or bittersweet chocolate chips
- Baking spray

Directions:
1. Preheat the air fryer to 325°F (or 330°F, if that's the closest setting).
2. Whisk the flour, oats, baking soda, and salt in a bowl until well combined.
3. Using an electric hand mixer at medium speed, beat the sugar, oil, tahini, maple syrup, and vanilla until rich and creamy, about 3 minutes, scraping down the inside of the bowl occasionally.
4. Scrape down and remove the beaters. Fold in the flour mixture and chocolate chips with a rubber spatula just until all the flour is moistened and the chocolate chips are even throughout the dough.
5. For a small air fryer, coat the inside of a 6-inch round cake pan with baking spray. For a medium air fryer, coat the inside of a 7-inch round cake pan with baking spray. And for a large air fryer, coat the inside of an 8-inch round cake pan with baking spray. Scrape and gently press the dough into the prepared pan, spreading it into an even layer to the perimeter.
6. Set the pan in the basket and air-fry undisturbed for 16 minutes, or until puffed, browned, and firm to the touch.
7. Transfer the pan to a wire rack and cool for 10 minutes. Loosen the cookie from the perimeter with a spatula, then invert the pan onto a cutting board and let the cookie come free. Remove the pan and reinvert the cookie onto the wire rack. Cool for 5 minutes more before slicing into wedges to serve.

Buttery Shortbread Sticks

Servings: 10
Cooking Time: 22 Minutes
Ingredients:
- ⅓ cup caster sugar
- 1 2/3 cups plain flour
- ¾ cup butter

Directions:
1. In a suitable bowl, mix the sugar and flour.
2. Add the butter and stir until it makes a smooth dough.
3. Cut the dough into ten equal-sized sticks. With a fork, lightly prick the sticks.
4. Place the sticks into the lightly greased baking pan.
5. Set the cook time to 12 minutes.
6. At 355 degrees F/ 180 degrees C, preheat your air fryer.
7. Arrange the pan in preheat air fry basket and insert it in the air fryer.
8. Place the baking pan to cool for about 5-10 minutes.
9. Serve.

Chocolate Croissants

Servings: 8
Cooking Time: 24 Minutes
Ingredients:
- 1 sheet frozen puff pastry, thawed
- ⅓ cup chocolate-hazelnut spread
- 1 large egg, beaten

Directions:
1. On a lightly floured surface, roll puff pastry into a 14-inch square. Cut pastry into quarters to form 4 squares. Cut each square diagonally to form 8 triangles.
2. Spread 2 teaspoons chocolate-hazelnut spread on each triangle; from wider end, roll up pastry. Brush egg on top of each roll.
3. Preheat the air fryer to 375ºF (191ºC). Air fry rolls in batches, 3 or 4 at a time, 8 minutes per batch, or until pastry is golden brown.
4. Cool on a wire rack; serve while warm or at room temperature.

Glazed Donuts

Servings: 2 – 4
Cooking Time: 25 Minutes
Ingredients:
- 1 can [8 oz.] refrigerated croissant dough
- Cooking spray
- 1 can [16 oz.] vanilla frosting

Directions:
1. Cut the croissant dough into 1-inch-round slices. Make a hole in the center of each one to create a donut.
2. Put the donuts in the Air Fryer basket, taking care not to overlap any, and spritz with cooking spray. You may need to cook everything in multiple batches.
3. Cook at 400°F for 2 minutes. Turn the donuts over and cook for another 3 minutes.
4. Place the rolls on a paper plate.
5. Microwave a half-cup of frosting for 30 seconds and pour a drizzling of the frosting over the donuts before serving.

Molten Chocolate Almond Cakes

Servings: 3
Cooking Time: 13 Minutes
Ingredients:
- butter and flour for the ramekins
- 4 ounces bittersweet chocolate, chopped
- ½ cup (1 stick) unsalted butter
- 2 eggs
- 2 egg yolks
- ¼ cup sugar
- ½ teaspoon pure vanilla extract, or almond extract
- 1 tablespoon all-purpose flour
- 3 tablespoons ground almonds
- 8 to 12 semisweet chocolate discs (or 4 chunks of chocolate)

- cocoa powder or powdered sugar, for dusting
- toasted almonds, coarsely chopped

Directions:

1. Butter and flour three (6-ounce) ramekins. (Butter the ramekins and then coat the butter with flour by shaking it around in the ramekin and dumping out any excess.)
2. Melt the chocolate and butter together, either in the microwave or in a double boiler. In a separate bowl, beat the eggs, egg yolks and sugar together until light and smooth. Add the vanilla extract. Whisk the chocolate mixture into the egg mixture. Stir in the flour and ground almonds.
3. Preheat the air fryer to 330°F.
4. Transfer the batter carefully to the buttered ramekins, filling halfway. Place two or three chocolate discs in the center of the batter and then fill the ramekins to ½-inch below the top with the remaining batter. Place the ramekins into the air fryer basket and air-fry at 330°F for 13 minutes. The sides of the cake should be set, but the centers should be slightly soft. Remove the ramekins from the air fryer and let the cakes sit for 5 minutes. (If you'd like the cake a little less molten, air-fry for 14 minutes and let the cakes sit for 4 minutes.)
5. Run a butter knife around the edge of the ramekins and invert the cakes onto a plate. Lift the ramekin off the plate slowly and carefully so that the cake doesn't break. Dust with cocoa powder or powdered sugar and serve with a scoop of ice cream and some coarsely chopped toasted almonds.

Mixed Berry Crumble

Servings: 4
Cooking Time: 11 To 16 Minutes

Ingredients:

- ½ cup chopped fresh strawberries
- ½ cup fresh blueberries
- ⅓ cup frozen raspberries
- 1 tablespoon freshly squeezed lemon juice
- 1 tablespoon honey
- ⅔ cup whole-wheat pastry flour (see Tip)
- 3 tablespoons packed brown sugar
- 2 tablespoons unsalted butter, melted

Directions:

1. In a 6-by-2-inch pan, combine the strawberries, blueberries, and raspberries. Drizzle with the lemon juice and honey.
2. In a small bowl, mix the pastry flour and brown sugar.
3. Stir in the butter and mix until crumbly. Sprinkle this mixture over the fruit.
4. Bake for 11 to 16 minutes, or until the fruit is tender and bubbly and the topping is golden brown. Serve warm.

Graham Cracker Cheesecake

Servings: 8
Cooking Time: 20 Minutes

Ingredients:

- 1 cup graham cracker crumbs
- 3 tablespoons softened butter
- 1½ (8-ounce / 227-g) packages cream cheese, softened
- ⅓ cup sugar
- 2 eggs
- 1 tablespoon flour
- 1 teaspoon vanilla
- ¼ cup chocolate syrup

Directions:

1. For the crust, combine the graham cracker crumbs and butter in a small bowl and mix well. Press into the bottom of a baking pan and put in the freezer to set.
2. For the filling, combine the cream cheese and sugar in a medium bowl and mix well. Beat in the eggs, one at a time. Add the flour and vanilla.
3. Preheat the air fryer to 450°F (232°C).
4. Remove ⅔ cup of the filling to a small bowl and stir in the chocolate syrup until combined.
5. Pour the vanilla filling into the pan with the crust. Drop the chocolate filling over the vanilla filling by the spoonful. With a clean butter knife, stir the fillings in a zigzag pattern to marbleize them.
6. Bake for 20 minutes or until the cheesecake is just set.
7. Cool on a wire rack for 1 hour, then chill in the refrigerator until the cheesecake is firm.
8. Serve immediately.

Almond Shortbread Cookies

Servings: 8
Cooking Time: 1 Hour 10 Minutes

Ingredients:

- ½ cup salted butter, softened
- ¼ cup granulated sugar
- 1 teaspoon almond extract
- 1 teaspoon vanilla extract
- 2 cups all-purpose flour

Directions:

1. In a large bowl, cream butter, sugar, and extracts. Gradually add flour, mixing until well combined.
2. Roll dough into a 12" x 2" log and wrap in plastic. Chill in refrigerator at least 1 hour.
3. Preheat the air fryer to 300°F.
4. Slice dough into ¼"-thick cookies. Place in the air fryer basket 2" apart, working in batches as needed, and cook 10 minutes until the edges start to brown. Let cool completely before serving.

Peanut Butter-banana Roll-ups

Servings: 4
Cooking Time: 20 Minutes
Ingredients:
- 2 ripe bananas, halved crosswise
- 4 spring roll wrappers
- ¼ cup molasses
- ¼ cup peanut butter
- 1 tsp ground cinnamon
- 1 tsp lemon zest

Directions:
1. Preheat air fryer to 375°F. Place the roll wrappers on a flat surface with one corner facing up. Spread 1 tbsp of molasses on each, then 1 tbsp of peanut butter, and finally top with lemon zest and 1 banana half. Sprinkle with cinnamon all over. For the wontons, fold the bottom over the banana, then fold the sides, and roll-up. Place them seam-side down and Roast for 10 minutes until golden brown and crispy. Serve warm.

Zucchini Bread With Chocolate Chips

Servings: 12
Cooking Time: 15 Minutes
Ingredients:
- ¼ teaspoon salt
- ½ cup almond milk
- ½ cup maple syrup
- ½ cup sunflower oil
- ½ cup unsweetened cocoa powder
- 1 cup oat flour
- 1 cup zucchini, shredded and squeezed
- 1 tablespoon flax egg; 1 tablespoon flax meal + 3 tablespoons. water
- 1 teaspoon apple cider vinegar
- 1 teaspoon baking soda
- 1 teaspoon vanilla extract
- ⅓ cup chocolate chips

Directions:
1. At 350 degrees F/ 175 degrees C, preheat your air fryer.
2. Layer a suitable baking dish that will fit the air fryer with parchment paper.
3. In a suitable bowl, combine the flax meal, zucchini, sunflower oil, maple syrup, vanilla, apple cider vinegar and milk.
4. Add the oat flour, baking soda, cocoa powder, and salt. Mix until well combined.
5. Add the chocolate chips.
6. Pour over the baking dish and cook for almost 15 minutes or until a toothpick inserted in the middle comes out clean.

Cinnamon Crunch S'mores

Servings: 12
Cooking Time: 10 Minutes
Ingredients:
- 12 whole cinnamon graham crackers
- 2 (1.55-ounce) chocolate bars, broken into 12 pieces
- 12 marshmallows

Directions:
1. Halve each graham cracker into 2 squares.
2. Place 6 graham cracker squares in the air fryer. Do not stack. Place a piece of chocolate onto each. Cook for 2 minutes.
3. Open the air fryer and add a marshmallow onto each piece of melted chocolate. Cook for 1 additional minute.
4. Remove the cooked s'mores from the air fryer, then repeat steps 2 and 3 for the remaining 6 s'mores.
5. Top with the remaining graham cracker squares and serve.

Vegan Brownie Bites

Servings: 10
Cooking Time: 8 Minutes
Ingredients:
- ⅔ cup walnuts
- ⅓ cup all-purpose flour
- ¼ cup dark cocoa powder
- ⅓ cup cane sugar
- ¼ teaspoon salt
- 2 tablespoons vegetable oil
- 1 teaspoon pure vanilla extract
- 1 tablespoon almond milk
- 1 tablespoon powdered sugar

Directions:
1. Preheat the air fryer to 350°F.
2. To a blender or food processor fitted with a metal blade, add the walnuts, flour, cocoa powder, sugar, and salt. Pulse until smooth, about 30 seconds. Add in the oil, vanilla, and milk and pulse until a dough is formed.
3. Remove the dough and place in a bowl. Form into 10 equal-size bites.
4. Liberally spray the metal trivet in the air fryer basket with olive oil mist. Place the brownie bites into the basket and cook for 8 minutes, or until the outer edges begin to slightly crack.
5. Remove the basket from the air fryer and let cool. Sprinkle the brownie bites with powdered sugar and serve.

Hasselback Apple Crisp

Servings: 4
Cooking Time: 20 Minutes
Ingredients:
- 2 large Gala apples, peeled, cored and cut in half
- ¼ cup butter, melted
- ½ teaspoon ground cinnamon
- 2 tablespoons sugar
- Topping
- 3 tablespoons butter, melted
- 2 tablespoons brown sugar
- ¼ cup chopped pecans

- 2 tablespoons rolled oats*
- 1 tablespoon flour*
- vanilla ice cream
- caramel sauce

Directions:
1. Place the apples cut side down on a cutting board. Slicing from stem end to blossom end, make 8 to 10 slits down the apple halves but only slice three quarters of the way through the apple, not all the way through to the cutting board.
2. Preheat the air fryer to 330°F and pour a little water into the bottom of the air fryer drawer. (This will help prevent the grease that drips into the bottom drawer from burning and smoking.)
3. Transfer the apples to the air fryer basket, flat side down. Combine ¼ cup of melted butter, cinnamon and sugar in a small bowl. Brush this butter mixture onto the apples and air-fry at 330°F for 15 minutes. Baste the apples several times with the butter mixture during the cooking process.
4. While the apples are air-frying, make the filling. Combine 3 tablespoons of melted butter with the brown sugar, pecans, rolled oats and flour in a bowl. Stir with a fork until the mixture resembles small crumbles.
5. When the timer on the air fryer is up, spoon the topping down the center of the apples. Air-fry at 330°F for an additional 5 minutes.
6. Transfer the apples to a serving plate and serve with vanilla ice cream and caramel sauce.

Sage Cream

Servings: 4
Cooking Time: 30 Minutes
Ingredients:
- 7 cups red currants
- 1 cup swerve
- 1 cup water
- 6 sage leaves

Directions:
1. In a pan that fits your air fryer, mix all the ingredients, toss, put the pan in the fryer and cook at 330°F for 30 minutes. Discard sage leaves, divide into cups and serve cold.

Apple-blueberry Hand Pies

Servings: 4
Cooking Time:7 To 9 Minutes
Ingredients:
- 1 medium Granny Smith apple, peeled and finely chopped
- ½ cup dried blueberries
- 1 tablespoon freshly squeezed orange juice
- 1 tablespoon packed brown sugar
- 2 teaspoons cornstarch
- 4 sheets frozen phyllo dough, thawed
- 8 teaspoons unsalted butter, melted

- 8 teaspoons sugar
- Nonstick cooking spray, for coating the phyllo dough

Directions:
1. In a medium bowl, mix the apple, blueberries, orange juice, brown sugar, and cornstarch.
2. Place 1 sheet of phyllo dough on a work surface with the narrow side facing you. Brush very lightly with 1 teaspoon of butter and sprinkle with 1 teaspoon of sugar. Fold the phyllo sheet in half from left to right.
3. Place one-fourth of the fruit filling at the bottom of the sheet in the center. Fold the left side of the sheet over the filling. Spray lightly with cooking spray. Fold the right side of the sheet over the filling. Brush with 1 teaspoon of butter and sprinkle with 1 teaspoon of sugar.
4. Fold the bottom right corner of the dough up to meet the left side of the pastry sheet to form a triangle. Continue folding the triangles over to enclose the filling, as you would fold a flag. Seal the edge with a bit of water. Spray lightly with cooking spray. Repeat with the remaining 3 sheets of the phyllo, butter, sugar, and cooking spray, making four pies.
5. Place the pies in the air fryer basket. Bake for 7 to 9 minutes, or until golden brown and crisp. Remove the pies and let cool on a wire rack before serving.

Dark Chocolate Cream Galette

Servings: 4
Cooking Time: 55 Minutes + Cooling Time
Ingredients:
- 16 oz cream cheese, softened
- 1 cup crumbled graham crackers
- 1 cup dark cocoa powder
- ½ cup white sugar
- 1 tsp peppermint extract
- 1 tsp ground cinnamon
- 1 egg
- 1 cup condensed milk
- 2 tbsp muscovado sugar
- 1 ½ tsp butter, melted

Directions:
1. Preheat air fryer to 350°F. Place the crumbled graham crackers in a large bowl and stir in the muscovado sugar and melted butter. Spread the mixture into a greased pie pan, pressing down to form the galette base. Place the pan into the air fryer and Bake for 5 minutes. Remove the pan and set aside.
2. Place the cocoa powder, cream cheese, peppermint extract, white sugar, cinnamon, condensed milk, and egg in a large bowl and whip thoroughly to combine. Spoon the chocolate mixture over the graham cracker crust and level the top with a spatula. Put in the air fryer and Bake for 40 minutes until firm. Transfer the cookies to a wire rack to cool. Serve and enjoy!

Coconut Cream Roll-ups

Servings: 4
Cooking Time: 20 Minutes
Ingredients:
- ½ cup cream cheese, softened
- 1 cup fresh raspberries
- ¼ cup brown sugar
- ¼ cup coconut cream
- 1 egg
- 1 tsp corn starch
- 6 spring roll wrappers

Directions:
1. Preheat air fryer to 350°F. Add the cream cheese, brown sugar, coconut cream, cornstarch, and egg to a bowl and whisk until all ingredients are completely mixed and fluffy, thick and stiff. Spoon even amounts of the creamy filling into each spring roll wrapper, then top each dollop of filling with several raspberries. Roll up the wraps around the creamy raspberry filling, and seal the seams with a few dabs of water.
2. Place each roll on the foil-lined frying basket, seams facing down. Bake for 10 minutes, flipping them once until golden brown and perfect on the outside, while the raspberries and cream filling will have cooked together in a glorious fusion. Remove with tongs and serve hot or cold. Serve and enjoy!

Apple Pie Crumble

Servings: 4
Cooking Time: 25 Minutes
Ingredients:
- 1 can apple pie
- ¼ cup butter, softened
- 9 tablespoons self-rising flour
- 7 tablespoons caster sugar
- Pinch of salt

Directions:
1. Preheat the Air fryer to 320°F and grease a baking dish.
2. Mix all the ingredients in a bowl until a crumbly mixture is formed.
3. Arrange the apple pie in the baking dish and top with the mixture.
4. Transfer the baking dish into the Air fryer basket and cook for about 25 minutes.
5. Dish out in a platter and serve.

Chocolate Molten Cake

Servings: 4
Cooking Time: 10 Minutes
Ingredients:
- 3.5 ounces (99 g) butter, melted
- 3½ tablespoons sugar
- 3.5 ounces (99 g) chocolate, melted
- 1½ tablespoons flour
- 2 eggs

Directions:
1. Preheat the air fryer to 375°F (191°C).
2. Grease four ramekins with a little butter.
3. Rigorously combine the eggs, butter, and sugar before stirring in the melted chocolate.
4. Slowly fold in the flour.
5. Spoon an equal amount of the mixture into each ramekin.
6. Put them in the air fryer and bake for 10 minutes
7. Put the ramekins upside-down on plates and let the cakes fall out. Serve hot.

Chocolate Banana Brownie

Servings: 4
Cooking Time: 16 Minutes
Ingredients:
- 1 cup bananas, overripe
- 1 scoop protein: powder
- 2 tablespoons unsweetened cocoa powder
- ½ cup almond butter, melted

Directions:
1. Before cooking, heat your air fryer to 325 degrees F/ 160 degrees C.
2. Using cooking spray, spray a baking pan that fits in your air fryer.
3. In a blender, mix the bananas, protein powder, cocoa powder, and the almond butter together until smooth.
4. Spread the better onto the baking pan.
5. Cook the brownie in the preheated air fryer for 16 minutes.
6. Serve and enjoy!

Butter Cheesecake

Servings: 6
Cooking Time: 28 Minutes
Ingredients:
- For crust:
- 2 tablespoons butter, melted
- ¼ teaspoon cinnamon
- 1 tablespoon swerve
- ½ cup almond flour
- Pinch of salt
- For Cheesecake:
- 1 egg
- ½ teaspoon vanilla
- ½ cup swerve
- 8 oz. cream cheese

Directions:
1. At 280 degrees F/ 140 degrees C, preheat your air fryer.
2. Grease its air fryer basket with cooking spray.
3. Add all crust ingredients into the bowl and mix until combined. Transfer crust mixture into the prepared baking dish and press down into the bottom of the dish.

4. Place dish in the preheated Air Fryer and cook for 12 minutes.
5. In a suitable bowl, beat cream cheese using a hand mixer until smooth.
6. Stir in vanilla, egg, and salt and stir to combine.
7. Pour cream cheese mixture over cooked crust and cook for 16 minutes.
8. Allow to cool completely.
9. Slice and serve.

Grilled Spiced Fruit

Servings: 4
Cooking Time: 3 To 5 Minutes
Ingredients:
- 2 peaches, peeled, pitted, and thickly sliced
- 3 plums, halved and pitted
- 3 nectarines, halved and pitted
- 1 tablespoon honey
- ½ teaspoon ground cinnamon
- ¼ teaspoon ground allspice
- Pinch cayenne pepper

Directions:
1. Thread the fruit, alternating the types, onto 8 bamboo (see Tip, here) or metal skewers that fit into the air fryer.
2. In a small bowl, stir together the honey, cinnamon, allspice, and cayenne. Brush the glaze onto the fruit.
3. Grill the skewers for 3 to 5 minutes, or until lightly browned and caramelized. Cool for 5 minutes and serve.

Curry Peaches, Pears, And Plums

Servings: 8
Cooking Time: 5 Minutes
Ingredients:
- 2 peaches
- 2 firm pears
- 2 plums
- 2 tablespoons melted butter
- 1 tablespoon honey
- 2 to 3 teaspoons curry powder

Directions:
1. Preheat the air fryer to 325°F (163°C).
2. Cut the peaches in half, remove the pits, and cut each half in half again. Cut the pears in half, core them, and remove the stem. Cut each half in half again. Do the same with the plums.
3. Spread a large sheet of heavy-duty foil on the work surface. Arrange the fruit on the foil and drizzle with the butter and honey. Sprinkle with the curry powder.
4. Wrap the fruit in the foil, making sure to leave some air space in the packet.
5. Put the foil package in the basket and bake for 5 to 8 minutes, shaking the basket once during the cooking time, until the fruit is soft.
6. Serve immediately.

Plum Apple Crumble With Cranberries

Servings: 6-7
Cooking Time: 25 Minutes
Ingredients:
- 2 ½ ounces caster sugar
- ⅓ cup oats
- ⅔ cup flour
- ½ stick butter, chilled
- 1 tablespoon cold water
- 1 tablespoon honey
- ½ teaspoon ground mace
- ¼ pound plums, pitted and chopped
- ¼ pound apples, cored and chopped
- 1 tablespoon lemon juice
- ½ teaspoon vanilla paste
- 1 cup cranberries

Directions:
1. On a flat kitchen surface, plug your air fryer and turn it on.
2. Gently coat your cake pan with cooking oil or spray.
3. Before cooking, heat your air fryer to 390 degrees F/ 200 degrees C for about 4 to 5 minutes.
4. Mix the lemon juice, sugar, honey, mace, apples, and plums in a medium sized bowl.
5. Place the fruits onto the cake pan.
6. In a second medium sized bowl, mix thoroughly the rest of the ingredients and add the fruit mixture on the top. Transfer to the cake pan.
7. Bake the apple crumble in the preheated air fryer for 20 minutes.
8. When cooked, remove from the air fryer and serve warm.

Chocolate-almond Candies

Servings: 4
Cooking Time: 2 Minutes
Ingredients:
- 1-ounce almonds, crushed
- 1-ounce dark chocolate
- 2 tablespoons peanut butter
- 2 tablespoons heavy cream

Directions:
1. At 390 degrees F/ 200 degrees C, preheat your air fryer.
2. Chop the dark chocolate bar and put it in the preheated air fryer mold.
3. Add peanut butter and heavy cream.
4. Stir the mixture and transfer in the air fryer.
5. Cook it for 2 minutes or until it starts to be melt.
6. Then line the air fryer tray with parchment.
7. Put the crushed almonds on the tray in 1 layer.
8. Then pour the cooked chocolate mixture over the almonds.
9. Flatten gently if needed and let it cool.
10. Crack the cooked chocolate layer into the candies.

Honey Donuts

Servings: 8
Cooking Time: 8 Minutes
Ingredients:
- 1 cup coconut flour
- 4 eggs
- 4 tablespoons coconut oil, melted
- 1 teaspoon baking soda
- ⅔ cup apple cider vinegar:
- 1 teaspoon cinnamon
- 3 tablespoons honey
- a pinch of salt

Directions:
1. Let the air fryer pre-heat to 350 degrees F/ 175 degrees C.
2. Spray oil on a baking tray, spray a generous amount of grease with melted coconut oil.
3. In a suitable bowl, add apple cider vinegar, honey, melted coconut oil, salt mix well, then crack the 4 eggs, and mix it all together.
4. In another bowl, sift the coconut flour, baking soda, and cinnamon so that the dry ingredients will combine well.
5. Add the wet ingredients in a bowl and mix with the dry ingredients until completely combined.
6. Pour the prepared batter into the prepared donut baking pan. And add the batter into cavities.
7. Let it air fry for 10 minutes or 8 minutes at 350 degrees F/ 175 degrees C, or until light golden brown.
8. Serve right away and enjoy.

Easy-to-make Almond Cookies

Servings: 8
Cooking Time: 15 Minutes
Ingredients:
- 1 and ½ cups almonds, crushed
- 2 tablespoons Erythritol
- ½ teaspoon baking powder
- ¼ teaspoon almond extract
- 2 eggs, whisked

Directions:
1. In a bowl, whisk all of the ingredients well.
2. Scoop 8 servings of the mixture and then arrange them to the cooking pan lined with parchment paper.
3. Cook them at 350 degrees F/ 175 degrees C for 15 minutes.
4. Serve cold.

Tasty Berry Cobbler

Servings: 6
Cooking Time: 10 Minutes
Ingredients:
- 1 egg, lightly beaten
- 1 tablespoon butter, melted
- 2 teaspoons swerve
- ½ teaspoon vanilla
- 1 cup almond flour
- ½ cup raspberries, sliced
- ½ cup strawberries, sliced

Directions:
1. At 360 degrees F/ 180 degrees C, preheat your air fryer.
2. Add sliced strawberries and raspberries into the air fryer basket.
3. Sprinkle sweetener over berries.
4. Mix together almond flour, vanilla, and butter in the bowl.
5. Add egg in almond flour mixture and stir well to combine.
6. Spread almond flour mixture over sliced berries.
7. Cover dish with foil and place into the air fryer and cook for almost 10 minutes.
8. Serve and enjoy.

Coconut Rice Cake

Servings: 8
Cooking Time: 30 Minutes
Ingredients:
- 1 cup all-natural coconut water
- 1 cup unsweetened coconut milk
- 1 teaspoon almond extract
- ¼ teaspoon salt
- 4 tablespoons honey
- cooking spray
- ¾ cup raw jasmine rice
- 2 cups sliced or cubed fruit

Directions:
1. In a medium bowl, mix together the coconut water, coconut milk, almond extract, salt, and honey.
2. Spray air fryer baking pan with cooking spray and add the rice.
3. Pour liquid mixture over rice.
4. Cook at 360°F for 15minutes. Stir and cook for 15 minutes longer or until rice grains are tender.
5. Allow cake to cool slightly. Run a dull knife around edge of cake, inside the pan. Turn the cake out onto a platter and garnish with fruit.

Low-carb Peanut Butter Cookies

Servings: 24
Cooking Time: 10 Minutes
Ingredients:
- 1 cup peanut butter
- 1 whisked egg
- 1 teaspoon Liquid stevia drops
- 1 cup sugar alternative

Directions:
1. Mix all the recipe ingredients into a dough.
2. Make 24 balls with your hands from the combined dough.

3. On a cookie sheet or cutting board, press the dough balls with the help of a fork to form a crisscross pattern.
4. Add six cookies to the basket of air fryer in a single layer. Cook in batches.
5. Let them Air Fry, for 8-10 minutes, at 325 degrees F/ 160 degrees C.
6. Let the peanut butter cookies cool for 1 minute, then with care, take the cookies out.
7. Keep baking the rest of the peanut butter cookies in batches.
8. Let them cool completely and serve.

Zucchini Bars With Cream Cheese

Servings: 12
Cooking Time: 15 Minutes

Ingredients:
- 3 tablespoons coconut oil, melted 6 eggs
- 3 ounces' zucchini, shredded 2 teaspoons vanilla extract
- ½ teaspoon baking powder
- 4 ounces' cream cheese
- 2 tablespoons erythritol

Directions:
1. Whisk the coconut oil, zucchini, vanilla extract, baking powder, cream cheese, and erythritol in a bowl, then pour in the cooking pan lined with parchment paper.
2. Cook at 320 degrees F/ 160 degrees C for 15 minutes.
3. Slice and cool down.
4. Serve and enjoy.

Recipes Index

A

Air Fried Bell Peppers With Onion ... 41
Air Fried Broccoli ... 38
Air Fried London Broil ... 77
Air Fried Mussels With Parsley ... 80
Air-fried Potato Salad ... 42
Albóndigas ... 72
Almond Shortbread Cookies ... 93
Apple & Turkey Breakfast Sausages ... 28
Apple Pie Crumble ... 96
Apple Rollups ... 17
Apple-blueberry Hand Pies ... 95
Arancini With Sun-dried Tomatoes And Mozzarella ... 16
Asparagus, Mushroom And Cheese Soufflés ... 47
Avocado Buttered Flank Steak ... 74
Avocado Fries ... 41
Awesome Chicken Taquitos ... 35
Awesome Lemony Green Beans ... 13

B

Bacon And Broccoli Bread Pudding ... 24
Bacon Butter ... 15
Bacon Pickle Spear Rolls ... 15
Bacon With Shallot And Greens ... 77
Bacon Wrapped Pork With Apple Gravy ... 74
Baked Eggs ... 29
Baked Jalapeño And Cheese Cauliflower Mash ... 36
Baked Parmesan Eggs With Kielbasa ... 30
Baked Ricotta ... 18
Banana-strawberry Cakecups ... 29
Barbecued Baby Back Ribs ... 70
Barbecued Chicken Thighs ... 54
Basic Corn On The Cob ... 35
Basil Tomatoes ... 51
Bbq Pork Chops With Vegetables ... 68
Bbq Pork Ribs ... 20
Beef And Mango Skewers ... 12
Beef And Pork Sausage Meatloaf ... 69
Beef Kebabs ... 75
Beef Taco Chimichangas ... 78
Bell Pepper & Lentil Tacos ... 50
Better-than-chinese-take-out Pork Ribs ... 71
Blackened Red Snapper ... 82
Blistered Tomatoes ... 34
Bourbon-bbq Sauce Marinated Beef Bbq ... 77
Breaded Avocado Tacos ... 49
Breaded Chicken Patties ... 55
Breaded Italian Pork Chops ... 67
Breaded Parmesan Perch ... 83
Breakfast Chimichangas ... 31

Broccoli & Parmesan Dish ... 48
Brown Rice And Goat Cheese Croquettes ... 39
Buffalo Bites ... 13
Buffalo Cauliflower ... 11
Buffalo Chicken Taquitos ... 63
Buffalo French Fries ... 12
Bunless Breakfast Turkey Burgers ... 25
Butter Cheesecake ... 96
Buttered Broccoli ... 50
Buttery Shortbread Sticks ... 92
Buttery Stuffed Tomatoes ... 41

C

Cajun Fish Cakes ... 84
Cajun Fish Sticks ... 85
Cajun Sweet Potato Tots ... 19
Cal-mex Turkey Patties ... 58
Caramelized Carrots ... 49
Caraway Seed Pretzel Sticks ... 33
Caribbean Skewers ... 83
Carrot Orange Muffins ... 26
Cayenne-spiced Roasted Pecans ... 11
Celery Chicken Mix ... 63
Cheddar & Egg Scramble ... 31
Cheddar Biscuits With Nutmeg ... 27
Cheddar Soufflés ... 25
Cheddar-garlic Drop Biscuits ... 35
Cheese Turkey Meatloaf ... 61
Cheeseburgers ... 75
Cheesy Enchilada Stuffed Baked Potatoes ... 48
Cheesy Spinach Dip(1) ... 11
Cherry Beignets ... 24
Chicken & Fruit Biryani ... 54
Chicken & Pepperoni Pizza ... 58
Chicken Burgers With Blue Cheese Sauce ... 64
Chicken Fajita Poppers ... 57
Chicken Fajitas ... 61
Chicken Salad With White Dressing ... 59
Chicken Scotch Eggs ... 28
Chicken Strips ... 53
Chicken Tenderloins With Parmesan Cheese ... 56
Chicken Wings With Bbq Sauce ... 61
Chipotle Drumsticks ... 62
Chives Omelet ... 24
Chocolate Almond Crescent Rolls ... 29
Chocolate Banana Brownie ... 96
Chocolate Coconut Brownies ... 91
Chocolate Croissants ... 92
Chocolate Molten Cake ... 96
Chocolate-almond Candies ... 97
Cholula Avocado Fries ... 12

Cholula Onion Rings	37
Cilantro Sea Bass	81
Cinnamon Apple Crisps	15
Cinnamon Chicken Thighs	64
Cinnamon Crunch S'mores	94
Cinnamon Pear Oat Muffins	25
Cinnamon Sweet Potato Fries	18
Cinnamon-stick Kofta Skewers	70
Coconut Cream Roll-ups	96
Coconut Rice Cake	98
Cod Nuggets	83
Collard Green & Cod Packets	85
Corn On The Cob	46
Corn Pakodas	36
Corn With Coriander And Parmesan Cheese	15
Cornflakes Toast Sticks	26
Country-style Pork Ribs	71
Crab Rangoon	86
Cranberries Pudding	91
Creamy Eggs And Leeks	31
Creamy Spinach With Nutmeg	37
Creole Pork Chops	77
Creole Seasoned Okra	35
Creole Tilapia With Garlic Mayo	85
Crispy & Healthy Kale Chips	18
Crispy Breaded Beef Cubes	11
Crispy Cajun Dill Pickle Chips	17
Crispy Chicken Cordon Bleu	56
Crispy Chicken Parmesan	61
Crispy Chicken Strips	65
Crispy Duck With Cherry Sauce	53
Crispy Lamb Shoulder Chops	74
Crispy Smelts	87
Crispy Steak Subs	70
Crispy Wings With Lemony Old Bay Spice	45
Cuban Sliders	14
Curried Brussels Sprouts	39
Curried Cauliflower	47
Curried Chicken With Fruit	57
Curry Peaches, Pears, And Plums	97

D

Dark Chocolate Cream Galette	95
Delicious Zucchini Crackers	15
Dill Eggs In Wonton	23
Duck Breast With Figs	59

E

Easy Air Fried Salmon	86
Easy Glazed Carrots	50
Easy Scallops With Lemon Butter	81
Easy Tex-mex Chimichangas	71
Easy-to-make Almond Cookies	98
Egg Peppers Cups	26
Eggless Mung Bean Tart	24
Eggplant Chips	16

Eggs Salad	30
English Pumpkin Egg Bake	23
English Scones	23

F

Fajita Flank Steak Rolls	74
Falafels	46
Fiesta Chicken Plate	63
Fingerling Potatoes	42
Fish Nuggets With Broccoli Dip	80
Flank Steak With Tamari Sauce	75
Flavorful Spiced Chicken Pieces	57
French Fries	37
Fried Catfish Nuggets	89
Fried Goat Cheese	19
Fried Herbed Chicken Wings	53
Fried Shrimp	88

G

Garlic And Oregano Lamb Chops	76
Garlic Edamame	14
Garlic Provolone Asparagus	40
Garlic Steak With Cheese Butter	68
Garlicky Mushrooms With Parsley	40
German Chicken Frikadellen	57
Giant Vegan Chocolate Chip Cookie	91
Glazed Donuts	92
Gluten-free Nutty Chicken Fingers	64
Golden Fried Tofu	50
Graham Cracker Cheesecake	93
Green Beans And Potatoes Recipe	36
Grilled Spiced Fruit	97
Grilled Steak With Salsa	72

H

Ham And Corn Muffins	28
Ham Tilapia	80
Hasselback Apple Crisp	94
Herb-roasted Turkey Breast	56
Holiday Breakfast Casserole	30
Homemade Pork Gyoza	78
Honey Donuts	98
Honey Pork Links	73
Honey Rosemary Chicken	60
Hot Cheese Bites	14
Hot Okra Wedges	39

I

Indian-style Chicken With Raita	57
Italian Bruschetta With Mushrooms & Cheese	11
Italian Seasoned Easy Pasta Chips	46
Italian Shrimp	83

J

Jalapeño & Mozzarella Stuffed Mushrooms	19
Juicy Beef Kabobs With Sour Cream	76

K

Kale & Lentils With Crispy Onions 51
Kale Chips With Tex-mex Dip 14
Katsu Chicken Thighs 65
Kid´s Flounder Fingers 83
Korean Brussels Sprouts 20
Korean Short Ribs 70
Korean-style Chicken Bulgogi 65
Korean-style Fried Calamari 83

L

Lamb Meatballs 76
Lemon Broccoli 38
Lemon Butter–dill Salmon 86
Lemon Fennel With Sunflower Seeds 40
Lemon Parmesan Chicken 58
Lemon Shrimp And Zucchinis 88
Lemon-dill Salmon With Green Beans 84
Lemon-pepper Chicken Wings 64
Lemony Cabbage Slaw 33
Lentil Fritters 46
Lime Bay Scallops 81
Lobster Tails 87
Low-carb Peanut Butter Cookies 98

M

Maple Butter Salmon 87
Marinated Beef And Vegetable Stir Fry 67
Marinated Rib-eye Steak With
Herb Roasted Mushrooms 72
Maryland-style Crab Cakes 88
Mashed Potato Tots 34
Mediterranean Air Fried Veggies 36
Mediterranean Fried Chicken 58
Mediterranean Sea Scallops 82
Mediterranean Stuffed Chicken Breasts 53
Medium Rare Simple Salt And Pepper Steak 27
Mexican Twice Air-fried Sweet Potatoes 49
Mexican-style Shredded Beef 69
Mini Meatloaves With Pancetta 77
Mixed Berry Crumble 93
Mixed Pepper Hash With Mozzarella Cheese 27
Molten Chocolate Almond Cakes 92
Mushroom & Cavolo Nero Egg Muffins 30
Mustard-crusted Fish Fillets 80

N

Nashville Hot Chicken 54
No-guilty Spring Rolls 19

O

Okra Chips 14
Old Bay Cod Fish Fillets 86
Old Bay Fish `n´ Chips 89
Olive & Pepper Tapenade 18
Open-faced Sandwich 37

Orange Curried Chicken Stir-fry 62
Orange Trail Oatmeal 25
Original Köttbullar 73

P

Pancake For Two 22
Pancetta Mushroom & Onion Sautée 43
Paprika Duck 55
Parmesan Asparagus 39
Parmesan Chicken Fingers 60
Parmesan Chicken Meatloaf 60
Parmesan Crusted Chicken Cordon Bleu 59
Parmesan Sausage Egg Muffins 28
Parmesan-crusted Pork Chops 69
Peanut Butter-banana Roll-ups 94
Perfect Grill Chicken Breast 56
Pizza Portobello Mushrooms 45
Plum Apple Crumble With Cranberries 97
Pork Meatballs 75
Pork Pot Stickers With Yum Yum Sauce 16
Potato And Prosciutto Salad 69
Potato Chip-crusted Cod 81
Potato Pastries 20

R

Ratatouille 37
Rice And Eggplant Bowl 38
Rice And Meatball Stuffed Bell Peppers 73
Rich Spinach Chips 41
Ricotta Veggie Potpie 49
Roasted Eggplant Slices 33
Roasted Fennel Salad 35
Roasted Thyme Asparagus 38
Rosemary Garlic Goat Cheese 14
Rosemary Potato Salad 40
Rosemary Roasted Potatoes With Lemon 43

S

Sage Cream 95
Salty Lamb Chops 73
Scalloped Potatoes 35
Seafood Spring Rolls 81
Sesame Chicken Tenders 62
Sesame Orange Tofu With Snow Peas 48
Sesame-crusted Tuna Steaks 84
Shrimp "scampi" 87
Simple & Tasty Brownies 91
Simple Cheddar-omelet 26
Simple Chicken Shawarma 54
Simple Curried Sweet Potato Fries 18
Simple Green Bake 33
Simple Rib-eye Steak 72
Simple Taro Fries 41
Snow Crab Legs 85
Sourdough Croutons 25
Southwestern Prawns With Asparagus 80

Spanish Garlic Shrimp	88
Speedy Baked Caprese With Avocado	33
Spice Chicken Pieces	55
Spiced Pork Chops	69
Spicy Celery Sticks	50
Spicy Corn On The Cob	42
Spicy Halibut Steak	86
Spicy Kale Chips With Yogurt Sauce	17
Spinach And Artichoke–stuffed Peppers	46
Spinach And Mushroom Mini Quiche	22
Spinach Bacon Spread	27
Spinach With Scrambled Eggs	23
Steak Bites And Spicy Dipping Sauce	76
Steak Fajitas With Vegetables	71
Steamed Green Veggie Trio	34
Strawberry And Peach Toast	23
Strawberry Tarts	22
Stuffed Bell Peppers With Mayonnaise	38
Sweet And Sour Pork	67
Sweet And Spicy Pork Ribs	67
Sweet And Spicy Tofu	33
Sweet Corn Bread	47
Sweet-and-sour Polish Sausage	77

T

Tacos	51
Tasty Berry Cobbler	98
Tasty Pork Chops	67
Tender Country Ribs	78
Tender Pork Ribs With Bbq Sauce	68
Thyme Lentil Patties	51
Thyme Scallops	82
Tilapia Teriyaki	85
Toasted Coconut Flakes	91
Tomato & Basil Bruschetta	13
Tomatoes Hash With Cheddar Cheese	29
Tortilla-crusted With Lemon Filets	82
Trimmed Mackerel With Spring Onions	87
Truffle Vegetable Croquettes	40
Tuna Wraps	84
Turkey & Rice Frittata	54
Turkey And Cranberry Quesadillas	63
Turkey Casserole With Cheddar Cheese	30
Turkish Mutabal (eggplant Dip)	36
Two-cheese Grilled Sandwiches	51

V

Vegan Brownie Bites	94
Vegan Buddha Bowls(2)	45
Vegetable Quiche	27
Vegetarian Eggplant "pizzas"	47
Vegetarian Quinoa Cups	22
Veggie Burgers	45
Veggie Salmon Nachos	16
Vip´s Club Sandwiches	62

W

Western Omelet	29

Y

Yellow Squash	42
Yummy Bagel Breakfast	28

Z

Za'atar Garbanzo Beans	13
Zucchini Bars With Cream Cheese	99
Zucchini Bread With Chocolate Chips	94
Zucchini Chips With Cheese	12
Zucchini Chips	12
Zucchini With Parmesan Cheese	13

Printed in Great Britain
by Amazon